JAMES DUBRO

Mob Rule

Inside the Canadian Mafia

JAMES DUBRO

Mob Rule

Inside the Canadian Mafia

Macmillan of Canada
A Division of Canada Publishing Corporation
Toronto, Ontario, Canada

CANADIAN CATALOGUING IN PUBLICATION DATA

Dubro, James, date.
　Mob rule : inside the Canadian Mafia

Includes index.
ISBN 0-7715-9686-3

1. Volpe, Paul. 2. Mafia — Ontario. 3. Organized crime — Canada. I. Title.

HV6453.C33V63 1985　　364.1′06′0713　　C85-098875-6

DESIGN: Artplus/Brant Cowie

Macmillan of Canada
A Division of Canada Publishing Corporation
Toronto, Ontario, Canada

Printed in Canada

To my colleagues on the Connections *team, to the memory of my father, and to all the innocent victims of organized crime.*

Good morning to the day; and, next, my gold!
Open the shrine, that I may see my saint.
Hail the world's soul, and mine! . . . Dear Saint,
Riches, the dumb god, that giv'st all men tongues:
That canst do nought, and yet mak'st men do all things;
The price of souls; even hell, with thee to boot,
Is made worth heaven!

Volpone, in the opening scene of Ben Jonson's *Volpone, The Fox*

Contents

PREFACE

I N THE LAST YEAR there has been a lot of media coverage of the Italian government's crackdown against the Mafia under Italy's new tough anti-Mafia laws. Pope John Paul II himself has in no uncertain terms condemned the Mafia by name and condemned as well its concept of "omertà", the Mafia code of total silence that forbids its members to talk to outsiders. Omertà is ruthlessly enforced, and a member who talks risks death. In the United States an all-out offensive has been launched by the FBI and federal strike forces against mob bosses, using a hitherto rarely used section of the U.S. criminal code adopted in 1970 and popularly known as the R.I.C.O. statutes (Racketeer-Influenced and Corrupt-Organization Act). R.I.C.O. allows the government to make a case against a Mafia member merely on the basis of having evidence that he belongs to an organization involved in continual criminal activity known as the Mafia and run by a commission of bosses. Five of the bosses and some of their underlings have been indicted in New York City alone.

But all this activity is on the American and international stage. Canada has no R.I.C.O. statute, and there are no anti-Mafia laws here similar to those in Italy. Yet the Mafia is alive and well, indeed it is thriving, in Canada. And it has been here since the turn of the century under one guise or another. But not-withstanding this, there are still a lot of myths about organized crime and the Mafia.

Underworld reaction to my August 1984 article in *Toronto Life* entitled "Life Inside the Mob", which featured a portrait of the late Toronto mobster Paul Volpe on the cover, reinforced one important fact: Toronto is, has been, and always will be a mob city. Having worked on the CBC's celebrated series *Connections: An Investigation into Organized Crime* (a co-production of the CBC and Norfolk Productions) as its research director and associate producer for five years, from 1974 until 1979, and on other organized-crime stories as an investigative journalist for CBC Television's flagship current affairs program, *the fifth estate*, for three years (where I was responsible for the exclusive interview with hit man Cecil Kirby broadcast in 1984 as well as other organized-crime stories, including one on Chinese gangs in Canada), I was more than familiar with the scope of mob activities in Canada. Still, I was staggered by the number of organized-crime members and their associates (known as "rounders" in the street world, because they hang around mobsters) who came out of the woodwork to comment directly or indirectly on my *Toronto Life* article. Not that the mob itself likes publicity, but rounders, mob associates, and mob groupies, of which there are thousands in the Toronto area alone, like to feel part of the action, and my article on the mob was the first bit of non-sensationalistic reporting the underworld has had for some time. I was struck by the many congratulatory calls from mob circles, and their frequent insistence that they be allowed to correct or add the most minute details to the retelling of old mob stories. One reason for this outpouring from organized crime itself is that in the article I struck a chord that has not been articulated for some time: namely, how the mob really works.

People inside the mob world were tired of the Hollywood clichés of *The Godfather* and the oversimplifications in the media (especially television), which depict all organized crime as being controlled by an all-powerful Mafia. As insiders know, this is not how organized crime works in the 1980s, especially in the major metropolitan areas such as Toronto. Displacing this mythic view with the hard reality of a fractured, highly factionalized multicultural mob operating in Ontario was so unusual that the mob responded in kind by contacting me.

If this book serves one purpose, it is to present the facts about organized crime in North America as they are, not as they were or as some people, including many of those in the media, would like them to be. The clichés of cheap fiction have somehow permeated most of the coverage of organized crime in our society, at least the coverage that anyone is paying attention to.

The focus of this book is the criminal career of Paul Volpe, from the early 1960s until his murder in late 1983. Volpe is the archetypal Canadian mobster of the period, and a major part of this book deals with how, why, and with whom he operated. There is also an attempt to recapture some of the lost history of organized crime in Canada, going back to the extortions of the Black Hand in the first decade of the twentieth century, long overlooked by other journalists in the crime area. The rest of the book delineates the deadly struggle in Canada between the "old mob", represented by Toronto-born criminals such as Volpe, and the "new mob" of tougher, leaner, Italian-born mobsters like Remo and Cosimo Commisso and Domenic Racco, who have been moving in on the older group in a fight for territory and mob supremacy. There is also a look at certain interesting mob characters, and suggestions of what might be done by society to curb the power and activities of the mob. Ontario is emphasized over Quebec and British Columbia (though Quebec and Vancouver mob characters invariably come into the picture as they relate to the situation in the rest of Canada), as there have already been several books on aspects of organized crime in Quebec as well as the highly publicized Quebec Crime Probe reports of the seventies. Amazingly, this is the first serious book-length study dealing primarily with the mob in Canada outside Quebec, but this book is by no means the final word on the subject of the Mafia in Canada.

Furthermore, this book is not an attempt to glamorize criminal life or exaggerate the importance and influence of gangsters. The simple fact is that the most colourful characters of the underworld are Damon Runyonesque individuals with a natural intelligence, imagination, and sense of humour, and possessed of an earthy street wit that takes many in. However, one should not be deceived by this. The worst in the underworld have no respect for human life and order murders and savage beatings as casually as others order a pizza. There are elements of the best and the worst of the underworld in Paul Volpe and his associates.

In compiling the research for this book it has been essential for me to protect the identities of several people inside the mob world (members, associates, spouses, and relatives) whose information I have good reason to believe is accurate. Every attempt has been made to verify details from mob informers, and information has been included in this account only if its source has a long track record of reliability, or I have been able to check out the data through other sources. Wherever possible I will try to indicate the nature of the source, if not the actual name. Without the assistance of these courageous informers, this book would not have been possible.

Parts of certain chapters appeared in other forms in *Toronto Life* and *Hamilton This Month*, and I thank these publications for permission to reprint this material. I also acknowledge with gratitude Norfolk Productions for kind permission to use some *Connections* research material and to reprint transcripts of certain interviews.

There are many people I must thank who helped me in some way in preparing this book:

Peter Herrndorf, Marq de Villiers, and Stephen Trumper, the publisher and editors of *Toronto Life*, for their encouragement.

Ron Haggart, Robin Taylor, Gordon Stewart, and *the fifth estate*, for bearing with me.

Peter Moon in Ontario and Michel Auger in Quebec for all they have so intelligently written on the subject over the past two decades.

Rick Archbold, for invaluable advice at the initial stages of the book.

My sister, Beverly Lacey, my brother, Dan, and my aunt, Rita Lyons, who have all helped in countless ways over the years.

Special thanks for assistance at some point during the long research period to: Chief Doug Burroughs and Deputy Chief Bill Teggart, Peel Regional Police; Inspector Kent Laidlaw, Halton Regional Police; Howard Morton, Crown Attorney's Office; Inspector James "the Bear" McIlvenna, RCMP; Staff Sergeant Robin Ward, RCMP; Cal Beacock, Ontario Police Commission; Staff Inspector Tom Macleod, Staff Inspector Robert Stirling, and Sergeant Charles Maxwell, Metropolitan Toronto Police Force; Sergeant Al Cooke, Criminal Intelligence Service Ontario; Colonel Clinton Pagano and Major Robert Winters, New Jersey State Police; Commissioner Archie Ferguson and Staff Superintendent Bruno Dorigo, Ontario Provincial Police; Deputy Commissioners Thomas Venner and Hank Jensen, RCMP; lawyers Earl Levy and Eddie Greenspan; and, of course, former Commisso enforcer and hit man Cecil Kirby.

In addition there are many other police sources who cannot be named here, for one reason or another, whom I also wish to thank.

I also wish to thank the Hamilton Public Library, the Centre for Investigative Journalism (CIJ), Investigative Reporters and Editors (IRE), and Wayne Narciso and Eileen Morrow of *Hamilton This Month*.

Friends or journalistic colleagues who encouraged me or gave me invaluable assistance: Jon Lidolt, Professor Ian Chapman,

Richard Wizansky, Kitson Vincent, Rob Roy (who in addition did some important research), Martha Porter, Beverly Wilson, Professor Joseph Wearing, Professor Kenneth Maclean, Claire Weissman Wilks, Richard Malone, Fred Peabody, Marlene Perry, Virginia Nelson, Edward Leitz, Gerald Robinson, J.-P. Charbonneau, Jonathan Kwitny, Joseph McGrath, Nedleigh Lynch, Judge Richard Noren, Jane Stone, Louis Lopardi, Robin Rowland, Philip Mathias, John Sawatsky, Tom Renner, Richard Nielsen, Wade Rowland, and most emphatically, *Connections* co-producers and my good friends, Bill Macadam and Martyn Burke.

And of course my tireless Macmillan editor, Macmillan lawyers Dennis Lane and Kent Thompson, and my publisher, Doug Gibson.

INTRODUCTION

Organized Crime and the Mafia: Myth and Reality

The underworld is not an organization, but an environment, a "milieu" of crooks, bandits, dealers, outlaws of all description. Within the milieu a multitude of gangs, clans, or organizations exist or co-exist. Some are powerful, well-organized and stable; others are loose, haphazard and even temporary coalitions of odd-job criminals and journeyman crooks. The Mafia, as such, is a collection of gangs or families and feudal chiefs of Italian origin united by cultural, family and ethnic links, as well as by mutual interest. For various historical and cultural reasons the Italian clans of the Mafia have long been a dominating influence in the North American underworld. But they have no monopoly on criminality.

Jean-Pierre Charbonneau, in *The Canadian Connection*

Mafia is a process, not a thing. Mafia is a form of clan-cooperation to which its individual members pledge lifelong loyalty.... Friendship, connections, family ties, trust, loyalty, obedience – this was the glue that held us together.

Joe Bonanno, New York City original Mafia family father, in his memoirs, *A Man of Honor*

Do not ever yield to the temptation of criminal and Mafia violence.... And how could you forget the phenomenon of criminal and Mafia activity and the worrying form of omertà and corruption which they generate? ... Have the courage to wipe out omertà ... a practice which promotes squalid complicity dictated by fear.

Pope John Paul II, October 7, 1984, during a tour of southern Calabria

There has always been organized crime. In the centuries before the birth of Christ, in ancient Egypt, Greece, and Rome, pirates organized into bands and roamed the seas. Julius Caesar himself, in his early career, was captured by pirates and had to pay a ransom of fifty talents (several hundred thousand dollars in today's currency) to regain his freedom. He then proceeded to gather a naval force and capture and punish the pirates. In the first century before Christ, Caesar's colleague on the First Triumvirate, Marcus Crassus, was heavily involved in real-estate fraud and arson for profit in Rome. And we all know about Ali Baba and the forty thieves, and Robin Hood and his Merry Men, to say nothing about the sundry groups of organized criminals that people the pages of Dickens's novels (Fagin and his associates come to mind). Organized crime has existed as long as civilization; indeed it may be an inherent aspect, albeit negative, of creatively building a society. Organized crime is probably an even older profession than prostitution.

In his Victorian book on the underworld published in 1862, Henry Mayhew refers to habitual criminals, some of whom were born in families involved in organized crime: "Thousands of our felons are trained from their infancy in the bosom of crime; a large proportion of them are born in the homes of habitual thieves and other persons of bad character, and are familiarized with vice from their earliest years; frequently the first words they lisp are oaths and curses."

In North America organized crime was here from the very beginning. Long before waves of immigrants in the late nineteenth century brought in the Mafia from Sicily and Calabria, the Chinese secret criminal societies from Hong Kong and China, and various crime-based groups from other countries, organized crime was a major factor in the United States and Canada. One need only look at the Wild West and characters such as Jesse James, Billy the Kid, and all the rest to see this all-too-obvious fact. A 1984 book, *Pirates and Outlaws of Canada, 1610-1932* by Harold Horwood and Ed Butts, profiles three centuries of colourful Canadian contributions to the organized-crime world.

"Organized crime" as a term has been so overused and abused in North America over the past several decades that it has ceased to have much impact or any real meaning. The same applies even more to the word "Mafia" and the concepts of "connections" and "respect" as they relate to criminal activity. Yet in order to appreciate the structure and extent of the underworld in Canada and the United States, it is necessary to carefully define these and other terms in a way that has real meaning.

"Organized crime" is easy to define. It is, as the official Canadian police definition goes, "two or more persons consorting together on a continuing basis to participate in illegal activities, either directly or indirectly for gain." Nothing about the Mafia! Ralph Salerno, an American organized-crime expert who frequently advises Canadian enforcement authorities on the subject, sharpens the focus a bit in his definition of "organized crime": "We say that organized crime will constitute a self-perpetuating group that will go on in a continuing conspiracy for many years, even if the original members of the conspiracy die, go to prison or elect to retire. There will be a continuum of the organization over a long period of time with the use of force or fear as part of the ongoing methodology."

Organized crime in Canada, as in the United States, is not just the preserve of one or two ethnic groups. There is much more to organized crime than the criminal association known variously as the "Mafia", the "Cosa Nostra", the "Black Hand", "N'Dranghita", or the "Honoured Society". In North America just about every major ethnic group has participated in a major way in organized crime over the years: Irish, English, Italians, Jews, French Canadians, blacks, Chinese, gypsies, Chicanos, and many others.

There is a popular sociological theory, originated by the noted American criminologist Francis Ianni, that explains how organized criminal activity has developed and passed on in North America from one ethnic group to another based on how long the group has been here, the language and cultural knots that tightly bind the group, and the degree to which the group assimilates into the prevailing culture. So the Irish gangs of the late nineteenth and early twentieth centuries faded into respectability as the Jewish hoods and Italian gangsters became more prevalent in crime in large American cities in the 1920s and '30s. There is much merit to this so-called "ethnic succession", which helps explain the rise and fall of various criminal groups in North America in the twentieth century.

Yet in many ways "organized crime" is really a lot less complicated than the academics and sociologists make it out to be. Former mob boss Vinnie "the Fat Man" Teresa put it best when he said on the 1977 CBC-TV show *Connections* that organized crime is very simple. "It is," he said, "just a bunch of people getting together to take all the money they can from all the suckers they can."

Everyone agrees that "organized crime" exists, but there has been considerable academic debate and controversy about the nature and indeed the very existence of "the Mafia" in North America. Some prominent sociologists, such as Daniel Bell of Harvard University, Dwight Smith of the State University of New York, and Gordon Hawkins of Australia, have written thoughtful and influential essays on the lack of proof of a highly structured group known as "the Mafia".

Belief in the "myth" of the Mafia, Professor Bell argues in his essay included in his well-known book *The End of Ideology*, "is like belief in the myth of the power of Wall Street.... There is a feeling in North America that someone is pulling all the complicated strings to which this jumbled world dances." Professor Hawkins adds, in his essay entitled "Organized Crime and God", that "belief in the existence of the Mafia requires a leap of faith much like belief in the existence of God." Professor Smith, in his article "Mafia: The Prototypical Alien Conspiracy", argues that people want to believe in conspiracy theories, especially when the conspiracies are run by foreigners. The reason for this scepticism on the part of some leading academics is twofold. First, the Hollywood, pulp novel, and television hype on the subject of the Mafia was overdone in the 1930s, '40s, and '50s, creating an unrealistic image of the all-powerful gangsters in America à la *Little Caesar* and *Scarface*; and later films, as well as the various mobsters depicted in *The Untouchables*, one of the most popular TV shows ever, continued the trend. Second, and perhaps more importantly, documented scholarly studies and books on the subject were sadly lacking until the 1970s, leaving only sensational and often superficial newspaper and television reports and police themselves as the major sources of concrete information and documentation.

In recent years all of this has changed, although the sensationalistic elements remain in fiction and the media. The famed Valachi hearings in the United States in 1963 and 1964 revealed first-hand evidence of the internal workings of some of the "Mafia" families referred to as "Cosa Nostra" (literally, "our own thing") by Joe Valachi, a soldier in a New York City Mafia family. Valachi's testimony was covered widely by the press in the United States and Canada, and the details of the structure and operations of this Italian-based criminal association with branches in most major U.S. cities and associates in Canadian cities such as Hamilton, Montreal, and Toronto became well known. A widely read book and an Italian-made film version, starring Charles Bronson as Valachi, followed the Senate hearings, keeping the Mafia very much in the public eye for the next few years. Other Mafia defectors and informers surfaced after the U.S. Justice Department started the Witness Protection Program in the late sixties, which supplied former organized-crime members with a new identity and allowed them to build a new life with police protection, in exchange for their co-operation with the police and their testimony against their former colleagues in the mob. A similar program, albeit an ad hoc one, has since been established in Ontario and Quebec.

More importantly, evidence of the existence and structure of the Mafia has come from police wire-taps and bugs in the 1970s in both Canada and the United States. Transcripts of these recordings have been made available to scholars, journalists, and the general public through court cases and crime probes. The notable DeCavalcante wire-taps, based on a bug inside the office of Sam "the Plumber" DeCavalcante, a New Jersey Mafia boss in the middle 1960s, surfaced in a mid-'70s United States federal case against a mob boss in New Jersey on charges of conspiracy and were later published as a book. The long-running Quebec Commission on Organized Crime in the middle to late '70s released many wire-tap transcripts, both in reports and privately to journalists and professional crime-fighters. In Canada royal commissions, such as the Ontario Royal Commission into Certain Sectors of the Construction Industry in 1974 (popularly known as the Waisberg commission), have also been sources. Wire-tap evidence is the most convincing, as it allows the police, reporters, and scholars to listen to the Mafia leaders themselves discussing hierarchy and operations. The most famous bug in Canada was perhaps the one the police installed behind a milk cooler in the headquarters of senior Mafia leader Paolo Violi in Montreal.

Violi and his boss Vic Cotroni and their associates were overheard discussing Mafia leadership battles, planning murders, robberies, and other crimes, and discussing their interrelationship with similar groups such as the Bonanno family of New York City, which exercised some control over Violi and Cotroni. The evidence from these wire-taps was incontrovertible proof of the existence of a Mafia organization in Canada.

In examining evidence from U.S. wire-tap sources, *Wall Street Journal* reporter Jonathan Kwitny concluded in his 1979 book, *Vicious Circles: The Mafia in the Marketplace*: "It is difficult to understand how a reasonable person could read these transcripts [the DeCavalcante conversations in New Jersey with other Mafia leaders] – or similar transcripts from bugs on the offices of other Mafia leaders – and fail to conclude that there is across the United States a tight knit criminal organization with strict regulation of membership and conduct; that it exercises ultimate governing power over its members, superior to the power of country or blood family; and that its sole purpose is making money through illegal activity. The conversations include numerous references to Sicilian titles or names, such as *regime*, *caporegime*, *brigata*, and *consiglieri*, now familiar to readers of popular fiction. But these conversations were recorded while Mario Puzo was still an underpaid magazine editor. Many of the conversations were recorded before Joe Valachi surfaced. This is not life imitating art, as Professor Smith and his sociologist friends would have us believe. This is the real thing!"

Recently there have been two fascinating Canadian cases involving documents and wire-taps that help prove the existence of an organized Mafia-style group with initiation ceremonies, some hierarchy, and some organization. The first one is the case of Francesco Caccamo, a member of the Calabrian Mafia group in Toronto known as the "Siderno group". Caccamo was involved in a counterfeiting ring that this group was running between Vancouver, Washington State, and Ontario. During a search of Caccamo's home in 1971, while he was being arrested for the counterfeiting charge and illegal possession of a revolver, the police discovered a twenty-seven-page document written in Italian in an archaic script, entitled "Come Formare una Società", or, in English, "How to Form a Society". Experts in Italy were consulted (including Dr. Alberto Sabatino of the Italian police, who testified at the trial), and it was proven that the documents were rituals for a secret Italian criminal organization based in Calabria. On the basis of these documents Caccamo was convicted for possessing the gun for a purpose dangerous to the public peace. The judge also ruled that the papers were the rules and regulations of the Honoured Society, and that Caccamo was a member of it. The case went all the way up to the Supreme Court. Famed criminal lawyer Arthur Maloney acted as defence counsel at the trial, which upheld the conviction and the authenticity of the "Caccamo Papers".

A later sensational case in Hamilton, Ontario, arose from the conviction of three Hamilton men in a late-1970s fraud involving the take-over of a family pasta business. The Crown unsuccessfully attempted to prove before the sentencing, in July 1982, that the three men, Antonio Luppino, age fifty, John Luppino, thirty-five, and Geraldo Fumo, twenty-nine, were members of a Mafia organization in Canada. Inspector Dino Chiarot of the RCMP presented the court with transcripts and reports from four police investigations dating from 1966 to 1982, which included electronically intercepted conversations between Giacomo Luppino, the alleged leader of this Mafia group, two of his sons, and his late son-in-law Paolo Violi, the leader of the Montreal Mafia. The transcripts revealed threats of a gang war for control of Montreal, connections with well-known Mafia leaders in the United States, and discussions of the structure, rules, and code of ethics of a Mafia group called "N'drina" or "N'Dranghita" (the Calabrian Honoured Society). On the tapes, reference was made to dues being paid, and there were many references to Giacomo Luppino as the leader of the group, which was divided into "decimas", or groups of ten, each with its own leader or "capo decima". Fraud, loan-sharking, and obtaining protection money from the community (referred to by the Italian name "cammara" or "cammera") were all alluded to. In one conversation, Giacomo Luppino and Violi lamented the fact that the U.S. Mafia groups "go the American way, because they don't understand things." They were referring to the fact that the newer Mafia groups have modernized and have lost the old-country ways of operating. The importance of "respect", "trust", and "honour" were emphasized in the discussions. The tapes clearly indicated the existence of a Mafia group that has operated in Hamilton, Toronto, and Montreal since at least 1966, with considerable connections with similar groups in the United States.

It is important to note that in both these cases, the evidence of the existence of Mafia-style organizations did not convince everyone. Edward Greenspan, the Toronto criminal lawyer who acted for Caccamo in his deportation hearing and for the Luppinos in the Hamilton case, finds some of the evidence in these cases "laughable, and woefully inadequate". It seems that proving the existence of the Mafia in a court of law still cannot be done to the satisfaction of those demanding absolute proof beyond any reasonable doubt.

But what is "the Mafia"? It is this encompassing term that causes confusion for the general public. Joe Bonanno, the long-time, self-admitted "father" of one of the five major families in New York City (and one that has extensive ties to Canada), attempted to explain it in his recently published autobiography, *A Man of Honor*: "What Americans call 'Mafia' never was an institution, an organization, a corporate body.... It pleases policemen to think of some outlaws as belonging to one monolithic group, a secret society perhaps, which can be attacked and defeated, once and for all, just as one's enemy can in conventional war.... This is a psychologically pleasing projection; it gives the policeman hope he can win the war against crime if only he can destroy the 'monolithic' group which he imagines controls organized crime." Bonanno's analysis is of course self-serving, and the police did not invent or create the Mafia.

Scholars do not agree on the origin of the word "Mafia", though it is almost certainly Sicilian. According to the Quebec Crime Probe report of 1975, the term "Mafia" describes a state of mind, a feeling of pride, a philosophy of life, and a style of behaviour. It is the mark of a known and respected man, and derives from the Sicilian adjective "mafiusu", used since the eighteenth century to describe magnificent or perfect people. The *Oxford English Dictionary*, on the other hand, states that "Mafia" comes from a Sicilian dialect for "mah", which means "bragging".

In his own memoirs, Joe Bonanno says "Mafia" comes from an event in 1282 when Sicily was under French rule. It became the rallying cry of the resistance movement after a French officer raped a Sicilian girl, and her mother ran through the streets screaming "Ma fia! Ma fia!" ("My daughter! My daughter!")

Bonanno goes on to say that whether the story is true is irrelevant, as it speaks to him "to this day of the living ideals of personal honor, personal justice, and personal dignity."

In Sicily and later in Canada and the United States, "Mafia" has come to refer to an organized international body of criminals of Sicilian origin. The term is now a convenient handle for the present dominant force in organized crime in North America, brought in by immigrants from Italy, namely the predominantly Sicilian, and more recently Calabrian, organized-crime groupings or "families". These families are held together by a certain code, which includes respect for senior family members and "omertà", a vow of silence about the activities and membership of the family. There is in addition a hierarchy, albeit flexible, and an initiation rite. "'The Family' should be viewed as an organism, a living tissue of binding personal relationships," says Joe Bonanno, "and the code of conduct prescribed by the Family is not written in any book.... Our tradition is mightier than any book.... We pass down the knowledge personally from generation to generation.... My tradition goes by many names in this country; some prefer the term 'Mafia', others like *cosa nostra*.... These are all metaphors.... The reason there is no formal term to describe it is that there never was a formal organization to describe.... We're talking about a tradition, a way of life, a process."

The Quebec Crime Probe reports of the late 1970s give detailed wire-tap evidence of a highly structured, organized Mafia family operating in Montreal under the leadership of Vic Cotroni, the Godfather, with considerable ties to the United States Mafia families. Bonanno himself admits that he controlled the Montreal family and that Stefano Magaddino, the old don of Buffalo, controlled part of Toronto in the 1950s and '60s. "It has long been acknowledged in my world that certain families and their Fathers had spheres of influence outside their own resident cities," he states. For example, Toronto had long been recognized as being within Magaddino's sphere of influence. Montreal, on the other hand, was considered in the domain of the Bonanno family. "In my world," Bonanno continues in his autobiography, "we often arrived at such arrangements so as not to step on each other's toes and thus avoid territorial disputes." But Bonanno belongs to the old world of Sicilian-born dons, known in the mob as "mustached Petes". This is a disappearing breed in North

America. Now the dominant forces in the Mafia families are mostly American- or Canadian-born criminals who rely less on the old traditions and values and more on brute force and intimidation to maintain their "families" and a degree of respect. Even in the underworld there is a generation gap.

In Canada, according to the Quebec Crime Probe report of 1975, "this new class of the underworld is a group of individuals continuously and secretly conspiring together on a permanent basis with a view to profiting from several types of crimes." And this group goes beyond the old-style Mafia and represents the whole spectrum of what is known as "organized crime", which is made up of criminals of many ethnic groups and backgrounds combining forces for various criminal conspiracies on a regular basis. Above all, knowing the right people, having "connections", is the most important requirement for the successful organized criminal. In many ways the word "connected", rather than the somewhat vague and emotive word "Mafia", is the right word to describe certain organized-crime leaders such as Paul Volpe. One veteran Ontario intelligence officer says: "There is no 'Mafia' in Toronto, just well-connected organized criminals of Italian descent who effectively use the 'myth' of the Mafia to enhance their own positions in the criminal world." In other words, the "mob".

By using the term "mob", it is possible to avoid the pitfalls of the academic debate on the existence of the Mafia and the sensitivities of some politicians and certain members of the Italian community about the use of the word "Mafia". Still it is important to realize that once all is said and done, there is a tightly knit group of Italian criminals operating in North America, and this group holds considerable sway in the underworld of criminal life. Allan Lawrence, when he was the attorney general of Ontario in the early 1970s, spoke for certain Italian constituents when he stated before a meeting of the Federation of Italian-Canadian Associations: "I want to assure you that there is no such monolithic monopolistic criminal activity." Strictly speaking this is true, though it begs the question of the existence of an Italian criminal group who control or have high profiles in the city's underworld.

The Italian criminal groups are also more feared than other organizations in the underworld. In spite of the academics such as Bell, Smith, and Hawkins, politicians like Allan Lawrence, and the sensitivities of certain members of the Italian community (I limit this to "certain members", as many vigorous fighters against Mafia-style groups have been Italians in the police forces, the business world, and the prosecutors' offices in the United States and Canada), these groups really do exist. Also, most of the real victims of the Italian criminal groups are Italians themselves. After examining all of the evidence now available, I think the average, fair-minded citizen has to conclude that there are indeed (and have been for some time) Mafia-type organizations operating in Canada and the United States that have some internal structure and considerable clout in the multi-ethnic criminal underworld.

After many years of careful research on organized crime, the Quebec Crime Probe in 1975 concluded: "The Italian element of the mob was a significant factor in organized crime.... Our contention that the criminal secret society ... through its historical foundations, as it exists in North America, is based on considerable information gathered over the years by hundreds of policemen, journalists and various researchers, and by a number of national or regional investigation commissions. Some of the best evidence gathered is certainly contained in the confessions of various members and close associates of this secret society. Also high on the list are the many conversations intercepted by the police."

The following is excerpted from the Quebec Crime Probe report of 1975. It states outright that the Mafia exists and is a major threat to society, and gives concrete examples of the structure of the Montreal Mafia groups.

There is in sober fact a highly structured criminal secret society in the United States, reserved for criminals of Sicilian and Italian ancestry: this organization is a direct descendant of similar secret societies which did and do exist in southern Italy, especially in Sicily. This statement is supported by many meetings between mafiosi leaders from all over America and elsewhere, particularly Italy....

Let us first analyse the structure of the Montreal organization within which Vincent Cotroni and Paolo Violi developed. In this way, we will be able to determine what kind of criminal gang is involved and how it can be compared in structure to other gangs known to belong to the Italian or American Mafia.

We have already seen that the Mafia is a secret society comprising regular members, bosses and associates. Its main characteristics are its special membership, open only to persons of Italian origin, and its formal hierarchy which determines the line of command and power in each unit, or family....

While the members of the Cotroni-Violi family are all of Italian ancestry, they are not, however, all Sicilians. In Montreal, Calabrians and people from other regions in the South of Italy can be found. We should further emphasize that Vincent Cotroni and Paolo Violi are themselves of Calabrian descent.

In the Cotroni-Violi gang, the term family is used in the same sense as in other Italian secret societies. Belonging to a select group gives members the feeling of being closely related.

We should remember the importance of the family for Italians. We know that they tend to multiply family ties among themselves. Therefore it is not surprising to learn that there are many real family relationships (by blood or marriage) and even more fictitious family relationships (godfather and "compare" relationships) among the members and even among the partners of the Cotroni-Violi family. Several members of the Cotroni-Violi family come from the same village or area in Sicily, Calabria or Campania.

We can therefore say that in many respects the Cotroni-Violi gang is a true family unit. In short, not everyone who wants to may enter the Cotroni-Violi family. The strict, selective method of admitting new members, which indicates that recruiting is done on a fairly systematic basis, points to the fact that this group constitutes more than an ordinary criminal gang. A system of recruitment, apprenticeship and rigorous selection of members is, as we have already mentioned, characteristic of most of the secret societies that have existed throughout history, including the Mafia.

Although some partners are of Italian descent, French Canadians, Jews, Anglo-Saxons, Slavs, Blacks and others can also be found. In reality, a large number of individuals and criminals of all sorts are involved with members of the Cotroni-Violi family, either as employees or as more or less independent partners. Evidence presented before the Commission proves that there are many people who not only recognize the moral authority of the leaders of the Cotroni family but who are also under their power. The Cotroni-Violi organization actually goes beyond the limits of the Italian family even though the family is the nucleus. Moreover, the family is the infrastructure of an association of criminals from different ethnic backgrounds.

In the criminal underworld one has power based on how many people respect your organization, your muscle, your connections, your ability to pull off major and sophisticated crimes, your ability to instil fear in the community, your leadership qualities – which inspire confidence and discipline, and some fear within your own group and fear within other criminal groups – and finally, admiration for the way you conduct yourself socially, with finesse and some sophistication. These are all elements that, added to a long track record of impressive "action", create a feeling of respect for certain criminal leaders in the mob.

A leader in the mob must be capable of great ruthlessness. A *Maclean's* reporter once said of Johnny "Pops" Papalia, an old-style, Hamilton-based Mafia leader, that he was "well mannered except when slugging someone with a blackjack." Or as a mob associate in the *Connections* series on organized crime put it when speaking about Paul Volpe and other mob leaders: "They're the nicest, classiest people in the world ... but just do something wrong or get out of line, that's how bad they are.... Just let them have something on you and they just put a hand around your throat and never let go." So fear is an integral part of mob "respect". But "respect" is more complicated than the dictionaries would have you believe. It is a peculiar combination of admiration for the individual, his character, coolness, achievements, of attention to his connections, and of fear of what he might do to you if you step out of line.

Another reason a mob leader is respected is that he provides, in an organized, business-like way, illegal services that certain sectors of the general public want, such as gambling, prostitution, loan-sharking, and the sale of soft drugs. In every large Canadian city, local bookmakers of all ethnic groups are involved in the mob through an elaborate lay-off system established to protect individual bookies from large losses. As Sergeant Tommy O'Brien of the New York City police department put it: "As long as people enjoy their service, and that is all it is, as long as people enjoy prostitution, untaxed cigarettes, after hours joints, gambling, as long as people enjoy that, there will always be mafia people, criminals who will supply them. It's like anything else

– if the general public wants it, they'll get it."

There is also a public perception that while mobsters can be violent, they generally only fight amongst themselves, causing no harm to society in general. This way of thinking allows many respectable people to socialize or hang around with mob leaders, which, in turn, adds to the respect in which they are held within the underworld and gives them a kind of credibility that would otherwise be lacking. These people forget or ignore the fact that the mob often extorts from innocent people, and that the mob is involved in other activities that are not as benign as are bookmaking, prostitution, and loan-sharking. These are the importation and distribution of hard drugs such as heroin, the fencing of stolen goods, extortion, armed robbery, kidnapping, and murder. The mob, through control of an industry or a product, can also substantially increase the price of everyday goods. Jonathan Kwitny, in *Vicious Circles: The Mafia in the Marketplace*, eloquently answers those in society who would defend or make excuses for the mob.

I have no dispute with prostitutes, pornography, football betting, cards, marijuana or other pursuits of the nonviolent adult population. This book is not the argument of a kill joy or religious moralist. It is rather, the argument of one of millions ... who would like to buy food, clothing, and other goods without paying an overcharge to support a network of thieves; who would like to patronize merchants who freely choose their products on the basis of quality and cost, without the interference of bribery and physical intimidation; who would like to take a job in any industry and join an honest labor union that would negotiate in the worker's best interest; who would like taxes reduced to cover only the actual cost of services of an honest government, without additional expenses for contracts puffed up by bribes, or for excessive repair work because sub-standard materials have been used on roads, buildings, and other projects; and who would like to expel from society a class of persons who live like kings but whose only contribution is to innovate new ways to steal from the wealth produced by hard-working citizens.

In reading this account of the mob in Canada it would be useful to keep this realistic perspective in mind. The mob is not here to make life easier for the average citizen. It exists primarily to exploit and profit from our weaknesses, and acts as a corrupting force in our society. As senior Crown attorney Howard Morton said in court in 1981, in a case involving the Commisso crime family of Toronto, "Organized crime exists in the Province of Ontario. It is not a myth created by law enforcement agencies. Regrettably it is a despicable fact of life. Organized crime is international in scope, difficult to detect and investigate because of the insidious manner in which it operates."

The strength of a Mafia leader is derived from smoke and mirrors. It is not so much having the power and respect as *acting* as if you have the power and respect. This is what Toronto mobster Paul Volpe did so consummately. He played the part of a mob leader well and, as a result, did have a lot of power and respect. However, this was an illusion more than a reality. In 1983 Volpe had no real muscle or massive organization to support him. Someone, most likely someone senior in the Toronto Calabrian Mafia, called his bluff. The smoke dissipated and the mirrors shattered and all that was left was the bullet-riddled body of Paul Volpe stuffed in the trunk of his own car. Where is the power, the respect?

This murder of a top gangster is not an isolated incident or a highly unusual one in organized crime in general or the Mafia specifically, now or in the past. In fact the tradition has been that if someone has a lot of power and respect in the mob, then he is extremely vulnerable to power plays and the machinations of rival mobs or upwardly mobile young Turks in his own organization. You only have to look at the body-strewn history of the mob in North America to see this point: from the murders of New York City Mafia chieftains Giuseppe Masseria and Salvatore Marazano in 1931 and the so-called consolidation of the Mafia under Lucky Luciano to the more recent shooting deaths of the highly respected Mafia bosses of Philadelphia (Angelo Bruno), New York City (Carmine Galente), Montreal (Paolo Violi), and Toronto (Paul Volpe) in the late seventies and early eighties. Respect breeds contempt in some, and in the mob that means you are dead.

Respect is an extremely fragile commodity in the underworld, one that can be shattered by a mere bullet. It is also in the mob a grossly exaggerated phenomenon, primarily because the Mafia is an illegal, underworld organization, and power is gained internally from respect rather than from legitimacy.

One of the things that distinguishes the mob from the legitimate world is its language. Mobsters, rounders, mob associates, and street people speak in a jargon that is all their own. It is a world where one lives either on the street or in the joint (that is, in the criminal underworld of the city or in jail). It is a world of "wise guys who take action" (professional criminals actively involved in criminal pursuits) and of "people" (mobsters) "on the lam" (hiding from the police). To "take out" someone means more than going out for a walk. It means "putting them to sleep with the fish" – or, in everyday parlance, murdering them. There are lots of euphemisms in the mob. When an enforcer says that you have to pay him "or you owe me nothing," he doesn't mean you don't have to pay. Rather, he means that if you don't pay you will be "taken care of", which is to say you will be beaten or killed. A "torch job" is an arson, not a song; a "Bay Street loan shark" is a higher species than a mere loan shark; he wears business suits and operates with a higher class of people without getting his hands dirty. When you "know people" you are considered well connected in the underworld. You don't say, "My uncle is a Mafia don," but rather, "My uncle knows people." When you "take the beef" you are not ordering a Big Mac, but going to jail for a crime that others either did or helped you with. When you are "taking something down" it is a crime you are working on, not an Aspirin. And so on. This street language can also be non-verbal. For instance, when a mobster puts his hand on his heart, it is not to indicate heartburn, but to signal that the person who has just come into the room is okay. Such body language is an integral part of the "street" way of carrying on business with the minimum of interference from outsiders. It is highly efficient and exclusive, the result of what Marshall McLuhan would call an "oral" rather than an "anal" tradition, a tradition where things do not have to be written down and analysed to be understood.

In the world of good guys versus bad guys, it can be a bit unsettling to discover that all is not black and white, that a mobster may be more interesting, colourful, and even appealing than the average member of the police force (though there are colourful cops, too). Part of this is rooted in their backgrounds and traditions. The bad guys in this case come from an oral tradition and speak with a salty street vernacular; they are generally outgoing, gregarious, and open – everything seems to flow naturally. Most of us, including the police, are from a more restrained, Anglo-Saxon tradition, more introspective and, in Canada, more uptight, tending to speak and act in a less spontaneous manner; in the case of the police and the government bureaucracies in general, things do not really exist until they are on paper in the form of memos, reports, and so on. Those in the underworld are constantly exploiting this tendency in the legitimate or "straight" world to their advantage, and are often able to keep one step ahead of the forces of law and order, by hook or by crook. The street world, simply put, cuts out the paperwork.

Paul Volpe and some of the other mobsters presented in this book have a certain charisma and charm, but it should never be forgotten that this is a veneer; behind this appealing human face lies a diabolical cunning that is constantly plotting our demise and looking for ways to exploit our weaknesses. In the language of the street, they are always looking to "take us for a walk" or scheming how to take advantage of natural weaknesses in us for their own monetary gain. The bottom line in the underworld, as one of its inhabitants cynically said, is that "money talks and bullshit walks."

Mob figures exist not to provide us with entertainment, but to make easy money by taking someone in some way. Former mobster Chuck Carlo put it this way: "The name of the game is to make money ... nothing else matters.... So how did I make my money? I made it through scheming, conning, treachery, crime." Vincent Piersante, the head of Michigan's organized-crime strike force, who has spent a lifetime monitoring and combating organized crime, eloquently sums up the character of a top crime figure: "Probably the most charming individuals that you could be fortunate or unfortunate enough to meet in your lifetime. They are well disciplined, well groomed, and have an understanding of human nature that I think is so much greater than most people that you meet. But you have to remember that even though they exude a benevolent paternalism ... they are easy to get personal favours from, easy to get personal loans from ... that the basis for their status is the fact that they are willing to participate in such evil acts as murder. Some of these charming individuals that I know are really there because they are stone killers."

CHAPTER ONE

The Old Walton Street Crowd: Paul Volpe's Early Years

SATURDAY, JANUARY 29, 1927, was unseasonably balmy for midwinter in Toronto. The city's bootleggers, hotel prowls, high-graders, and Black Hand extortionists were operating with their usual efficiency, and professional thieves pulled a major fur heist at the Lewis Fur Company at 215 Church Street in the downtown area. Several blocks away, on Walton Street, just off Yonge and Bay streets, Elizabeth Volpe gave birth to her seventh son. The seventh son of the seventh son, according to folklore, is the child of the Devil.

Paul Volpe never knew his father, an impoverished tailor who had recently moved to Toronto with his family from New York City. The two eldest Volpe children, Patsy and Johnny, had stayed on in the States, one in Connecticut and one in New York City. Not long after Paul's birth, Volpe's father abandoned Elizabeth and left her to bring up the remaining children, five sons (Frank, Eugene, Albert, Joseph, and Paul) and one daughter, Laura. It was a very humble home.

It was in the heart of what was then the Italian immigrant community, an area running between Yonge and Bay streets and Gerrard and Dundas in downtown Toronto (a couple of blocks north of the Eaton Centre and behind the current site of the Chelsea Inn), and part of what was known as "the Ward". At the time, this was a very colourful residential area of immigrants, writers, and artists, and it had a reputation as the city's Bohemian quarter – a reputation it held from the 1920s until the '50s – a sort of poor man's Greenwich Village. The streets were lined with charming Victorian houses.

The Orde Street Public School, established in 1914 (and today still functioning as a school), stood behind the old police station that is now part of the Ontario College of Art, on College Street just west of University Avenue, and that is where Paul Volpe went to public school. On his way to and from school he would have taken in much of the richness and colour of the neighbourhood. Daily, Volpe would have passed the comparatively posh Murray Street area near Orde Street; perhaps he paused to admire the splendour of the homes and cars of the well-to-do who lived there, thinking that this was something to aspire to. What is now the Theatre-in-the-Dell was at the time a candy and grocery store, and it is likely that Volpe would have stopped in here on his way home.

The art-deco-style Ford Hotel was at the corner of Dundas and Bay. Across the street there was a seedy downstairs poolroom where lots of gambling, off-track betting, and other illegal action went on and where local bookies and other criminals used to meet. Mary John's was for years a popular restaurant at the corner of Elizabeth and Gerrard streets, and was famous for its inexpensive home cooking in a city that did not have a great number of good, reasonably priced restaurants. Ernest Hemingway used to eat at Mary John's regularly in the 1920s when he was working as a reporter for the *Toronto Star* and he lived along the street in a small apartment at 40 Gerrard Street West, in part of what was called Gerrard Village. Mandolin players used to perform in the streets to the delight of the area's children and residents. Just a few blocks away from where Paul Volpe was born, near Gerrard and University, "America's Sweetheart", 1920s film star Mary Pickford, was born. A smaller, modest version of the Women's College Street Hospital was also nearby in what is now the hospital centre of the city.

At the corner of Walton and Bay there was a butcher shop, which later expanded, moved down one block to Elm and Bay, and served as the first local supermarket, selling tobacco, food, and many household items including olive oil, brought in by the well-known Hamilton-based international bootlegger Rocco Perri. There was a restaurant with apartments above it at the northwest corner of Walton and Yonge. Also on Walton Street were Chinese whorehouses, which continued until the Second World War dried up the business ("The girls depended upon the volume," according to a long-time resident). It certainly was a stimulating neighbourhood to grow up in.

In the 1920s and '30s, the Volpe family lived on the poverty line. Their tiny house at 35 Walton Street was horribly rat-infested, and Paul later told stories of how his mother had to catch the rats and choke them to death with her bare hands to protect her children. She was that kind of woman: strong, resourceful, and dominant. Paul was always deeply attached to his mother, especially as a child, when he was, as the youngest son, a "momma's boy". Often young Paul would push his sister away so that he could hang onto his mother's skirts. This had at least one unfortunate lifelong effect on him. One day Mrs. Volpe accidentally dropped a cauldron of scalding water on the young boy, sending him to the hospital and giving him a scar on his chest that he bore all his life.

"Paulie", as he was affectionately called by his family and closest friends, was only twelve years old when the Second World War broke out. Later he was fond of saying that more than anything else, he wished he could have gone and fought for Canada as, according to Paul, his older brother Eugene Volpe did with distinction in military intelligence.* But Paul was just a teenager, and he was left behind to make his own way.

Leaving school about the time his brother Eugene went to fight for Canada, he lived and worked on the streets, soon becoming a toughened street kid. He did odd jobs, helped his mother, hung around with other punks, and generally lazed about, mixing with the colourful characters of the area. Paul remained a functional illiterate all his life; he could barely read or write. But he could certainly talk. Paul was always a real charmer, highly manipulative, seductively endearing, and a master of the "con" even as a teenager.

Physically he was a presence too. He was over six feet tall with heavy, oddly rounded shoulders. He looked just like James

---

*Patriotism is a recurring theme with many American and Canadian mobsters: Rocco Perri, the self-proclaimed King of the Bootleggers of the 1920s and '30s, said in a newspaper interview in 1939 that even though he was still technically an Italian citizen, he wanted to "fight for England" and Canada in the war, even against Italy, his homeland. Many American mobsters, notably Lucky Luciano, helped in the Allied invasion of Sicily in 1944.

Caan in *The Godfather* without his shirt on, according to one Volpe confidante. He had a medium build, a dark complexion, and a prominent nose that appeared to have been broken in his early youth, probably in a street fight. His appearance conveyed a sort of authority.

With his presence and charm, he survived on the streets, gaining street smarts through trial and error. He also helped out in the family bootleg business. But, being poor, uneducated, and Italian, he was the quintessential outsider in the WASP Toronto of the 1930s and '40s. He was to resent this outsider status all his life, and used it in later years to get sympathy and understanding. Many mobsters throughout North America share this resentment and motivation, including Jewish, Chinese, black, Puerto Rican, French-Canadian, and other gangsters who were treated as inferiors by the majority because of their ethnic backgrounds and the poverty in which they were raised.

Volpe's sexual initiation came about in 1942 as the war raged in Europe. In later years Volpe would tell certain intimates the details to prove that he was broadminded and experienced in many sexual things. The veteran Hollywood actor Michael Whalen, who had played the leading role as Shirley Temple's father in the celebrated 1930s classic film *Poor Little Rich Girl*, was in Toronto on a road show. He picked up the fifteen-year-old Paulie and a friend off the streets for a good time. According to Paul Volpe himself, the forty-three-year-old actor had a very brief sexual affair with the immature Paulie. There is no real indication that Volpe had any serious, long-term homosexual inclinations. To him this was a lark. He got some money out of it and a good time to boot. It was the normal experimentation of a teenager, especially one growing up on the streets of a large metropolitan centre.

Paul's homosexual period was short-lived, for by 1944 he was out fooling around with women. On one occasion, Paul picked up a beautiful CWAC and took her to Cherry Beach for a brief encounter (the Chinese whorehouses on his street being closed by this point). She was wearing a standard Canadian army-issue blouse, the large buttons of which unfortunately got entangled with Paul's testicles as he pressed in for the kill. Paul later told the story to intimates with a forced laugh as he remembered the discomfort he had for a week.

Also in 1944, Paul Volpe was involved in an unspecified incident on the streets that resulted in his being charged with "willful damage". This is the first offence to appear on his record, but it was trivial, tough, street-kid stuff. He was remanded.

About the time Paul Volpe was playing with CWACs and causing willful damage on the streets of Toronto, a significant event took place in southern Ontario's underworld. On April 23, 1944, Rocco Perri, who had ruled the bootleg trade in the 1920s and '30s and was now living in Toronto after spending several years interned under the War Measures Act as an enemy alien, went down to visit a cousin in Hamilton and mysteriously disappeared. He had told his host that he had a headache and was going for a walk to clear his head. He never returned. His body was never discovered, but most informed underworld and police sources reported that he was cement-coated and dumped into Hamilton Bay. This was one of the final acts of the bootlegging wars of the 1920s and '30s. A year later Louis Wernick, a Perri crime underling who was heavily involved in bootlegging and drug importation in Toronto, Buffalo, and Hamilton, was found in a snowbank near Long Branch Race Track with five bullet wounds in his head and back. Two other underworld murders of Perri associates followed that year in rapid succession.

If Rocco Perri had not lived, it might have been necessary to invent him, if only for the sake of Canada's self-image. Perri was the first of the archetypal "dons" in Canada and, from 1916 to 1944, one of the most colourful of Hamilton's underworld figures. Perri provided the necessary transition between the less structured, somewhat random violence of the Black Handers, extortionists who preyed on hapless Italian immigrants, and today's powerful Mafia, whose tentacles pry into every aspect of southern Ontario's underworld activities of the 1980s.

Perri's vehicle to notoriety was, of course, Prohibition. "That great and noble experiment", Herbert Hoover once called it. With hindsight, however, it appears a fruitless attempt to legislate morality that only made criminals of ordinary people. It also made any of those willing to take a few risks extremely wealthy in a big hurry. If most of the population already felt like criminals, it requires no great leap of faith to understand the idolatry, the fascination, and the popular myths that grew to surround men like Rocco Perri, Al Capone, Bugs Moran, or Detroit's Purple Gang.

But Prohibition offered the same opportunity to many people. Why were Al Capone and Rocco Perri to become so prominent? They owed their success to a lucky convergence of factors that, as it turned out, did not all depend on fate. Given the opportunity, Perri proved that he shared the organizational skills, the ruthlessness, and the instinct for self-promotion and publicity that characterized Al Capone.

Perri, as we have seen, was a well-known figure in the Walton-Gerrard area. In the late 1920s and early '30s he used to come by regularly in his large Marmot to deliver barrels of olive oil and booze to local establishments. One veteran resident remembers that he used to give quarters to the children as he passed. It is very likely that the young Paul Volpe saw and looked up to this ostentatious, gregarious old bootlegger and crime figure as he made his rounds. But by 1944 the old bootlegger was a shadow of his former self, and he was easily taken out of the action. Perri had outlived his usefulness within the gangster community of his day in southern Ontario.*

Whether the youthful Paul Volpe took much interest in the demise of Rocco Perri and his associates is anyone's guess, but these events were certainly the talk of the neighbourhood. It was not long after this that the Volpe brothers themselves became heavily involved in bootlegging. This, of course, was post-Prohibition bootlegging, but there was still a market in strait-laced Toronto for off-hours booze. It was said that a prescription from a doctor was needed to get any alcohol at a reasonable hour. Those who lived the fast life couldn't be bothered to buy their booze only on certain days at certain hours, and hence a new demand for bootleg liquor was created.

Paul was simply the delivery boy and general errand-runner for some of his older brothers. A party would ring up for booze, and within minutes young Paul Volpe would be at the door delivering the order. Although this may not have been the most auspicious start for a future crime leader, he did make a lot of interesting and useful contacts on his rounds. Everyone has to start somewhere. Paul Volpe just worked his way up the ladder, starting at the bottom.

---

*The story of the bootleg empire of Rocco Perri and the mob wars of the 1920s and '30s is a story in itself. The Addendum, Part I, details the rise and fall of this self-styled King of the Bootleggers, Canada's Al Capone.

In the late 1940s and early '50s, Walton Street, where Paul Volpe lived until 1955 and operated for decades thereafter (and where he owned property until the late '70s), was itself at the centre of some major underworld activity. It was a place where street people from all parts of the city, from Cabbagetown to St. Clair West and from out of town, came to hang around, make deals, conduct meetings, arrange card games and off-track betting, and generally socialize. Walton Street was definitely "downtown" without being the centre of the commercial area as it now is (though a sentimentalist like Paul Volpe continued to meet his people on Walton Street until the very end).

Walton Street was peopled with many interesting characters other than mobsters, many of whom later went on to distinguished careers in law, business, and politics. Of the Walton Street regulars, one became one of the most prominent real-estate entrepreneurs in Toronto, another a prominent radio personality, another a prominent provincial court judge, another a successful businessman who started a popular local dinner theatre, another a celebrated clothing magnate, another a construction tycoon, another a well-known boxing promoter, another a prominent city alderman, and yet another the leader of the major crime group in Toronto. This was the Walton Street mix.

Life on Walton Street in the old days was life in the fast lane – the exotic world of colourful street people with schemes on the brain – deals both criminal and marginally legal. There was Bassel's Restaurant, on Yonge across from Walton (it replaced Childs' Restaurant, a popular hang-out at Dundas Square and Yonge Street frequented by street people and musicians until it closed in the early 1950s). Bassel's was where the rounders and street people used to gather, arrange crap games, stock frauds, and scams, and, as they say on the street, "take action".

"Lou", an underworld informer interviewed in the CBC *Connections* series (disguised in a black hood), was close to all the Volpes and himself a part of the old Walton Street crowd. He described the area in a portion of the interview not used in the programs:

Volpe started on Walton Street. In the early fifties I was a downtowner hanging around Walton Street at Bassel's Restaurant. The Volpes were not organized crime then. They had a booze factory going, bootlegging. Later they bought a car wash on

Walton Street.... Paul was a nothing.... We'd go gambling....

Walton Street consisted of a tremendous amount of people. The Walton Street gang started at the corner of Walton and Yonge, directly across the street from Bassel's. Every house was a bootlegger or card games.... And eventually Frankie Nassau [also known as Nasso, a Toronto lawyer] *got involved on the street. Pucci used to hang around there as well as Sam Shirose* [two later Paul Volpe partners in real estate and gambling, respectively]. *Some of the Volpes were born on that street. And it became an Italian community. Walton Street belongs to the Volpes because they lived and grew up there.*

Staff Inspector Tom D. Macleod, a veteran Metropolitan Toronto policeman, recently retired, who had the Walton Street area as his beat at the time, confirms Lou's description. Macleod says the Walton Street area was the centre of the street and night life in the Toronto uptown area, while the King Edward Hotel and the Mercury Restaurant were favourites for rounders and more sophisticated street people downtown. "There was Tops Restaurant, Bassel's, and many second-hand stores in the area. Walton Street itself was lined with homes.... There was a Checker Cab outlet and a fish-and-chips joint where the Colosseum Restaurant now is.... Visiting Americans [including those of the underworld variety] used to congregate there.... Some used to call it Yongee [accenting the "e"] Street."

Florence Vale, the widow of renowned Canadian artist Albert Franck, who lived in the area at Gerrard and Elizabeth streets from 1946 until 1954, remembers a delightful mixture of charming old houses and "nice little shops with Dickensian-like paned windows and a door, and the Old Chelsea Shop was there, a wonderful old antique store." It was a wonderful neighbourhood. "Everyone was oh-so-friendly," she says. "There were all types of people, artists, writers, much like Greenwich Village." She remembers there was an old house, "a little bungalow, like a cottage," owned by Italians around the corner off Gerrard, where everyone used to get booze, which was referred to by everyone in the neighbourhood as "the bootlegger's". (This was possibly Volpe's place.) "We always had to have a bootlegger around, in those days, to get a bottle of liquor in the middle of the night."

The world of the Walton Street crowd of the late 1940s and

early '50s was an exotic one, and this was the world of Paul Volpe's youth. They included criminal characters and street people with names like "One-Eyed Connelly", "The Mope", "Wingy", "Hot Nuts Louie", Harry "the Hat" Hamilton, Lenny the Fireman, and so on. Also, the old Walton Street crowd practised what in the 1970s and '80s would be considered the "old values" in their criminal pursuits.

This was where Paul Volpe got his entrée to the criminal world, but it was Paul himself who was to create a criminal empire, carved out of the raw material of the exotica of Walton Street and the surrounding areas in downtown Toronto.

Even in the early 1950s, before Paul Volpe became a "name", he was known by people on the street and by police as someone who operated without regard to legal technicalities, especially in the bootleg trade, the fencing of stolen goods, and illegal gambling activities. Tom Macleod says of the Paul Volpe he knew in the early '50s: "He was a dapper individual, well built. He was an outgoing person and well known around the community. He was close to the community. We [the police] knew him.... He was involved in unlawful activity at the time: bootlegging, card games. He was easygoing, though he could handle himself on the street."

In November 1952, Detective Macleod had an unusual, though he says not entirely surprising, encounter with Paul Volpe. He and his partner, Constable Sam Priestly, were investigating an attempted stabbing incident at the King Edward Hotel late on the evening of November 11, 1952. When Macleod and Priestly arrived, hotel security staff at the scene were holding a suspect. They told the officers that a tall, athletic young man had subdued the knife-wielding attacker as he was stabbing a hotel detective, fifty-six-year-old Christopher Forrest, in the lobby of the hotel. The young man courageously intervened by grappling with the assailant, later identified as Karol Bardeur and described in the newspapers rather non-descriptively as a "forty-year-old new Canadian". Then the young man blocked the exit door with his foot, at considerable risk to his own life, as Bardeur tried to escape. He then left the scene without even giving his name. Christopher Forrest, the security officer, was taken to hospital with a stab wound, but he was in good condition as a result of the timely intervention.

The papers dubbed the young man the "Mystery Hero" in

their headlines on November 12, but it didn't take Detective Macleod long to find out from street people that the "mystery hero" was none other than the young bootlegger and well-known Walton Street resident Paul Volpe.

Volpe, it turns out, was meeting with lawyer Frankie Nassau in the lobby of the King Edward Hotel, where Nassau lived. Volpe witnessed the attack and leapt into action without thinking of his own safety. The Toronto *Telegram* of November 12, 1952, published a front-page photo of the hero, and quoted police as "lauding his quick-thinking action." Volpe himself was quoted as saying that he left the scene because "I thought there would be an investigation and I might get into trouble." Volpe was described in the papers as an "all-round athlete and contractor from 35 Walton Street." Though a defender of law and order (at least for the day), he didn't want to have to expose himself to official scrutiny. In this incident Paul Volpe, at the age of twenty-five, certainly demonstrated that he was impulsive and capable of great physical courage, and that, even at this early period, he was distrustful of the police.

Paul was a hero for only a few days, for he had real reason to be apprehensive of the police. As it turns out, they were in the process of closing in on the Volpes' illegal bootleg operation. Paul Volpe, the delivery boy, magnanimously offered to take the rap for the family and protected those of his brothers who were involved by pretending to be the sole owner of the bootlegging business. As a result, in early 1953, Volpe served sixty days of a ninety-day sentence for bootlegging in Mimico Reformatory.

However, the days of the Volpe bootleg business were coming to a close, as the risks of prosecution and jail increased. Also, the neighbourhood was quickly changing to a commercial area and people were selling out and moving. The family decided to go legit, so they put their bootleg profits into a car wash, which they opened up on Walton Street in 1954 (the front entrance was on Gerrard Street near what is now the Chelsea Inn). They also bought a house on Pricefield Road in Rosedale, where the Volpe family moved in 1955. The upwardly mobile Volpes were finally on the social ascent, and Paul Volpe and his family were very proud of living in Rosedale, even though it wasn't the best part of Rosedale. Meanwhile, the car wash thrived.

His arrest and imprisonment gave Paul Volpe time for thought. He was still searching for direction, and from 1953 to 1956 he did try a number of legitimate jobs, though he continued to build up contacts and connections for a criminal thrust as well. In early 1954, he took his share of the bootleg profits and opened up a paving business with a friend named David Steiner. But there were major cash-flow problems with the business. Volpe and Steiner didn't really have enough capital or business expertise to keep things going, and the company soon folded. In 1955 Paul worked in the pit at the car wash, actually washing cars, though police now confirm that there was a lot of criminal action taking place on the side there as well.

In 1956 his older brother, Albert Volpe, became a stockbroker and stock promoter, and he soon opened a small brokerage firm; among others, a now prominent Toronto restaurateur worked for him as a salesman there. Paul decided to try the stock business, too, and he studied for and took the stockbroker's examination. But it was hopeless. Because of his lack of education, and especially his near illiteracy, Paul flunked the test, and at this point organized crime as a career option began to look far more attractive.

Sometime between 1953 and 1956, according to his later testimony before a royal commission, Paul Volpe had befriended a young Italian immigrant from Hamilton named Vincenzo "Jimmy" Luppino. This was to be an important contact, for Jimmy Luppino's father was a Mafia don from the old country. He was a respected figure in certain areas of Calabria, and as a result had some respect in Hamilton and Toronto as well.

In 1957 Paul Volpe made a decision that was to change his life. He decided to abandon all attempts at a legitimate career. (In a much later conversation with a mob enforcer during an extortion that was being secretly taped by police in 1965, Paul Volpe admitted that legitimate businesses required too much up-front money and "that's the trouble with legitimate businesses.... I don't like them.") Also, he decided to break away from his brothers and establish his own identity. Since he couldn't make it, or didn't want to make it, in the conventional sense, he consciously chose a career as a criminal. "Better to reign in hell than serve in heav'n," as Satan says in Milton's *Paradise Lost*. A "seventh son of the seventh son", as he often used to refer to himself, a child of the Devil as folklore has it, it was natural for Paul to be a rebel and join the underworld. He was living up to his name as well, for *volpe* in Italian means "fox", and it took all the cunning he could muster for Paul Volpe to survive and prosper in the criminal world. Paul Volpe, if he was anything in his life, was certainly as crafty, dissembling, and carnivorous as any fox of the quadruped variety. Paul was also attracted by the easy money, the glamour, and the covert nature of a life of crime. Becoming an outlaw was romantic, exciting, and the major gamble of Paul Volpe's life.

Since he had decided on a criminal career, the natural model for Paul Volpe, coming from the milieu he did, was of course the legendary Mafia.

CHAPTER TWO

The Black Hand

I TALIAN ORGANIZED-CRIME activity was not new to Ontario. There is much evidence of major Mafia-style crime activity in the United States as far back as 1890, and in Ontario as early as 1906.

The Hamilton, Niagara Peninsula, and Toronto areas have been the centre of mob activity in English Canada since the first years of the twentieth century. Here the Black Hand and other Italian gangs were involved in extortions, bombings, and murders involving people from as far away as Italy and New York City. In a series of over fifty murders, rival Italian gangs littered the streets with bodies in the fight for control of territory.

While Prime Minister Laurier proudly announced in 1904, "Canada shall fill the twentieth century," those in the southern Ontario underworld might just as accurately have predicted that "the twentieth century will be filled with the Mafia in Canada." Certainly the new century saw the emergence of powerful organized-crime groups in southern Ontario based upon Italian Mafia structures. It all started with the Black Hand, an organization from the old country that had surfaced in the United States in the Gay Nineties and reached Canada in the first decade of the century.

In 1890 the chief of police of New Orleans, David Hennessy, began investigating Black Hand activities in his city, where there was an ongoing rivalry between two Black Hand gangs from Sicily, one run by Carlo Matranga and the other by the Provenzano brothers. At the height of his investigations, Hennessy returned home one night at eleven. As he was unlocking his front door, he was shot six times. Hennessy took ten hours to die, but the only word he uttered was "dagos". He had touched a raw nerve. And while the city of New Orleans responded with horror and an all-out crackdown on the gangs, it showed as well that the Black Handers were willing to go to great lengths to instil fear and avoid arrest. Nineteen Sicilian mafiosi, proven to be members of a secret organization known as the Mafia "beyond a shadow of a doubt", according to the grand jury, were arrested as co-conspirators in the murder, but because of insufficient evidence they were later released. An angry New Orleans mob, however, was not as gracious, and eleven of the accused Mafia members were killed, two lynched on city lamp-posts and nine shot to death. It was mob rule over *the* mob rule!

It is a mistake to look at the Black Hand as a highly organized or structured phenomenon, even though Black Handers were bold enough to kill the chief of police and others who got in their way. Noted criminologist Francis Ianni puts it this way in his essay "Mafia and the Web of Kinship":

In the early days of the Italian ghettos the crimes reported in the press were, in fact, Italian crimes.... Almost as soon as they arrived the Italians brought public notice to crime in the ghetto through the Black Hand: a series of threats, murders, maimings, and bombings as a means of extorting money from fellow immigrants.... What seems clear from all of the evidence is that the Black Hand, which lasted about fifteen years (from the turn of the century to the First World War), was a cultural but not an organizational offshoot of Mafia and was completely Italian in origin and character.

At the turn of the century, when the great Italian operatic singer Enrico Caruso performed at the Metropolitan Opera House in New York City, he was forced by the Black Hand to pay huge sums of money upon threat of death. He secretly paid approximately $1,000 of each $10,000 he earned at the Met to Black Hand leaders in New York to get them off his back. However, after he was asked for $15,000 from the Black Handers, Caruso finally went to the police, who eventually arrested two Italian "businessmen" who were behind the extortions. These early Mafia bosses in New York City in the early years of the century were much like the young Don Corleone as presented in Mario Puzo's novel *The Godfather*. They were gentlemanly thugs, respected and feared in the Italian immigrant community.

Violence was frequent in the United States. In 1909, Lieutenant Joseph Petrosino, the most knowledgeable New York City cop working on the Black Hand organization there, was sent by the city's police commissioner on a secret mission to Sicily to follow through his leads on ongoing criminal activity in New York City. On March 13, 1909, the Black Hand struck, and Lieutenant Petrosino was shot down in the streets of Palermo in broad daylight.

It was in the same year that the Black Hand first came to public notice as a Canadian-based phenomenon as well. In fact, the arrest and trial of five Black Handers was one of the major news events in Canada that year.

There were two sensational and interrelated cases in Hamilton in 1909, involving the head of the Black Hand organization in southern Ontario, Joseph Taglerino (also known as John), and five of his subordinates, Carmelo Colombo, Ernest Speranzo, Sam Wolfe, Ralph Rufus, and Joseph Courto. Up to this point the "Black Hand" had simply been seen in Canada in newspaper stories about murders and other events in such faraway places as New Orleans, New York City, and Italy.

The trials that took place in Hamilton between October and December 1909 brought together an impressive array of legal talent. Taglerino's lawyer was Louis Vincent McBrady, a prominent Toronto lawyer who was vice-president of the Toronto Reform Association, and the counsel for three of the other Black Handers was Thomas Cowper Robinette, KC. T. C. Robinette was famous at the time for his flamboyant courtroom manner, his defence of the underdog, especially in the immigrant Italian and Jewish communities, and his defence (albeit unsuccessful) of the notorious police killer Fred Rice in 1901. (T. C.'s son is J. J. Robinette, later to become the dean of Canadian trial lawyers with a reputation for brilliance in his own right. J. J. was born in 1906, the year the first Black Hand letter is known to have appeared in Canada.) The judge in this early Black Hand case was The Honourable Mr. Justice Colin George Snider, a former president of the United Empire Loyalists' Association and the head of the Royal Commission for the Revision of the Ontario Statutes in 1906.

It was a hot case. On March 9, 1909, Hamilton Crown attorney S. F. Washington personally attended at Queen's Park in Toronto to brief the premier, Sir James Whitney, and the attorney general, James J. Foy, on the situation. The closed-door meeting dealt with "certain crooks supposed to have their headquarters in Hamilton," according to the Hamilton *Spectator* of March 10, 1909.

The events that led up to the Black Hand trials of 1909 had begun in 1906 when an Italian fruit dealer from Hamilton, one Salvatore Sansone (spelled in the newspapers of the time "Sanzone") of North James Street, received a letter demanding a thousand dollars in extortion money. Sansone knew from the old country what this meant. Mafia writer Frederic Sondern, Jr., in his essay "How the Mafia Came to America", describes the Black Hand extortion technique this way:

Mafia extortion gangs simply used the imprint of a hand as a signature on their warnings, ransom notes, and other demands. In Sicily for decades they had signed with a skull, a dagger or a hand. In America they discovered – and they have always been clever psychologists – that the hand was for some reason the most effective symbol. The first targets of the brotherhood were prosperous Italian farmers and merchants, who understood the Mafia's capabilities. A Long Island truck farmer would receive a notice to leave a hundred dollars in cash in a certain place, or else. The note was written in the unmistakable Mafia style of the Sicilian dialect and signed with The Hand – the Mano Nera. If he failed to meet the deadline, a stenciled black hand would appear on a fence or a side of the house. That was the final warning.

The early Black Hand extortions in Hamilton followed the same pattern. According to the testimony of Taglerino's subordinate Ralph Rufus, Taglerino ordered him to write threatening letters to Sansone from his home in Toronto containing threats on Sansone's life and signed "Revolver". Joseph Courto, another Taglerino underling, testified that Ernesto Speranzo wrote the first such letter to Sansone under direct orders from Taglerino;

he later posted it himself from Niagara Falls. According to trial accounts, Taglerino broke down and cried in the prisoner's dock as Courto gave his evidence.

In the first trial, which took place in Hamilton in October, the three Taglerino underlings were found guilty of attempted extortion. They did not have much chance of acquittal. Police, aided by Sansone, had caught them red-handed in the act of extortion on Dundas Street in Hamilton – and had arrested them on the spot. Sansone testified that he had been hounded by various members of the Black Hand for three years. In a later, related trial, Taglerino and his subordinates were tried and convicted of extortion. The letters, signed with the Black Hand, figured prominently in the evidence against them.

Poor Sansone never quite got over his fear of revenge from the Black Hand for his co-operation with the police and his testimony against them. As late as March 1910, the Hamilton *Herald* featured an article headlined: "Sanzone Worried; Italian Has Not Got Over the Black Hand Scare." To get the flavour of the fear prevalent in the Italian community in Hamilton at the time it is worth quoting part of the *Herald* piece:

Although the three Black Hand men who attempted to extort money from Salvatore Sanzone, the North James Street fruit dealer, are now lodged behind prison bars, apparently the last has not been heard of them or their friends. The wealthy Italian fruit dealer whose life they threatened is living in constant dread of some of the convicted men's friends seeking vengeance on him or his children.

Since the three Black Hand men were found guilty and sentenced to long terms in Kingston Penitentiary, Sanzone has been, according to his relatives, in fear of Black Hand men molesting his children. Day in and day out, despite the weather conditions, Sanzone accompanies them to the separate schools they attend and at the noon hour and closing hour he always calls for them.

Shortly after the Black Handers were captured, Sanzone was seized with heart trouble, and he has been under medical care ever since. The fear that his children will meet with harm as a result of his assisting in the capture of the trio has been playing on his mind and relatives of his say he is almost a physical wreck....

Only Italians and the police are acquainted with the steps

members of the Black Hand organization take to seek revenge on those who inform on them, and Sanzone is guarding his children night and day in case some attempt may be made to harm them or lure them away with malicious intent. (emphasis mine)

Such was the grim state of affairs in the Italian community in southern Ontario in 1910. But things got worse.

By the late teens and early '20s the Black Hand in southern Ontario was involved in a series of bombings and murders. One day in March 1921, Monaco Natale (or Natale Monaco, as the newspapers seem to have got the first and last names reversed with some Italian names and also frequently erred in spellings) received a letter demanding a thousand dollars. The stationery depicted a black hand and was marked with a cross. Natale was instructed to take the money to the GTR Bridge on John Street in Hamilton, where he would be met by a Black Hander who would accept the extortion payment. Natale failed to comply. Two and a half months later, at one o'clock in the morning, a bomb rocked Natale's house at 7G Sheaffe Street. The windows were blown out and the glass was driven deep inside the bedroom, but miraculously no one was injured. The explosion was of such force that it was heard in remote parts of the city of Hamilton.

The Black Hand bombings in Hamilton reached their peak with the Simcoe Street bombings of 1922–23. On September 17, 1922, the home of Vincenzo Napoli at 32 Simcoe Street West was bombed. On October 4, 1922, the home of Mrs. Pauline Lombardo of 36 Simcoe Street West was bombed. Mrs. Lombardo's next-door neighbour had been receiving Black Hand letters, and the October 4 bombing was apparently intended for him. Mrs. Lombardo, an elderly Sicilian immigrant, is quoted as saying that she did not believe that she was marked by the Black Hand fraternity. Detective Goodman of the Hamilton police department said that the Black Handers definitely blew up the wrong house. "There is no reason why the home of this widow should be attacked.... They are after this house I believe," he is quoted as saying in front of 34 Simcoe Street in the Hamilton *Herald* on October 5.

The misdirected bomb affected everyone on the street, including victims who were not even Italian, let alone the subject of the extortion. Fifty windows in all were shattered. Mrs. James

Cook of 46 Simcoe was thrown out of her bed by the force of the explosion and lost the front windows of her house. Like many residents of Simcoe Street, Mrs. Cook decided that this second bomb blast in three weeks was the final outrage: "I've had enough of this kind of thing," she exclaimed to a Hamilton reporter, "and if someone wants a bargain in a good home send them to me." Miss C. Lawlor of 364 Bay Street, another unintended victim, was a non-Italian living in a predominantly Italian area. (It is important to note that Italian immigrants were the main targets for victimization of the Black Hand terrorists because they understood the tradition and were less likely to go to the authorities.) Miss Lawlor had just finished paying for the replacement of her windows from the earlier bombing when the new blast occurred, destroying ten more windows. Miss Lawlor, who had recently buried a brother and had just returned from hospital after a serious illness, declared that if something was not done to guaran tee the safety of Simcoe Street "all will be forced to abandon their property." She was a nervous wreck from the shock and felt that she had "reached the limit." This poor Englishwoman, who lived around the corner from Simcoe Street, hardly understood Italian, let alone the meaning of the "Black Hand" tradition of the old country.

There is no doubt that a "reign of terror" prevailed in Hamilton in the early 1920s. One newspaper said that "Italians throughout the city are considerably outraged" at the series of bombings perpetrated by the Black Hand Society. The judge in a case against some of the bombers denied bail on the basis that "men who would blow up another's house would do just about anything." Four weeks after the arrest of four of the bombers, the chief witness against them mysteriously disappeared.

The Simcoe Street bombings reached their climax on March 27, 1923, when the home of Sebastino Notto of 33 Simcoe Street was levelled. On that day the bombed-out remains of Notto's home were featured on the front pages of the Hamilton papers. The headlines screamed: "Terror Reigns Amongst Italians" and "Havoc Wrought by Black Hand This Morning." A family of twelve (the youngest a baby of fifteen months) were asleep in the house when a bomb, placed on the ledge of the front window, exploded at one o'clock, demolishing the entire front room of the house. Miraculously no one was injured but everyone was terribly shaken. Interviewed by the Hamilton *Herald*, Mr. Notto commented with some pathos: "No home ... nine kiddies ... cold." Asked if he knew of anything which might have prompted what the papers called the "bomb outrage", Notto plaintively replied, "Mebbe think me know something but I never talked – done nothing." No other explanation was offered by a clearly frightened Sebastino Notto.

On the same day as the Notto bombing, four men were arrested and charged with vagrancy. They were Joseph Restivo, Charles Bardinaro (another name for Calogero or Charlie Bordonaro, the old don of Hamilton, who was the father of Paul Volpe's long-time close friend, lawyer Harold Bordonaro, and one of Volpe's sponsors into the Mafia), and William Pasquale, all of Hamilton, and Joseph Scibetta of Buffalo. (The Scibettas later became one of the leading mob families in the Hamilton-Niagara region and even as recently as May 1985, when he died, Joseph's brother Santo Scibetta was a highly respected Mafia figure in Hamilton.) They were also held on a warrant that implicated them in the bombing of Vincenzo Napoli's house at 32 Simcoe Street in 1922. This ended the Simcoe Street terror, but bombings continued elsewhere throughout the city and the Italian community in Hamilton was justifiably alarmed.

On August 17, 1924, a seven-room house at 23 Murray Street, Hamilton, was blown to bits, leaving, according to newspaper accounts, "charred remains only where Sam Guallino's residence stood." This followed an arson job that had occurred only a week earlier at the home of Mrs. Guallino's brother, W. Agra (or Agro), at Bay and Stuart streets. According to the Hamilton *Herald*: "The Italian settlement was thrown into a turmoil when news of the explosion [at Guallino's house] spread. It turns out," the paper continues, "that Black Hand letters were received by friends and relatives of Guallino during the past three months.... Police believe the explosion to be the work of blackhanders." This was all too credible an explanation to the Hamiltonians of 1924 who had been through so many sensational Black Hand bombings and extortions over the past fifteen years. All quite routine, really.

A new ingredient in the Guallino bombing was that Guallino was deeply involved in the bootleg trade, as the remains of kegs of wine found in his cellar indicated. "Police guards have had their hands full this morning restraining spectators from hauling off the kegs," explained the Hamilton *Herald* reporter. This was at the height of the bootlegging gangland warfare that broke out in Canada and the United States.

In the decade between 1914 and 1924 there were also at least twenty sensational murders in the Italian community, mostly as a direct result either of Black Hand activity or of Italian criminal infighting over the lucrative bootleg trade. This chain of murders started with the murder of Hamiltonian Peter Basile in 1914. He was found in Lockport, N.Y., "riddled with bullets". The Basile family had been deeply involved in bootlegging even before the passage of the Ontario Temperance Act of 1916, and were one of the first organized criminal groups in the field. Consimina and Patsy Basile were shot to death in 1918, and in 1924 Joseph Basile, described in the papers as "a James Street North restaurateur, convicted bootlegger, and suspected highgrader," was shot to death in Buffalo in broad daylight. Joseph Basile was killed at the height of the gangland war in 1924. Shortly before his death, Basile's car had been impounded by Ontario Temperance Act officials for illegally carrying whisky, and Basile's wife had been charged with high-grading gold. The Hamilton *Spectator* of May 30, 1924, reports that Basile "was a marked man ... done to death by members of a gang of rum runners." Proof that he was marked was adduced by the fact that "no effort was made to engage him in conversation" before the murder: "Whatever the grudge they [the murderers] bore him, there was apparently no excuse, no recompense in the dead man's power to offer." So much for the Basile family.

But in the early 1920s, there were other mob murders in southern Ontario apart from those involving the Basile crime family. At eleven on the night of June 4, 1922, a farmer named Gordon Joyce was walking peacefully along a lonesome road near Oakville, Ont. Suddenly his quiet reflection was interrupted by the sounds of a man moaning. Joyce searched about in the dark and finally stumbled upon a shadowy figure vainly attempting to crawl out of a nearby ditch. The man was bleeding profusely from a gunshot wound in the head and babbling unintelligibly in Italian. Joyce called for help, but the mortally wounded stranger died within the hour without identifying either himself or his assailant.

It was later determined that the dead man was Tony Leala of Toronto, also known as "Frank Cico" or "Frankie Cici", a Sicilian immigrant who was a member of an organized gang of Italian bootleggers operating out of 121 St. Patrick Street in Toronto. Leala's murder had been the second gangland slaying in the Toronto-Hamilton area within a few weeks. Several weeks earlier in mid-May another Italian gangster associated with bootlegging, one Jimmy Lauria (also known as Loria, Luria, or Lorio) of Railway Street, Hamilton (the same street from which Johnny "Pops" Papalia, a long-time leader of the Mafia in Ontario since the late 1950s, currently operates), was found murdered in the Beverly swamp. Papers of the "secret Italian society", as it was described by the newspapers and police, the Black Hand, were found on Lauria's body.

The Hamilton *Herald*, under the headline "Loria's Murder Makes Total 20," reported on May 22, 1922, that "evidence accumulates that Loria was the victim of a vendetta, one killing in a chain of slayings numbering half a hundred in all, extending from Syracuse, New York, to Guelph, Ontario, and centering about Welland and Hamilton ... laid at the door of the Camorra or Black Hand."

Twelve days later, the Hamilton *Spectator* headlined Tony Leala's death with "Another Victim of Terrible Italian Vendetta," and gave details of the police theory that the victim was shot in the head in an automobile and thrown out onto the side of the road near Oakville to die. Inspector Springer of the Ontario Provincial Police is quoted as saying that there was a connection between the two murders: "They were similarly carried out and it looks as if the long series of killings that have been perpetrated of late have been the work of one organized gang of Italians, either members of some secret order or working as wholesale bootleggers." The newspaper then went on to describe a recent police dispatch from Buffalo, where similar murders had taken place, that stated that a gang known as the Good Killers, Italians engaged in rum-running, were involved in a dispute with the Toronto-Hamilton gang. It was further revealed on June 7, 1922, that Leala had been known to police and that he had been suspected by associates of being a "stool". The "rumour in the Italian quarter in Toronto was to the effect that three men were out to get him for his alleged intimacy with the police."

In 1924 alone there were four major mob killings in southern Ontario as well as the murder of Ontario mobster Joe Basile in Buffalo, connected with the bootleg business. Things had clearly gotten out of hand, even by southern Ontario's standards. There were so many gangsters, gangs, and murderers in the streets of southern Ontario during this period that the *Toronto Star* of November 17, 1924, contained the following romantic, if over-written, description of the situation, datelined Hamilton:

The ridge of hills which encircle Burlington Bay and run eastward past Stoney Creek into Niagara Peninsula, are composed of red clay that again and again have been made still more red by human blood.

Hamilton mountain has become a place of skulls, a mountain of human sacrifice. It is like one of the stone pyramids on which the bloodthirsty Aztec priests cut the throats of innumerable victims. Canada needs an Edgar Allan Poe to write the murders of the Rue St. James and to solve the mystery of Hamilton's many Marie Rogets....

On the steep slopes of this famous ridge of death on Saturday morning about one half mile east of Stoney Creek, was found the brutally battered body of Fred Genesee, a missing Hamilton taxi driver. Again there was a trail of blood on the red soil underneath the red autumn leaves. Again traces of sanguinary struggle were scrawled on the mountain side like hieroglyphics on an Egyptian pyramid. And again the hieroglyphics of homicide were indecipherable.

So far the Hamilton police force has produced no Poe or Sherlock Holmes. Again and again they have been baffled by the inscrutable mountain which frowns above them like an inscrutable enigma.

Not only are the Hamilton murderers invisible but they seem to have the magical power of making the bodies of their victims also invisible. Someone rambling the mountain in idle curiosity stirs a bundle of rags with his foot. It is a decomposed corpse. Or he kicks at a white stone and finds it is a skull rolling down the hill. Bones or carrion flesh, that is generally the first intimation that Hamilton has another gruesome mystery. And it is ironical that it has been more often the boy scouts than the police who have unearthed it.

This macabre and melodramatic description of life in southern Ontario in 1924 does succeed in graphically underlining the hard fact that southern Ontario has had a long history of Mafia brutality. A lot of this has to do with the proximity of the Buffalo and northern New York State mobs and their interrelationships and activities with the mobs in southern Ontario. Mobsters in the States and their Canadian equivalents gradually updated the techniques and structures of the Italian organized-crime groups of the 1920s to accommodate their criminal activities in the '30s and beyond, right up until the '80s.

The Mafia in Ontario, as we have seen, has been alive and well since the turn of the century. In fact, southern Ontario has been, for over eighty years, *the* mob capital of English Canada.

This is the tradition and world that Paul Volpe had chosen to enter.

CHAPTER THREE

Initiation into the Mafia

BY THE 1950s, as Paul Volpe was preparing to enter the real underworld, organized crime had entered a new era in southern Ontario. With the end of Prohibition and the assimilation and education of the older Italian immigrants, the influence of the bootleg empires and the Black Hand groups waned. However, the end of the Second World War brought a new influx of immigrants to Canada from Sicily and Calabria, many of whom were uneducated and steeped in the criminal traditions of their areas, and thus vulnerable to the pressures of Mafia-style organizations.

The American Mafia had expanded quite a bit since the bootlegging days. Under Lucky Luciano of New York, twenty-four Mafia families were organized in the United States in the early 1930s under the direction of a "ruling commission", which arbitrated all disputes and included the most powerful of the American mob bosses, most of whom got their start during Prohibition. The activities of these crime families now included importation of heroin, off-track betting, gambling, loan-sharking, frauds, union activities, extortion, and contract killing. By the late 1940s and early '50s some of the more powerful of the American Mafia families also expanded their territory into Canada.

This was particularly true of one of the five ruling Mafia families in New York City, the so-called Bonanno family, named after Don Joe Bonanno who founded the group and was himself on the commission. The Bonanno family exerted its influence in Canada through Montreal, where Bonanno established close ties with Vic Cotroni, the Godfather and founder of the Mafia in Montreal, by sending up his underboss, the ruthless Carmine Galente, to establish a firm controlling hand. Galente used Montreal as a base for the importation and distribution of heroin from Europe and also assisted Vic Cotroni in the running of his local crime family.

But there were others with Canadian interests. The mob family that has controlled Buffalo and northern New York State since the 1940s, the Magaddino family, named after its founder, Don Stefano Magaddino, has for a long time exerted an influence in the mobs of southern Ontario. Don Stefano Magaddino was known locally as "the Undertaker" because of the Magaddino family cover business, which, conveniently enough, was a funeral parlour. In addition to this power base in the north, Magaddino was also for a long time the head of the ruling commission of the Mafia, a role that carried with it more honour than real power, as the American Mafia has always been rife with internal discord and rivalries that no one man or group could ever hope to control. Only in theory were the American Mafia families under the ruling commission, as the Mafia structure has always been very feudal and requires a group of senior, respected people to arbitrate disputes. But like the United Nations, each major power bloc within the Mafia has only submitted itself to the ruling commission when it has been convenient to do so.

Magaddino, since his early bootlegging and gambling days in the late 1930s and early 1940s, had long had an interest in and an influence on southern Ontario, especially in the Toronto-Hamilton area and the Niagara Peninsula. From a southern Ontario point of view, Magaddino was the most influential of the American dons both because of his proximity (Buffalo is just across the Canadian border) and his seniority in the American mob structure. Don Stefano allied himself with a number of southern Ontario mobsters, many of whom worked for him as well as with other American Mafia families.

One of Magaddino's major Ontario underling-allies was Johnny "Pops" Papalia of Hamilton. In addition to his alliance with the Magaddino family of Buffalo, Pops built up his own empire in the Toronto-Hamilton area. He also involved himself in a major way with an international heroin importation ring run by Bonanno underboss Carmine Galente out of Montreal (with Vic Cotroni's able assistance) and out of New York City (with the assistance of other Bonanno aides and Mafia soldiers). Since the early 1950s Papalia has been one of the most influential and ruthless of mob bosses in southern Ontario, well "connected" with senior mob people in New York City, Buffalo, Montreal, Italy, and Toronto, to say nothing of Hamilton, where he lived, and other smaller mob outposts in southern Ontario. The story of Johnny Papalia is as important in organized crime in southern Ontario in the 1950s and early 1960s as that of Paul Volpe is in organized crime in southern Ontario in the late 1960s and 1970s.

Johnny "Pops" was the son of a bootlegger named Anthony Papalia who came to Canada in 1900 and, like many other Italian underworld types, settled in the Hamilton-Niagara Peninsula area. Johnny was born in the Italian ghetto on Railway Street in 1924, a year, as previously mentioned, that saw at least five mob murders in or near the city over bootleg booty and many bombings in the Italian community caused by Black Hand extortion gangs. Indeed, as we have seen, one resident of Railway Street, Jimmy Lauria, a bootlegger, was found murdered in 1922 in the Beverly swamp. Clearly this environment played a role in Papalia's future career. Like Paul Volpe, Johnny dropped out of school at an early age (at the eighth grade) and made his way in the tough street world of Hamilton. Early in his career Pops was involved in bootlegging as well as more violent activities such as extortion and enforcement work. In 1954, while running Crown Taxi on James Street North in Hamilton with his brother Domenic, he was mentioned in the press when one of his drivers, Tony Coposodi, was murdered. Clearly while he was running the taxi company, he was also undertaking more serious business, most likely including drug importation, enforcement work, and gambling. Throughout his long criminal career, which stretches from the late 1940s and continues today, Pops has always utilized cover businesses operating simultaneously with his criminal enterprises. Some of these businesses provide revenue and places to have meetings, and also act as convenient vehicles for laundering money gained through criminal activity.

At first Papalia was allied with the Sylvestros of Guelph, Ontario, who had been involved in bootlegging with Anthony

Papalia and Rocco Perri in the old days. In the 1950s Pops moved to form his own group with support from Don Stefano Magaddino of Buffalo. He was heavily involved in drug importation, including the smuggling of heroin, which Italian criminals shipped through Marseilles, France, in what was loosely known as the "French Connection". In 1949 Pops was arrested outside Union Station in Toronto selling capsules of heroin. For this, the first of his many major convictions in a criminal career that was to span five decades, he got two years in prison.

In the mid 1950s Pops became part of a regular extortion ring in Toronto. The group beat up stockbrokers who hadn't paid their protection payments to organized crime. At the time the five-foot-eight Papalia, though not an impressively built figure like Volpe, was known for his brutal enforcement techniques. As we have seen, one crime reporter said of Papalia that "he was soft-spoken and well-mannered – except when slugging someone with a blackjack.... He was also very ambitious."

Pops was very big in Hamilton (and to a lesser extent in more populous, though harder-to-handle, Toronto) when Paul Volpe entered the organized-crime field in the 1950s, but there were other Mafia groups around southern Ontario as well. There was Don Giacomo Luppino of Hamilton, who had come to the Hamilton area from a power base in the mob in southern Calabria, and some of his sons, including Jimmy and Natale of Burlington and Hamilton. There were the Sylvestros and the Cipollas (also known as Sipollas) of the Guelph area, who also operated in and around Toronto, and a mob led by old Don Calogero "Charlie" Bordonaro (alias Charles Bardinaro) of Hamilton. There were other, smaller Sicilian groups dealing in drugs, groups of Sicilians in southern Ontario, and a host of smaller Italian mob groups involved in gambling, loan-sharking, and other criminal enterprises in Ontario.

In addition to the many Mafia-style families in the southern Ontario area, there were as well the independent, non-Italian criminal organizations such as the gambling empires run by Maxie Bluestein of Toronto and the one run by the so-called "Three Thieves". Hamilton was (and still is to many mafiosi) the headquarters of the Mafia in Ontario. Toronto was always considered too large, disparate, and broken up to be handled by one family, and hence it became a more opportune ground for independents and new Mafia groupings; and Italians then, as now, were not the only ones interested in or organized enough to run effective organized-crime operations. Most of these independents at the time operated in the field of gambling. The "Three Thieves" were three bookmakers, Joseph McDermott, Vincent "Pete" Feeley, and James Ryan, who operated a lucrative gambling casino near Cooksville, Ontario. All three had been involved in the underworld throughout the 1940s and knew their way around the streets of the cities and towns of southern Ontario. "The Three Thieves" and their gambling activities were featured in the 1963 report of the Roach commission on gambling, set up by the Province of Ontario – a report that concluded, ironically enough, that organized crime was not a major threat in Ontario.

This optimistic view stimulated one of the best pieces of investigative reporting in Canadian journalism, a massive five-part series in *Maclean's* in the summer and fall of 1963 by journalist Alan Phillips on the make-up and extent of organized crime and Mafia activities in Canada. The series included an extensive history of the operations and activities of the various crime groups in the 1950s. Johnny "Pops" Papalia was prominently featured in Phillips's articles as were the Cotroni family of Montreal, the Magaddino family of Buffalo, Maxie Bluestein of Toronto, and dozens of other Toronto and Hamilton mafiosi and organized criminals operating at the time. The only reference to the Volpes was this oblique one, which incorrectly labels Paul's older brother Eugene as the boss of the group. "A large loose knit group in Toronto headed by a local car wash operator who served in army intelligence in World War II and became a postwar gold smuggler.... He is still wanted by police in Detroit.... A fast moving Mafia group." The reference is to Eugene Volpe, who had done some high-grading (gold operations) after the war. But Eugene never headed the group – Paul did.

For Paul Volpe, having decided on a criminal career, chose to try the Mafia, in spite of the complexities of the Mafia scene in Ontario. First, in 1957, he began visiting New York City regularly, to establish connections in Mafia circles. In late 1957 he connected with a mafioso named Vito de Filippo, a middle-rank member of the Bonanno crime family in New York City. (Joe Bonanno had always had Canadian aspirations even outside of the Montreal connections with Cotroni, maintained through his underboss Carmine Galente. When Don Stefano Magaddino later complained at a Mafia commission meeting that "Bonanno was planting flags all over the place," he had Bonanno's Toronto dealings and relationships in mind as well as his many Montreal connections and businesses. This complaint led eventually to the temporary replacement of Joe Bonanno as head of the Bonanno crime family, his kidnapping, and his two-year banishment from New York City.)

From Paul Volpe's point of view, the relationship with Vito de Filippo and the Bonanno family was to have a profound effect on his life. Volpe realized that working for Vito gave him invaluable entrée into the secret world of the traditional Sicilian Mafia, a connection that could help establish him in his home base in Toronto. As a native-born Canadian, Paul Volpe didn't naturally possess the old-world, secret-society traditions. He didn't even speak Italian, let alone understand the intricacies of the Mafia societies, and he had been born and bred and was now based in the more cosmopolitan, sophisticated world of Toronto, rather than in the tightly knit Hamilton Italian community. Through Vito de Filippo, Volpe found out that success in the criminal underworld depended a lot on building up a larger-than-life image and becoming a "name" to be reckoned with. This required connections to top criminals, establishing "respect" through both contacts and intimidation, and an ability to put together a well-oiled criminal machine. The Mafia was to be his ticket to success. Joe Bonanno, in turn, was using Volpe, through de Filippo, to take a little power away from Magaddino by establishing a stronger power base in Canada.

From 1957 to 1959 Paul travelled back and forth to New York City with increasing frequency. Sometimes he would go back to New York City just a few days after returning to Toronto. Volpe treated de Filippo with great respect, as a boss, and during this period Vito occasionally even came up to consult with Paul in Toronto. Vito de Filippo was, simply put, Paul Volpe's Mafia tutor.

In 1959 Volpe got involved in some phoney stock deals and tried to muscle in on Hamilton. He had a base there through his connection with Jimmy Luppino and his father, the respected Don Giacomo Luppino. But this turned out to be a tactical mistake. Volpe rubbed some people, including Johnny Papalia, the wrong way in Hamilton; he was still, in Hamilton and in Mafia terms, an outsider, and he was moving too fast without a major base of support and without any muscle or back-up. One Hamilton crime faction put the heat on Volpe by warning him to back off, and he was forced to hide in New York City for over three months until things cooled down and he had worked out a game plan. He returned to Toronto later in 1959.

At this point, Volpe decided to concentrate his efforts on using his connections in the United States, in Quebec, in Hamilton, and in other southern Ontario cities to establish his base of criminal operations in the more open, laid-back Toronto world of organized crime. Volpe used his New York City ties to the Bonanno family, through Vito de Filippo, to ingratiate himself with members of the Magaddino family of Buffalo, which still controlled certain areas of Toronto and Hamilton. When drug courier Albert Agueci, a member of Magaddino's family who was working with the "French Connection" drug importation team, which included Johnny "Pops", was on the lam in Toronto in 1960, Paul Volpe helped find a safe place for him to hide from the police.* In this way Paul Volpe was able to solidify his position in Toronto. Volpe also made a special trip to Montreal with Jimmy Luppino to pay his respects to the Godfather, Vic Cotroni, and to get his blessing for his Toronto undertaking. He further increased his respect by becoming quite close to Harold (born Ignazio) Bordonaro, a Hamilton lawyer secretly in the Mafia, who was the son of Calogero (Charlie) Bordonaro, one of the old dons of Hamilton who were active participants in the extortions and bombings in the early 1920s.

Finally, in 1961, after many years of making all the right moves and connections, Volpe was really "in". Sponsored by Charlie and Harold Bordonaro and by Giacomo and Jimmy Luppino, Paul was formally initiated into the Mafia in a ceremony in Hamilton. He burned a piece of paper (said to represent the Virgin Mary) and pledged allegiance and a vow of silence (omertà). This was two years before New York City mafioso Joseph Valachi gave his famous testimony and described his own

---

*Agueci was later brutally murdered for openly criticizing his boss, Don Stefano, for not supporting his wife and kids while he was in jail for heroin importation undertaken for the Magaddino family. What remained of his tortured, acid-soaked body was found in a ditch in northern New York State. Thirty pounds of flesh had been carved from his body while he was still alive. Through this ritualistic and savage killing, Don Stefano was sending a clear message to all in the family about the consequences of breaking with the sacred Mafia tradition of omertà. But this murder was several years after Paul Volpe helped Agueci out on behalf of Magaddino.

initiation ceremony into what he called "la Cosa Nostra" (literally, "our own thing"). The two ceremonies, Volpe's and Valachi's, were remarkably similar, though they were in two different cities and at different times.

From this point on Volpe concentrated on putting together the best mob he could in the Toronto area, and for the next three years he shuttled between Toronto and Hamilton, consulting the Bordonaros and Luppinos as well as other mob bosses in the area. The trips to New York City ceased. The help of the Luppinos, the Bordonaros, and Vito de Filippo was useful in overcoming the initial resistance to his criminal thrust, but it required a lot more than public-relations work on Volpe's part to establish a beach-head and create his own crime family, for by the time of his formal initiation into the Mafia, the mob scene in southern Ontario was a minefield of rivalries and discord.

By the late 1950s Johnny "Pops" had built up quite a criminal empire in the Toronto-Hamilton area, supplanting many old-time dons and independents operating in gambling, loan-sharking, extortion, and drug importation. Pops was on a real roll and had substantial backing from the major Mafia bosses in the United States and Montreal. Paul Volpe himself had given up any attempts to establish himself in the Hamilton-Niagara Peninsula area, even with the strong local alliances he had built up with the Luppinos and the Bordonaros, because he lacked a base there and feared the power and strength of the Papalia organization, with its strong connections with the Magaddino and Bonanno families.

In Toronto itself, the organized-crime picture was quite complex. As we have seen, Toronto had long been an "open city", that is, open to many different mob groups operating simultaneously in different areas. This allowed criminal entrepreneurs like Maxie Bluestein (alias Max Baker) to establish his considerable gambling empire in Toronto, while at the same time Paul Volpe established himself in extortion, loan-sharking, and frauds, and Johnny "Pops" continued his considerable action in Toronto in drugs, gambling, and extortion. Many other crime groups and independents as well were operating in Toronto harmoniously.

But all of this changed dramatically in 1961 when Pops decided to flex his muscles in Toronto with the support of Mafia dons in Buffalo, Guelph, and Hamilton, as well as with the help of members of his own organization in Toronto and Hamilton. This is when he decided to put Maxie Bluestein out of business. Pops wanted to do this to establish his own supremacy in mob circles in southern Ontario, as well as to gain control of Bluestein's lucrative gambling empire. The only problem was Maxie himself, who was "a stubborn old bugger".

In the late 1940s and early 1950s Max Bluestein had established himself as head of one of the largest and most profitable gambling operations in the Toronto area. He had several popular clubs, including the famous Lakeview Club on Eglinton Avenue West, which for a long time was the prime gambling joint in Toronto. In addition, Maxie always had major floating crap games going on. Essentially he was a one-man operation, though from time to time he did hire "connected" people, such as Volpe croupier Sam Shirose and others, on an ad hoc basis. But he was totally independent of the Mafia-run gambling joints and those games and clubs run by the "Three Thieves", and he desired no alliances or partners. Maxie also knew where his talent lay, and he limited himself to the gambling circuit and did not get involved in loan-sharking, extortion, frauds, or any other activities associated with organized crime, such as contract beatings and killings. According to his own testimony before the Roach commission in 1963, Bluestein took in about $10,000 a day in bets (in 1950s dollars). Quite simply, in the 1950s Maxie Bluestein ran the most lucrative gambling show in town.

However, in 1961, Maxie served three months in jail for keeping a common gaming-house, and those in the mob who had been planning his demise for a long time began to think that he was vulnerable. Maxie resisted all attempts by the Mafia to drive him out of business, and in early 1961, after his jail term, he was called into several conferences with Mafia chieftains to discuss a possible peaceful take-over of his games. In one such meeting at the Westbury Hotel in downtown Toronto (a few blocks up from Walton Street and Bassel's Restaurant) Maxie had a dramatic show-down. "Fred", a Toronto underworld source who appeared in the CBC television series *Connections* wearing a red hood, explained to researchers what happened:

He met with two parties from Buffalo and Johnny Papalia from Hamilton. They said it would be very nice if Maxie would work hand in glove with Johnny here. Max just put the thumbs down,

*and he says, "I have no partners, I work by myself." They wanted
to go a little further in the conversation, but Max just stood
up and walked out of the room. They came back to him on
a couple of other occasions to try to make another meet, but
he wouldn't hear of it. The situation just got more and more
aggravated until they had a meeting between themselves and
looked to make an example out of Maxie.*

But in spite of all of this intimidation and pressure, Maxie
continued to operate his gambling empire, publicly scorning the
Mafia and daring the gangsters to do anything to him. Finally,
the Buffalo Magaddino mob gave Johnny "Pops" the okay to
move physically against Bluestein. It all reached a climax at a
famous meeting on March 21, 1961, which took place at the
Town Tavern in Toronto, a well-known mob and rounder hang-
out at the time. Papalia had called the meeting to give Maxie
one more chance. It was all dramatic stuff, like the movies. All
of Papalia's people were in place at the Town as well as many
rounders and prominent criminal lawyers such as Wally Rose,
and the friends and allies of Bluestein. What happened that
night at the Town Tavern is a Toronto legend. The events that
followed caused a sensation in the media for months and led
to the establishment of the Royal Commission into Gambling
and Crime in Ontario. The writer and columnist Pierre Berton
firmly established his reputation as a journalist in his coverage
of the events, and people in the mob speak of it frequently
– as if it had happened yesterday. It was High Noon in Toronto.
And it is still unclear who, if anyone, won the contest. Alan
Phillips, who meticulously researched and reported on the events
of that evening in his *Maclean's* exposé of September 23, 1963,
describes what happened after Bluestein agreed to a face-to-
face "meet" with Papalia on March 21, 1961:

*The Town in downtown Toronto is a popular lounge and
restaurant. It had almost a hundred customers that night, many
of them hoodlums who were there by invitation. Papalia had
spread the word. He wanted Toronto's gamblers to know that
Bluestein had capitulated, or – if he still held out – to see the
consequences.*

*Bluestein came in after dining a few blocks away, sat as usual
on the restaurant side, and held court surrounded by friends.*

Gabourie and Weaver [two Papalia men] *joined him. From another table Papalia, sitting with Marchildon* [a Papalia lieutenant] *and Irwin* [a former heavyweight boxer working as an enforcer for the mob], *sent a waiter over to Bluestein with a drink.*

This was the time of decision. If Bluestein accepted the drink – "the hand of friendship" – he was accepting the syndicate as his partner. He had come prepared, at least, to talk, but there was the matter of prestige. In the rackets, as elsewhere, prestige increases with wealth and Bluestein, though he denies it, is more than a millionaire. He has interests in at least two hotels, a finance company, and perhaps as many as twenty apartment buildings. He had been a rackets boss when Johnny "Pops" had been working the street for Bluestein's close associate Harvey Chernick. Bluestein waved the drink away. "If some punk wants to talk to me," he rasped, "let him come to my table."

He had made his choice. Bluestein has nerve. As time passed his confidence grew. He told his friends to leave. "Go ahead, I can handle these punks," he assured them.

The lounge closed. One o'clock neared. Bluestein rose and strolled from the restaurant. At the hat-check counter Papalia and Weaver engaged him in conversation. They asked him to step in the lounge, now dark and deserted. Bluestein declined. As they talked, Gabourie, Marchildon, and Irwin were leaving their restaurant table and stealing through the lounge to come up behind Bluestein.

Bluestein pulled a thin-bladed fish knife. A black jack thudded against his head. Falling, he clutched at his nearest assailant – Marchildon – stabbing him eight times in the back. Iron bars swung on short ropes were smashing against his cheekbones and his forehead. Brass knuckles gouged his face and eyes. A broken bottle was thrust into his mouth. As he lay on the floor in a spreading pool of blood someone kicked his face.

Outside, customers trying to enter were intercepted by hoodlums. When police arrived they found no one who would tell them what had happened. Though the beating had taken place in plain sight, the Town's customers, staff and management, as Pierre Berton later reported in the Toronto Star *column, had been stricken by perhaps the most remarkable case of mass blindness in scientific history. Berton's column created pressure. A special police squad was put on the case, and on April 21 warrants were sworn out for Papalia, Marchildon, Weaver, and Gabourie. Johnny "Pops" had overreached. More people had learned his lesson than he intended.*

Since the Mafia's lifeline is its ability to instil fear in people – to make victims and potential victims fear what they can do – Johnny "Pops" and the Mafia, in the final analysis, lost the fight with Maxie Bluestein. Not only did Maxie stand up and fight, inflicting his own share of damage, but he showed everyone that all one had to do to overcome the Mafia *was* to stand up and fight, even if that meant risking your own life. Many on the street argue that Maxie was never the same after the terrible beating he received from Pops and his boys. But Bluestein did hold onto his stake in gambling in Toronto, and Pops did go to jail for the beating after many reluctant witnesses were shamed by Pierre Berton and others into coming forward. The fact is that Papalia didn't take over Bluestein's operations – or Mafia operations in Toronto. In fact he has never even taken over mob operations in his home town of Hamilton. Pops was put in his place by Max Bluestein in 1961, and Papalia was never as big as he once appeared to be. He had lost a lot of respect, a vital (and all too fragile) commodity for a Mafia boss.

Bluestein also stood up to Paul Volpe and other mafiosi over the years. Fred, the eye witness at the Town Tavern and long-time associate of the Volpe group, put it this way in his *Connections* interview:

Yes, he [Maxie] stood up to Pops, who was looking to take over his craps. He stood up to Paul Volpe on a couple of occasions. He called him a spaghetti. He called him a meatball prick on a couple of occasions. Well, he just stood up to them. As a matter of fact ... they really looked to make an example.... He gave it to three of them very bad; three of them were never the same after that beating they wanted to give him.

No matter how you look at it, Papalia was a loser. He went to jail for the beating and was also convicted while in jail of heroin importation for the Galente group. He ended up in prison from 1962 to 1968. With Pops out of the way, Volpe had a much easier climb to the top.

One thing Paul Volpe learned from the Town Tavern episode

was the importance of making alliances with, and even working with, non-Italian groups. In fact Volpe was to go even further, building a mob group that was multicultural in make-up, the first truly multicultural mob outfit in Canada. Volpe had natural management skills and was a born talent-spotter. Working in a Canadian context, he naturally went for the best people, regardless of their backgrounds, when structuring his crime family. Creatively, Volpe brought together under his leadership an ethnic mix of people with diverse talents and skills.

In 1961, the year that Paul Volpe was initiated into the Mafia and Maxie Bluestein was beaten up, the man who was to become his most serious rival arrived in Toronto from Italy with two of his brothers. This was Rocco (Remo) Commisso. The Commissos came to Toronto with the second wave of immigration from Italy, which started in the late 1950s and brought with it an influx of many Calabrian mafiosi (known as the Honoured Society in southern Calabria) who have since become prominent in the Ontario Mafia. Most of these mafiosi were from the area around Siderno Marina in Calabria, and so the criminal group has come to be known in Ontario and the eastern United States as the "Siderno group". Michele Racco, one of the most respected figures in the Mafia in Ontario, was the leader of the group in Canada from the late 1950s until his death in 1980.

The Commissos were all quite young when they arrived in their new home. Remo was only fifteen years old. But they had come from a long tradition of Mafia activities. Their own father was murdered in a Mafia vendetta in the streets of Siderno in the 1940s, and they had the background that would later help them to emerge as the main rivals for Paul Volpe's ever-expanding power and influence in southern Ontario. But that was much later. It is enough to note here that the Commissos arrived in Toronto in 1961, and that the other major Calabrian mafiosi were already in place at the time of Volpe's initiation into the North American Mafia. Later Paul Volpe would find it difficult to contend with the Italian-born crime element. Volpe's training and background as a native-born Canadian did not sufficiently prepare him for his struggles with the real Italian mafiosi that later would lead to his undoing.

The year 1961 was, indeed, a very important year in the history of organized crime in Ontario. Johnny "Pops" failed in his attempt to take over gambling in Toronto. The general public in Toronto was made dramatically aware of the extent of the mob's presence. The government was forced to do something and set up the Roach commission on gambling. Paul Volpe was formally initiated into the Mafia and started to build his own group in Toronto, using non-Italians in senior positions. The Commissos arrived off the boat from Italy. It was a banner year for the mob, setting the stage for the consolidation of power by Volpe and the Calabrian groups in the 1960s and '70s and the mob wars of the '80s. It was also reaffirmed, in 1961, in a sensational manner, that Toronto was and perhaps always would be an "open city" for organized crime, allowing many different organizations to operate simultaneously, if not always harmoniously.

CHAPTER FOUR

Diamond in the Rough: The Early Years of Nathan Klegerman

IN EARLY 1962 Viscountess Downe was visiting New York City from England. She was staying at a plush hotel near Idlewild Airport. A burglar broke into her room and stole jewels worth several hundred thousand dollars. In the same year a wealthy Dutch diamond merchant in Antwerp was pistol-whipped and robbed at gunpoint. Thieves made away with a number of diamonds worth a fortune. In Montreal, also in 1962, a wealthy woman was the victim of a break-and-enter at her fashionable Westmount home. Valuable jewels were stolen.

What do all these events have in common? All this stolen merchandise was fenced through the same organized-crime network in Toronto. All the stolen jewels ended up with Nathan Israel Klegerman, who ran an "investment" business on the second floor of a building at Spadina and College, above Tip Top Tailors. In fact, Viscountess Downe's jewels were being appraised by Klegerman in Toronto the very day after the robbery. Klegerman was in effect a major fence – much like Fagin, who disposed of the goods his boys stole in Dickens's *Oliver Twist* – only Klegerman specialized in diamonds and jewels. He took hot jewels from professional jewel thieves around the world and disposed of them by finding them a safe home where the police could not trace them. A canny deviousness, intelligence, tremendous efficiency, and great organizational skills were required to pull together this sophisticated international network of thieves. Klegerman possessed all these characteristics in spades, which is why he has always been a master criminal and con man extraordinaire. It was also these very characteristics that were to endear him to the freshly initiated Mafia member Paul Volpe, who still needed some long-range planning, a more sophisticated organization, and overall direction for his own criminal schemes.

Klegerman took the hot goods stolen from around the world and other jewels similarly collected through theft as collateral for "investors", who then gave Klegerman bags of cash to invest at a guaranteed high rate of return. Many of these investors were shady themselves, and others were simply wealthy men whom Klegerman knew from the Spadina/Walton areas, who were greedy and wanted a higher return on their money than they could get from the banks. They were not too concerned about how the money was invested, only that they be guaranteed a very high interest rate. Klegerman, in turn, either put the money out on the street (loan-sharking) or used it to purchase diamonds on the diamond exchange.

Nathan Israel Klegerman couldn't have presented a sharper contrast to Paul Volpe in background, style, and physical appearance. According to many sources it was Natie who helped Volpe prosper in the 1970s and early 1980s, for he was the proverbial "brains" behind many of the sophisticated frauds and he organized Volpe's loan-sharking empire. One source close to both Paul Volpe and Klegerman says of Natie: "He never comes across as someone sinister.... He is a blue-eyed angel, an innocent ... yet he has a real mind and a deadly cunning." One of his lawyers, Earl Levy, categorically denies this: "He was a puppy compared to the sharks he was dealing with.... He was well read, studied philosophy, and laughed at being called an organized criminal – 'We are disorganized,' he would say." Moreover, he didn't drink and never carried on with women, remaining loyal to his long-time wife, Frances. But there was no doubt that Volpe came to feel that Klegerman was essential to his crime network throughout their long criminal careers in Toronto. In a luncheon meeting with lawyer Earl Levy three days before his death in November 1983, Paul Volpe referred in passing to his respect and "great love" for Natie. There is no doubt that Klegerman added a whole new dimension to Paul Volpe's understanding of a crime organization and brought significant new, non-Italian talent into the Volpe orbit, thus changing the very nature of organized crime in Toronto.

Unlike Paul Volpe, Natie has never been much of a physical presence. Of medium height and weight, with blue eyes and brown hair, he was rather owlish in appearance, though his language was salty enough and down to earth. However, like Volpe, he had an open, engaging, gregarious manner in dealing with people, appearing all innocence. In reality, he was all con, and in this, again, he was very much like Volpe. Klegerman is the quintessential confidence man.

Nathan Klegerman was born of Orthodox Jewish parents on August 22, 1929, on Spadina Avenue near Baldwin Street in the wholesale-clothing district of downtown Toronto. In his youth Nathan aspired to be a rabbi, and he always valued knowledge and education. He always thought of himself as a bit of an intellectual (which he was, compared with the other people in organized crime), and he continued to work on a university degree in philosophy well into his forties, attending the University of Toronto in the mid-1970s while running Volpe's loan-shark empire and organizing diamond frauds and other sophisticated criminal schemes. Klegerman began his career innocently enough, as a furrier in Toronto, but quickly developed an all-consuming interest in the diamond trade, which was controlled by Orthodox Jews in New York City and Europe.

The diamond trade is a secretive world with its own rules and code of ethics; a lot of transactions there are sealed on little more than a handshake or an oral agreement. Deals are based entirely on a trust established among individual diamond merchants. In the diamond area of New York City, diamonds are bought and sold right in the streets, much as some criminals sell drugs right in the streets of Harlem (though the diamond trade is, of course, legal). The diamond trade has always been difficult to police because it is extremely easy to smuggle objects that are so small, yet so valuable. In addition, the dealers themselves adopt what might charitably be called defensive strategies, which keep their taxes and overhead down. (The diamond trade appears to be more over-taxed in Canada, leading to more evasive and secretive dealings by even the legitimate dealers.)

In this shady, murky ambience Klegerman operated for many

years as a diamond dealer himself, taking diamonds on consignment from dealers in Antwerp, New York City, Toronto, or elsewhere. Often he would buy and sell the diamonds legitimately. However, as often as not he would be simply playing a confidence game, thriving on the greed of the diamond dealers, who wished to maximize profits and minimize, avoid, or evade taxes.

One scam at which Klegerman was particularly adept was getting certain diamond merchants to place valuable stones with him on consignment, which Klegerman would then try to sell at a huge mark-up. Often Klegerman either would not pay the dealer the full amount he had agreed to or would defer payment endlessly so that the merchant was out of pocket for an extended time. Then Klegerman would put the money out on the street through loan-sharking, thus making money for himself, while the diamond merchant waited for either payment or return of the jewels. In the meantime Klegerman would use the jewels for collateral or resale. Klegerman, a master confidence man, was a genius at picking his victims, who themselves were often shady, with some sort of skeleton in their closet. Klegerman really was defrauding fellow bandits in the diamond rackets, and the "victim" was often as bad an apple as the "criminal". Klegerman thrived on the greed and loose morality of his victims. He was so clever a con artist, so consummate a liar, that in many cases, victims of Klegerman rip-offs went back to him later to place more jewels. Clients wanted to believe Natie; he sounded so sincere. But he has been, in reality, as sleek as a snake. The charm and apparent good will has been just a veneer.

The story of how Klegerman came to meet and become attached to Paul Volpe has all the elements of a 1930s grade-B gangster film, but it provides an insight into both men's characters and into their symbiotic relationship.

In 1962 Klegerman was happily running his fencing and "investment" empire from his office at College and Spadina in downtown Toronto. This corner, not far from where he was born, has always been one of Klegerman's favourite haunts. It used to be and still is partly a Jewish neighbourhood with a lot of local colour. It is about a block away from the University of Toronto, so there have always been many college types in the area. There are as well many bars (the famous Silver Dollar is nearby), some of them especially seedy, and inexpensive restaurants. The Bagel restaurant has always been a haunt of taxi drivers and interesting types, including Natie Klegerman, who used to meet some of his clients here. From 1960 until the late 1970s, his office, his headquarters for fencing stolen goods and lending money, was just across the street.

Before he met Paul Volpe, Klegerman was doing quite well financially, with a residence in the fashionable northwest area of Toronto. He seems to have established friendly relations with a network of hotel prowls, professional thieves who robbed hotel rooms in Toronto and elsewhere. Klegerman would act as a fence for these hotel thieves and their colleagues, helping them get rid of their hot goods. He was what was called, in the eighteenth century, "a receiver of stolen goods", engaging in activities much like Mr. Peachum's in John Gay's popular *The Beggar's Opera*. Klegerman didn't recycle the stolen goods into the open market. As we have seen, he used the goods, usually hard-to-trace jewels, as collateral for taking money from "investors", wealthy friends, and associates, often legitimate but greedy, who were looking for a higher rate of return than their banks offered. Natie offered them a guaranteed return of over fifteen per cent. What Klegerman was doing was a massive laundering operation for business people (those, for example, who wanted to hide some of their profits from tax people, business partners, or wives) and for criminals, as well as providing a convenient fence for professional thieves. It was a clever set-up, but it was to bring him unwanted attention.

Things started to go seriously awry early in 1962. It all began to fall apart when, unbeknownst to Klegerman, Tom Macleod, now a sergeant in the break-and-enter squad of the Toronto police (who significantly had considerable artistic talent), got a call at nine one morning from a source who wanted him to look at some "escaped" jewellery that had not been cleared by police for investment purposes and that he intended to dump later that day in a resale package with some investors. Macleod's "Deep Throat" wanted him to clear the jewels that morning. He did not want to risk arrest or worse, in the process of selling the jewels, and by contacting Sergeant Macleod and acting, in effect, as a police informer, he was taking out protection against incrimination in the future. He was a very street-wise and savvy jeweller, who was used to dealing with unsavoury types, while at the same time constantly protecting himself and still maximizing his profits in the transaction. He was a real middleman, used to skilfully unloading merchandise of dubious origin.

Sergeant Macleod met with the source in an automobile and looked over a huge quantity of jewellery, including exotic brooches and rings. Macleod noted that one piece was similar to something reported stolen in a robbery of a west-end home, but he really had no idea where the jewellery came from. Since the source had to dispose of the jewels that day, Macleod sketched the pieces free-hand. Macleod then circulated the drawings to the various investigatory agencies and police forces. He even got the *Globe and Mail* to publish some of his sketches. It was the beginning of an investigation that was to last over a year and take him to Greece, New York City, Montreal, and finally into the home of Nathan Klegerman in northwest Toronto.

Macleod's first positive response came from the Montreal police, who recognized one of the jewels as one stolen in an armed robbery (which had involved a shooting) in the Montreal area. Montreal police came to Toronto, and Macleod got search warrants of banks and locations in west Toronto as a result of Montreal police intelligence. He then went back to his source and found that the jewellery had been exchanged for collateral.

Finally, after investigating various leads, Macleod was led to the office of Nathan Klegerman's supposed mortgage investment business at Spadina Avenue and College Street in Toronto. From this office Macleod found out that Klegerman would invest cash (without asking questions), up to $100,000, for his clients. He invested millions, according to Macleod, though police were never able to determine who or how many people "invested" with Klegerman. Macleod seized a number of documents from Klegerman's office and home, as well as $400,000 (in 1962 dollars) in stolen jewellery and furs.

Direct evidence led to three specific charges being laid against Nathan Klegerman involving handling of stolen goods from robberies in New York City, Montreal, and Antwerp. In addition, Macleod seized a huge quantity of unset diamonds. Interpol later helped identify three of the diamonds as the property of the pistol-whipped diamond merchant in Antwerp. The merchant himself later came to Canada and identified the pieces beyond a shadow of a doubt, for there were certain identifying knots in the stones that proved that he bought them from a diamond merchant in the Netherlands. Montreal police positively identified jewellery taken from the Westmount home, and a diamond and platinum bracelet stolen from Viscountess Downe was also positively identified. Finally, in early 1963, Nathan Klegerman was arrested by Macleod and charged with three counts of possession of stolen property. When Macleod went to Klegerman's office at Spadina and College to make the arrest, Natie acted quite surprised. He was "unassuming, unimpressive physically, and non-committal," says Macleod.

At the time, being charged was the least of Klegerman's problems. Word of what had happened quickly spread on the street. Many of Klegerman's "investors", who included some pretty heavy underworld characters from Toronto and from as far away as New York City, were very upset, to say the least. They had lost their money or jewels, which had been personally guaranteed by Klegerman. Serious threats against Natie began to be heard on the street. In desperation, Klegerman pretended to be crazy and for a short time checked himself into a Toronto-area mental hospital. From here he sent out word that he needed help – physical, not emotional – from someone on the street who was well connected and could allay everyone's fears and explain the situation. Finally, Klegerman was introduced to one of the toughest "names" in Toronto at the time, Paul Volpe. Of course Klegerman had heard of Volpe, as he was a real comer in the criminal world of Toronto in the late 1950s and early 1960s and, after all, they had grown up and operated professionally only five or ten blocks away from each other; but to this point Klegerman had not had any business or social dealings with him. He decided to hire Paul Volpe, on the strength of his "connections" and his street image as a mafioso, to straighten out his complex and delicate situation. In one of their first meetings, Klegerman dramatically handed Paul Volpe a $1,000 bill as a down payment for his protection services. Volpe was impressed, as this was a considerable sum as a retainer, worth at least five grand in today's money. He agreed to help Klegerman.

Volpe delighted in the challenging task. He assigned a bodyguard, Tony Iatti, to Klegerman and secured Natie's personal security, as well as that of his wife and two children, by putting word out on the street that Klegerman was under his protection. When things had calmed down, Volpe contacted underworld people in Toronto and New York City to smooth things over for Klegerman. Then he made arrangements to fly down to New York City with Natie secretly, under false names and IDs, to talk directly to the hostile forces there. They travelled as "Paul Fox" of Buffalo and "John Smith" of Akron, Ohio. Things went well in New York City, and Klegerman was pleased with Volpe's work. When the danger from his irate "investors" seemed to have passed, Natie paid Volpe off handsomely, thanked him very much, and told him that his services were no longer required.

But this was not the end of either Klegerman's problems or his relationship with Paul Volpe and the Mafia.

Volpe decided he wanted to keep Klegerman under his muscle, for Volpe quickly saw him as an important man to have around in planning and organizing criminal operations, and Volpe has always been able to seize an opportunity when it presented itself. So Volpe let it be known on the street that Natie was no longer under his protection. Then he arranged for some of Klegerman's former "investors" to find him. According to a source close to Volpe at the time, "Paul made a phone call and he said, 'The umbrella is off, boys, take your best shot.' He knew they were going to beat him. I wouldn't be surprised if he arranged for him to be beaten." Klegerman, now out on bail, was savagely beaten in the elevator of his apartment building. Says Sergeant Macleod of the event, "We [the police] heard about it.... Many people [criminals] were upset with Klegerman." But Klegerman did not report this attack to the police. Instead, the very next day, he contacted Paul Volpe and put him on the payroll once again. So began a criminal relationship that was to last over twenty years.

Over the next year, from mid-1962 until mid-1963, between the time Paul Volpe went to Haiti to take over a casino and the time Nathan Klegerman was about to face a major trial and go to jail for five years of a six-year sentence, Paul and Natie became inseparable. Paul Volpe had quickly grasped the importance of Klegerman's cunning, and his ability to organize and think out new criminal schemes. It was Klegerman who was to help Volpe build an efficient organization that was multicultural in make-up and diverse in its activities. Volpe was persuaded not to use the Mafia model as it was practised in the United States, Italy, and hitherto in Canada by Italian gangsters who relied solely on a close-knit Italian group of criminals in a family-like relationship. Rather, Klegerman convinced Paul Volpe of the desirability of having an ad hoc alliance of individuals of varying ethnic backgrounds, talents, and abilities, who could be used only as events warranted. There were to be no permanent payroll problems. Volpe was to command respect through his Mafia status, but this was not to be a traditional Mafia organization. However, this organizational set-up of Volpe's and Klegerman's was in the future, for the two men, because of overlapping jail terms, were not out on the street at the same time again for almost a decade. In the meantime, Paul Volpe decided to try his hand on the international mob stage.

CHAPTER FIVE

The Haitian Interlude

I N MID-1963, while Klegerman was preparing to face a major trial, Paul Volpe went down to Haiti on the advice of his old friend and criminal mentor Vito de Filippo, to look into the possibility of purchasing a casino there. His international mob connections paid off, and Volpe found that a casino was within easy reach. He rushed back to Toronto and hurriedly raised the capital through his own sources in Toronto and with the help of various Mafia colleagues in New York City.

Paul Volpe's period in Haiti – from late 1963 until early 1965, and intermittently from then until he went to jail in 1968 on his first major conviction – was the most exciting international adventure Volpe ever undertook. Although he soon got to loathe living in Haiti, according to those who knew him well at the time, he did thoroughly enjoy running a casino and organizing gambling junkets, which he did with the help of Toronto and New York mafiosi and friends as well as with the able assistance of his brother Albert, who was later to run his own casino in Yugoslavia. It was the best of times and the worst of times for Paul Volpe.

But how did a street kid, born and bred in Toronto and schooled in the Mafia life-style of New York City, Buffalo, and the Toronto-Hamilton area, end up in this strange Caribbean island renowned at the time for the long-time dictatorship of François "Papa

Doc" Duvalier and the widespread practice of voodoo rites? Apart from his various continuing business ventures in the United States (especially in New Jersey and New York states), this Haitian interlude was Paul Volpe's only venture onto the international mob stage. It was the only sustained time he was off his home turf. He never went to Italy, the birthplace and home of the Mafia, or to the rest of Europe. In fact he never left North America, except during this Haitian period and for the occasional holiday jaunt to the Bahamas. Volpe's period in Haiti became the one big romantic adventure of his life.

A number of elements fell into place in late 1963 and early 1964 that led to Volpe's move to Port-au-Prince and his taking over the management of a local casino.

First, a lot of heat was coming from the police. Volpe had expanded his operational base to include money-lending activities, business frauds, and illegal card games and other gambling activities, as well as protection services. He ran most of his activities out of the family-owned car wash on Walton Street, where he felt most comfortable, though he maintained an apartment on Mount Pleasant Boulevard, near St. Clair Avenue and Yonge Street in Toronto. He had a girl-friend from whose downtown apartment he also used to operate. He had become one of the leading criminal characters in the area where he was born and bred, which was, of course, an area full of action and interesting characters looking for action. Volpe arranged big card games here, as well as other gambling operations. He always loved the ambience of the gambling world, where he also picked up quite a few loan-shark clients who were unable to pay their debts by evening's end. But there was a lot of competition for this gambling trade in the competitive organized-crime world of the Toronto-Hamilton area, both from other Mafia powers and from the independents such as Maxie Bluestein and the clubs in Cooksville and the Niagara region.

One day Paul Volpe discovered a suspicious-looking green truck next door to the car wash. He had the licence plates checked, and sure enough the truck was an RCMP surveillance vehicle. He knew this for certain, as, amazingly enough, not only was it registered, but the RCMP headquarters in Toronto was its listed address. So much for the undercover operations of the early days! Apparently the RCMP had been intercepting phone calls to Volpe from bugs placed in the company next door and were listening from the truck. Paul got the message. He was hot.

But the police were not his only problem. There were still those in the underworld who resented his sudden emergence as a leading criminal figure, notably Johnny "Pops", who was also involved in gambling activities in Toronto and who had recently been charged in a major drug-ring case involving senior members of the Bonanno family of New York City and the Magaddino family of Buffalo. Pops's people didn't have a lot of time for Paul, nor did several others in the Toronto-Hamilton crime world.

In addition to the attention of the police and fellow criminals, Paul Volpe was worried about the upcoming hearings of U.S. Senator McClellan's committee, which was about to hear the testimony of Joe Valachi, the first major defector from mob ranks. It was very possible that the names of senior American mobsters and their Canadian connections might come out. As it turned out, Paul Volpe and his brother Albert were indeed named by the committee, along with Johnny "Pops" and Dante "Danny" Gasbarrini of Hamilton (a convicted heroin trafficker at the time), as Canadian members of the Mafia syndicate allied to the Magaddino family in Buffalo. The Valachi hearings were to cause a sensation across the United States and Canada, for the media prominently covered the latest testimony as it occurred in Washington. When Lieutenant Mike Amico of the Buffalo police department's intelligence division testified, showing a chart of the Magaddino family that listed Paul Volpe and others as Toronto members, it was treated as a major news story in Canada. Of course Paul Volpe was associated with and allied to the Buffalo crime family, though he never really was a member of the Magaddino family in any formal sense. Neither were the others (Albert Volpe, Gasbarrini, and Papalia), though their association made good copy for the papers and the radio and television news. There were big headlines, and major police and media heat developed in Toronto and the United States. By that time, however, Volpe, who had foreseen the reaction, was down in Haiti on a scouting expedition for his casino, and he avoided this new pressure from law enforcement and the media. It also helped make his stay in Haiti a bit longer. His worst fears seem to have been well founded.

The combination of all these pressures and fears meant that

Paul Volpe leapt at the chance to go south when his old friend Vito de Filippo of the Bonanno family said he was getting away from the heat in New York City by taking over a casino in Haiti. At the time the Bonanno family was engaged in a major power struggle, popularly known as the "Bananna Wars", with other New York City families and with Buffalo's Stefano Magaddino. Old man Joe Bonanno was in hiding, and Carmine Galente, his underboss, was in jail for heroin importation.

So, for $10,000, Paul Volpe sold his share of the car-wash business (which was doing quite well, legitimately), talked his brother Eugene into selling his share and coming in with him financially (later these shares in the car wash would have been worth $100,000 as it continued to prosper), and entered into a partnership with Vito de Filippo under the auspices of the Bonanno family to take over the International Casino in Port-au-Prince, Haiti. Volpe and de Filippo also had financial backing from John "Peanuts" Tranalone, a senior member of the New York City family of Frank Costello, the so-called "Prime Minister" of organized crime in his day.

In the beginning they had the only casino in Haiti, in a renovated old hotel called the International in the heart of Port-au-Prince. Until Volpe and de Filippo took it over, it was only a nickel-and-dime operation, but Volpe helped turn it into a very profitable operation, selling everything from food to medicine on the premises. He and Vito managed to attract some of the gambling junkets from the States and Toronto. As the croupier and blackjack dealer for the casino, Volpe brought down his gambling organizer and card-game man in Toronto, Sam Shirose. Both mob and police sources say that Shirose is "one of the nicest guys you would ever want to meet," and a first-rate croupier. The venture had all the makings of a big score. There was only one thing that caused concern – the erratic behaviour of Haiti's leader, who, according to Paul Volpe himself, was the only person he ever truly feared.

Duvalier's rule was ruthless, and his personality was bizarre; he was into both heroin and voodoo in a big way. He had his own secret police, the "tontons", who terrorized the island. According to mobster Vinnie Teresa, writing in his autobiography, *My Life in the Mafia*, co-authored with veteran *Newsday* organized-crime reporter Tom Renner, "the tontons looked more like hoodlums than we did. They wore dark glasses, expensive sharp civilian clothes, and they all carried guns.... The biggest trouble with them is that they were animals."

Papa Doc was fascinated with the mob and loved working with it, and Volpe and de Filippo were not the first nor the last mobsters to be establishing themselves in Haiti. Later, Vinnie "the Fat Man" Teresa and members of the Gambino and Patriarca crime families, of New York and New England respectively, opened a second mob casino. They were invited to Haiti with the full backing and co-operation of Haiti's dictator. In 1967, three senior American mobsters came down to Port-au-Prince to set up this casino, one that ultimately cut seriously into the International's business. The delegation from the Gambino family of New York City and the Patriarca family of New England consisted of Vinnie Teresa, number three man in the New England mob, Dave Iacovetti, a senior soldier in the Gambino family, and Joseph (Joe Kirk) Krikorian, another Patriarca representative. They went directly to the presidential palace when they arrived in Haiti. Vinnie Teresa describes the scene in *My Life in the Mafia*:

The three men followed a gaudily uniformed officer down endless corridors lined with guards. The floors glistened, reflecting chandeliers. Finally the officer stopped at two huge doors and knocked, then entered, holding the door for the three mob representatives. A vast table covered by a white cloth occupied the center of the room. At the head of the table stood a small black man with white hair and a smartly tailored white military jacket emblazoned with rows of colored ribbons and shiny medals.... You could see he was a smart guy. He had a good education – you could tell when he talked. He was short, on the slim side, with tan, not dark black skin, and he wore glasses. Behind those glasses were piercing brown eyes – eyes that made you feel he was looking right through you, like he had X-ray eyes. We called them snake eyes. He'd never take those eyes off you.

Paul Volpe took the same route many times to meet Duvalier, and he was always terrified. One day he was summoned to the presidential office to explain his casino operation. Duvalier, of course, had demanded a certain percentage of the take (as well as certain bribes, one costing Volpe $50,000), and Volpe, like Vinnie Teresa at the second mob casino, El Rancho, skimmed money off the top before Duvalier's tontons collected the dictator's share. This was the only way to keep the business profitable, according to both Teresa and Volpe. On this occasion, Volpe feared that the unpredictable Duvalier had somehow found out about this skimming through his secret spy network. Volpe was pacing back and forth when the two huge doors opened and the short, ageing President for Life, resplendent in full military regalia, walked in and began the interrogation. Volpe noticed that Papa Doc had two .45s on his desk and talked to Volpe in an ominous whisper. "Mr. Paul," he started, "where is the map for the gold mine?" Papa Doc was referring to an old abandoned gold mine Volpe had suggested be reopened so that Volpe could work a gold fraud. His tone "really scared me," Volpe reported later.

In the middle of the meeting, according to Paul Volpe's own account of it to lawyer Earl Levy, Papa Doc shot himself up with heroin. Volpe became even more fearful. He was surrounded by the tontons in the palace of a dope-crazed dictator. "He was really terrified of Papa Doc and his guards," says Levy.

In another visit to the presidential palace, Volpe was explaining something to Duvalier and threw out his arms to demonstrate something. The tontons guarding Papa Doc immediately put two rifles to Volpe's head, thinking he was about to hit the dictator. Volpe himself later told this story to a Toronto policeman who was investigating his activities. He enjoyed talking about the good old days in Haiti.

Despite the threatening atmosphere, however, nothing really happened to Volpe except that eventually Duvalier's men did catch the skimming, and this cut into Volpe's profit margin. Duvalier seemed to favour the Teresa mob group over Volpe's – even though Volpe had paid Papa Doc an initial bribe of $50,000. Teresa explains why in his book:

Dave Iacovetti [the Gambino family rep and Vinnie's partner] *was very close to Papa Doc. In 1961 and 1962 he had cooked up a scheme to peddle illegal lottery tickets for the Republic of Haiti Welfare Fund Sweepstakes. It was a multimillion-buck scheme.... Each ticket resulted in a payoff to Papa Doc, who made a bundle out of that deal. But that wasn't all Dave did for the old man. When Papa Doc needed guns and the U.S. government wouldn't provide them – in fact the feds secretly*

*tried to overthrow Papa Doc – Dave arranged to have machine
guns and rifles and all kinds of ammunition smuggled into Haiti.*

Still Vinnie Teresa had to pay ten per cent of all the money
bet in his casino to Duvalier – not just ten per cent of the
profits. The money was, according to Teresa, "to be delivered
to him each night by one of his secret policemen." Teresa thought
Duvalier would have made an excellent criminal himself:

*Watching him, I thought he'd made a helluva con man. He
made all of us think that everything was hunky dory, but he'd
get his point across – he'd let you know he was Papa Doc,
the boss, and don't you ever forget it. He had a will of iron,
and he was as hard hearted as they come. His people were
starving, begging in the streets, but he lived in the lap of luxury.
All Papa Doc was interested in was how he could make more
money.... But those people he didn't like, those he didn't trust,
lived on the edge of a razor blade.... He thought nothing of
putting people up against the wall and shooting them without
any trial. He was worse than any crime boss I ever met, and
I've met more than a few.*

So Paul Volpe's fears, it turns out, were well founded. Duvalier
was a bit of a wild card in the whole casino operation.
   But what really makes or breaks such a casino business is
the quality of junkets being run. Teresa's casino was more
successful because it got the better junkets, a higher-class clientele.
Teresa explains how his gambling junket system worked. It was
similar to Volpe's system, though more sophisticated because
Vinnie's mob provided more resources and back-up:

*The idea was to fill a plane with as many as a hundred gamblers
with good credit ratings. The gamblers wouldn't have to pay
a dime. They would first fill out an application stating how
much credit they had, what banks they did business with, and
how much money they had invested in stocks and real estate.
The casino involved would then make a credit check. Once they
had the credit approved by the casino, they could board a junket
flight from Boston, New York or wherever.... All food,
accommodations, and airline tickets would be paid for them by
the casino. All they had to pay out was money for expenses*

*for telephone calls ... and whatever they spent gambling....
Everything at the casino was in the bag. Card sharks, dice
manipulators, all kinds of crooks.... They had women dealers
handling twenty-one card games with marked cards; switchmen
who moved mercury loaded dice in and out of the game to
control it.*

Volpe, of course, utilized all the tricks of the trade as well. The
casino, in addition, provided him with prospects for fresh loan-
shark victims. People who over-extended themselves gambling
were ready to receive the kind, helping hand of Paul Volpe with
a short-term loan to cover their losses or debts. Eventually these
people wanted out when they learned they still had to pay back
hundreds of times the original loan. In many cases they couldn't
pay, and they then found themselves faced with threats of physical
violence. Soon the rough stuff would begin. Thus the original
supplicants became the victims, and the International Casino
readily served up more and more willing yet hapless loan-shark
victims to Paul Volpe.

Having a casino was also a good way for Volpe to launder
some of his profits from loan-sharking, frauds, gambling, and
extortions in Ontario. One of the major problems for members
of organized crime is making dirty money clean without paying
huge taxes or having to expose themselves to prosecution. Later
in life Volpe accomplished this by putting nothing in his own
name, and allowing relatives and associates to front the money
for him. In the early 1960s, however, he didn't rely on fronts
as much, so it was necessary to launder money in more creative
ways. One thing he did was to falsify the take on the casino,
though he never paid any taxes in Canada (or in Haiti, for
that matter) on the casino profits. What he did was mingle
illegally obtained money with legally obtained money, thus
making dirty money clean. This type of laundering was better
suited to someone living in the United States or Canada. It was
of limited value to him in Haiti since the government took
most of its money under the table, rather than in taxes. Volpe
had to pay huge amounts to Papa Doc and his relatives, plus
give a percentage to the Bonanno family in New York City,
who were his partners through Vito de Filippo, and to other
New York City mob investors.

But despite all this, Volpe certainly made a buck or two in

his first year in Haiti. On one of his better days in Haiti, a corrupt Haitian immigration officer tipped him off that a tourist had arrived with $60,000 cash. Volpe dashed down to the airport in Port-au-Prince and managed to coax the unwitting tourist into the International, where he was unburdened of most of his cash.

He even allowed the Haitian government to use a picture of him for its tourist brochure. The brochure featured a happy group of people with Paul Volpe in the middle overlooking a roulette wheel at the International Casino and surrounded by all of the exotica of Haiti. Haiti, the land of fun and games! Not many countries would use a mobster in their promotional material.

Volpe also had to do favours for the New York bosses, especially since Frank Costello (through "Peanuts" Tranalone) and Bonanno (through de Filippo) had money in his casino. When Jimmy "Blue Eyes" Alo, a top Genovese family lieutenant, who was also the Mafia liaison to U.S. mob banker Meyer Lansky, was on the lam from the FBI in 1964, Volpe provided him with sanctuary at his place in Haiti. And Volpe was proud of it, too. The FBI rarely made it to Haiti, and if they did, they rarely made it out of Haiti. Here is Vinnie Teresa reporting what Papa Doc said about that, in the CBC-TV *Connections* program of 1979:

"If you see an FBI agent or federal agent on this island, that is tailing you or something, just point him out.... Just point them out to my men.... They'll put them in the dungeon and they will never see daylight again." And he meant that. He was no man to fool with. Smart, very, very shrewd. Very, very clever man. His son is a donkey.

After being in Haiti for a year, Volpe began to hate the place. The Haitian secret police kept so tight a control that the only way he could get any money out of Haiti was to send it in U.S. cash in packages with friends. Volpe's spirits were kept up by the steady stream of visitors from Toronto (some of whom were given these packages of cash to take back to Toronto for safety and for later use), including two of his brothers (Eugene and Albert), his girl-friend, his associates, and, of course, the junketeers. Furthermore, Volpe himself made several visits to

Toronto to break from the pressures of Haitian intrigues and to keep an eye on his Canadian interests.

So in 1965 Paul Volpe went back to Toronto to live, though he kept a financial interest in the International until late 1968, when he finally sold out. While he was living in Haiti, as we have seen, Volpe made frequent business trips back to Toronto to keep his organized-crime pot boiling. Now the situation was reversed. For the next three years, from 1965 to 1968, he would travel back and forth between Haiti and Toronto, but his prime residence was once again Toronto.

By 1968 Teresa's casino, El Rancho, was getting the real money junkets. Says Teresa of Volpe's casino: "The International was nickel and dime, and none of the good junkets ran in there. They all went to the El Rancho." The heavy burden of paying off and dealing with the irrational dictator made Volpe anxious to get out. When the tontons of Duvalier tuned in to his skimming operation, it really began to hurt financially. Volpe never succeeded in making the International the first-rate, world-class casino he hoped it would turn into. El Rancho was a gold mine compared to the International.

However, Haiti was to take on mythic stature in Volpe's mind as time went by. In the 1970s and even up until his death, he was fond of talking nostalgically about his days in Haiti with his underlings and associates. And he always dreamed of opening up another casino, somewhere, someday.

CHAPTER SIX

A Visit from "Mr. Palmer"

PAUL VOLPE came back to Toronto during the first week of March 1965 and attempted to pick up where he had left off in his criminal career in Hogtown. He was picked up at the airport by a well-known Toronto rounder and criminal associate and taken downtown. Clearly, Volpe had actively kept up his organized-crime contacts and operations in Toronto from the Caribbean and on the frequent visits he had made to Toronto while living in Haiti. He actually came back with more prestige and respect than he had had when he had gone down just a year and a half before. While away he had been named, along with Johnny "Pops" and his own brother Albert, as a Toronto member of Buffalo's Magaddino Mafia family. There were sensational headlines. Johnny "Pops" was safely in jail for the Bluestein beating and for heroin trafficking. The crime world of Toronto seemed to be ready for the taking, and Volpe was already becoming a legend on the street.

He wasted no time in getting down to business. In his second week back from the land of voodoo, at two o'clock on St. Patrick's Day 1965, Volpe went to have a drink at the bar at the Park Plaza Hotel in downtown Toronto with three others: his brother Albert, an enforcer he had brought up from Buffalo, and a stock promoter he was in the process of extorting. As Paul Volpe put his hand out to pick up his drink he suddenly found himself in handcuffs. He was told not to make a move. All the doors were covered. He was under arrest. Ironically, he realized, he had been far safer in the hands of the eccentric dictator Papa Doc than in his more civilized home town. When one of the arresting officers, Detective Ed Barkley, asked Volpe who his companion was, Paul introduced the policemen to Pasquale Natarelli, a vicious Buffalo enforcer, as simply "a guy who comes into the car wash".

The police took Volpe downtown and pushed him into a room with four heavy-set officers. Thinking that he was about to be beaten, Volpe asked if he could take off his overcoat, as it was brand-new and he didn't want to get it torn or stained with blood.

"Go ahead and take your best shot," Volpe bravely told his captors.

The police present were amused: "Take it easy, Paul, sit down and relax. Do you want a cigarette?"

Volpe, used to the brutal methods of the mob and the more direct approach of Papa Doc's tontons, was surprised; this was to be a civilized interrogation. But he was even more surprised to be in this predicament at all only two weeks after returning to Toronto.

What had happened was this. Albert Volpe had been working for years on some stock promotions (which were legal, though sometimes just on the line) with a promoter named Dick Angle, who, though he didn't know it, was himself being taken by the more experienced promoter, Albert Volpe. One source close to both the Volpes and Angle at the time described the situation at the point Paul Volpe got involved: "By this time Albert was wining and dining Dick Angle, who had taken a house in Nassau, the Bahamas. He had taken Angle for close to $80,000 on con pretences.... Cons do it with stocks. Albert was pretty good at that. So he drained Dick Angle pretty well, but Paul thought there was still some potential there ... so he figured he could get something out of Dick Angle, make a score." Albert Volpe at first balked and told Paul to leave Angle alone, that there was "no more to be squeezed out of him." Paul Volpe convinced Albert that there was room for a more imaginative scam with lots of money for them through Dick Angle. He also felt that they could use Angle to work with them, helping them to organize some additional stock frauds, since Angle was one of the best stock promoters in the business at the time. Reluctantly, Albert Volpe delivered Angle unto his brother.

Paul's first scheme had to do with a gold mine in Haiti. This was the same abandoned gold mine that he had discussed with Papa Doc Duvalier earlier. Angle was supposed to give Paul Volpe $17,500 for his share of this worthless gold mine, though, of course, Angle did not know it was worthless at the time. Angle was to write a prospectus and run a stock promotion on it. Paul Volpe and Angle had met in the Bahamas about this scheme while Paul was still living in and operating out of Haiti. It was a rather far-fetched plan, poorly organized and thought out. Basically it was an excuse for Paul Volpe to hit Angle up for money – for Paul Volpe to get his hands on the score.

However, the scam was so badly organized that even Angle became aware of this deception and eventually changed his mind about the scheme's potential. He refused to pay the $17,500. But Volpe would not let Angle off so easily. When Paul Volpe had someone on the hook, he always followed through and took maximum advantage. He made it plain to Angle that he "owed" this money, and that if he didn't pay it there would be consequences. Since at the time the threats were being made from Haiti, Angle ignored them and simply didn't pay. He decided that he didn't want to have anything further to do with the Volpes. He was not to have that choice.

It was arranged by Volpe associates on Bay Street that the price of shares in a company owned by Angle would come down sharply. Angle was told that his company would be taken over by the Volpe interests (which included Eugene and Albert as well as Paul) if the money "owed" Paul Volpe wasn't paid.

At this point Angle received a visit from a mysterious stranger who called himself "Mr. Palmer" and said he was from Buffalo. "Mr. Palmer" was actually Pasquale Natarelli, a heavy-duty mob enforcer and arsonist who was a member of the Magaddino crime family of Buffalo. He demanded the $17,500 from Dick Angle to prevent a take-over of Angle's company.

A series of meetings furthering the extortion then followed. They took place in the week of March 9-17, 1965, and involved Paul Volpe, Albert Volpe, Eugene Volpe, Angle's lawyer Jack Gilbert, Dick Angle, Pasquale Natarelli, and Natarelli's associate and fellow enforcer from Buffalo, one "Cicci".

On March 9, 1965, Angle met first with Albert and Paul Volpe, Natarelli, and Cicci, in Room 1031 at the Park Plaza Hotel in Toronto. Natarelli started the conversation: "You'd better come up with the money or blood will run in the streets of Toronto. I've got an army behind me." Dick Angle was absolutely terrified. The fourth man, Cicci, who was quite nasty-looking, made some menacing motions with a fork. Angle later said, "[I] would have sold my soul to get out of that room."

This was in the days when certain stock promoters and brokers were being beaten with baseball bats right on Bay Street by mob enforcers. Morton Shulman, a high-profile crusading NDP member in the provincial legislature, was to make several of these blatant extortions on Bay Street public in the legislature in the early 1970s, including the beating of stockbroker Billy Ginsberg. Angle had a real reason to be scared. Volpe and his boys had gone too far; they had done too effective a job in frightening this victim. Angle had few alternatives left, and he reached for the most obvious solution to save both himself and his family, who had also been threatened by Volpe's goons.

In a major departure from his previous handling of the extortion, Angle finally went to the police. At first, certain high-ranking police officials, including the chief of police at the time, didn't want to believe that Paul Volpe was really a member of the Mafia or a major criminal. Junior officers who worked the street finally persuaded the brass that this case was worth pursuing and that Volpe was an important criminal. A major police operation was begun under the command of a veteran intelligence and morality officer, Inspector Robert Stirling of the Metro Toronto Police Force. Part of the police operation on Volpe involved taping telephone conversations and wiring Angle for his meetings with the Volpes and "Mr. Palmer" and his associate. When police later realized who it was that Volpe had brought up from Buffalo, they were all, according to Inspector Stirling, "quite shocked". Natarelli was a very high-level mafioso, and his appearance in Toronto on behalf of Paul Volpe was proof positive that Volpe was a major Mafia member. But police didn't realize this until after the arrests, as Natarelli used the cover name of "Palmer" throughout the extortion.

At Angle's next meeting with Paul Volpe, a week later, the

following conversation took place, secretly recorded by a hidden body-pack Angle wore under his suit:

VOLPE: I've stuck my ass out 40,000 miles for you, and I mean I stuck it out. [Sticking "his ass out" was one of Volpe's favourite expressions; it meant he felt he was owed something for his trouble.]
ANGLE: Let me ask you something. When I was up to the room Monday night and you knew I was nervous ...
VOLPE: I tried to cool you down, didn't I?
ANGLE: The guy sits there tapping the fork.... [Cicci did this to keep Angle anxious.]
VOLPE: You're lucky he didn't have an ice pick in his hand. I know how this guy performs.

Of course Volpe knew how Cicci and Natarelli performed. This is exactly why he brought up two of the meanest enforcers from Buffalo's Magaddino family to help extort Dick Angle.

In a subsequent conversation, Paul Volpe increased the psychological pressure on Angle by threatening Angle's wife and child as well as his lawyer, Jack Gilbert. Volpe's strategy, often employed by mobsters, was to make his victim feel totally insecure through intimidation of the people around him. Volpe later had a meeting with Jack Gilbert in his office and demanded that he make his client pay up. In a later conversation with Angle, Volpe insisted that the lawyer be brought to him in New York City to meet with him and some of his connections in the New York mob.

VOLPE: Bring him there, all right? Tell him any fucking thing you want. Bring him.
ANGLE: But I have got to have an excuse.
VOLPE: I don't care what you do. Bring him to me. Bring him to New York for me.... If he raises his fucking voice, he won't come back ...
ANGLE: That's what you want me to do?
VOLPE: Yeah. I'd like to have you do that. You want to bring him?
ANGLE: I'll see what I can do.
VOLPE: Yeah, bring him to New York for me.
ANGLE: Who's he going to meet? I mean, I've got to say something, Paul.

VOLPE: He's going to meet somebody and maybe not come back.

At this point Angle agreed to pay Volpe the $17,500 at a meeting the next day in the Park Plaza Hotel's plush Prince Arthur Lounge. Police officers mixed with the crowd of lunch-time drinkers as Angle, still wired, Paul Volpe, Albert Volpe, and "Mr. Palmer" sat down. The police were listening in on radio mikes outside the bar. The conversation started with Angle asking "Palmer" if his troubles would be over after he made the payment. Natarelli was trying to impress Angle with the power of the Mafia and laid it on quite thick:

NATARELLI: Look, I mean, I don't know how the hell else to convince you, Dick. Look, look, with us, it's like having City Hall behind you ... you can't make a mistake.... I don't care, I don't care who you ... what you do, how you do it, who you hurt. You know Dick, with us you're always right.... From this moment on, you can go home and sleep like a baby, with peace of mind, all right? Untroubled, believe me, because if you get in trouble you'll know that our word is bigger than a police .45 or all the money in the world. Are you listening?
ANGLE: This money will take care of it?
NATARELLI: It will.
ANGLE: No trouble?
NATARELLI: No expenses. It's all right.... Paul, Al, and the Volpes can call on anybody from the States or Canada for help. I want you to know that. But as you just said, you are through, you are absolutely finished, you've got peace of mind. Go home and sleep like a baby. Nobody at any time will bother you. You get in touch with me, and we'll take anybody that's on your back right off.

Angle then asked Paul Volpe if the payment of $17,500 would take the pressure off his lawyer, Jack Gilbert, as well. At first Volpe hedged, sensing he might be able to suck some money out of Gilbert or get more out of Angle. "Palmer" simply stated that "anything Paulie says is all right with me." Volpe told "Palmer" what a rough time Gilbert had given him in his office: "He's a mother-fucker, the way he spoke to me in the office." Natarelli asked Volpe, "Why didn't you slap him across the kisser?" Volpe replied, "I shoulda given him a fucking shove," but ironically he added, "I thought he had a tape going.... I would've done it if I had been out of the room." Finally, Volpe agreed to "see that Gilbert's off the hook."

Within minutes of this, as Paul Volpe and Natarelli were about to have their drinks, the police moved in: "Fellas, don't move out of the seats you're in. You're under arrest." This time *Angle's* secret tape machine did do Volpe in.

And so the Volpes and Magaddino family lieutenant Pasquale Natarelli were arrested for extortion on March 17, 1965. The bail for Paul, Albert, and Eugene (who was also arrested separately) was a cool $360,000. But the Volpes raised the money in cash later the next day through friends and associates, and were back out on the street. Albert Volpe fled to Europe, where he stayed to avoid the trials, running a casino in Athens and later in Yugoslavia. Natarelli was later charged in Buffalo with a number of major crimes after the defection of mobster Paddy Calabrese. Paddy was a soldier in Natarelli's mob family who squealed to police and was able to implicate Natarelli in some major arsons and frauds in Buffalo. Natarelli was sentenced to twenty years in jail in the States. Because of this the Toronto Crown attorney eventually dropped the charges against him in Toronto.

Paul Volpe stayed to face the music. But the ensuing series of legal battles that finally ended up putting him in jail lasted three and a half years, from 1965 until mid-1968, and involved a record five trials for the same crime.

In the first trial, which took place in 1966, a mistrial was declared when a juror, obviously intimidated by the situation, stood up suddenly – midway through the trial – and dramatically announced that he really didn't understand English well enough to follow all the arguments and testimony. The second trial ended with a hung jury. Eleven jurors voted for conviction and one juror stubbornly held out for acquittal even in light of all the evidence. It later turned out that this juror's mortgage was held by a Volpe associate, real-estate agent Dave McGoran.

In the third trial, Paul Volpe instructed McGoran to reach into the jury with a bribe. The juror that McGoran contacted told police. McGoran was later charged and convicted of tampering with a jury. He got nine months in jail. Meanwhile a third mistrial was declared. The fourth trial ended up miraculously with a verdict of not guilty. But the Crown appealed the verdict to the Supreme Court of Canada, which ordered yet another new trial because it found that the judge had misdirected the jury.

In the meantime, after the fourth trial, Dick Angle had moved to the United States, where he lived in hiding under police protection. Albert Volpe remained on the lam in Europe, and Natarelli was in jail for his New York State convictions.

Paul Volpe, after his acquittal, went down to the Bahamas with his long-time girl-friend for a short holiday. In the Bahamas, Volpe ran into James Crossland, the Crown attorney who had conducted the case against him. Volpe invited James Crossland and his wife to join him for a drink. They did, and stayed for several drinks. No bribe was offered. James Crossland later became a provincial court judge, and Paul Volpe always claimed that Crossland was "in his pocket". But he wasn't. They had just met to have drinks. Paul Volpe was always trying to influence and befriend people like Crossland: Crown attorneys, judges, and members of Parliament. Volpe never missed a chance at influence-peddling and making contact with those in power. Even though, in reality, they were of marginal value at best, Paul Volpe always boasted about his judicial and political connections. Knowing influential people helped his image. But in this instance, as in others where he mingled with political and judicial figures, Volpe created problems for the prominent individual concerned; these people were then usually investigated by the police if they were seen with Volpe or if someone reported the incident. Paul Volpe used to say, jokingly, that if he wanted to get back at some distinguished figure, all he had to do was to make sure to be seen with him.

After the Supreme Court ordered a new trial, Paul Volpe knew that someone would have to go down on this one. He wanted to spare his older brother Eugene, who was only minimally involved anyway, the pain and indignity of jail. In a deal with the Crown negotiated by his lawyers, Volpe pleaded guilty at the fifth trial in exchange for the reduction of charges against Eugene Volpe. After all, as Paul himself pointed out, Eugene was not that heavily involved in organized crime (though he had helped in the Angle extortion and had done some bootlegging, fencing, and high-grading in the past). It was a noble gesture on Paul Volpe's part – at least so he thought himself.

Paul Volpe now knew he was going to jail. Three days before the fifth trial was to take place, on June 17, 1968, Volpe married Lisa Dalholt, a Creeds model whom he had met two years earlier and had been going with on and off for a year. Paul Volpe really had a sense of timing. To marry the Danish model, he dumped his girl-friend of sixteen years, who had just testified for him as a character witness in his trials.

About a week before he was to go to jail in 1968, Volpe claims he went down to a southern Ontario city at the request of a senior Conservative back-room man to help get a certain prominent Tory candidate re-elected in the upcoming 1968 federal election. There is no other evidence that this incident actually took place. Volpe's claim is that in exchange for some money and his help in getting out the Italian vote in the riding, he was told that the grateful politician would help him avoid jail for the Angle extortion. He didn't receive the help, even though he claims he "worked his ass off to get the guy re-elected." He was very bitter about this for years after.

Finally, on June 21, 1968, the Crown accepted the plea of guilty from Paul Volpe in court. This was over three years after the terrified Dick Angle had originally gone to the police.

Paul Volpe was sentenced to the maximum jail term for the offence – two years in jail – after his lawyer failed in his negotiations for a reduced sentence. But the recently married Volpe was relieved after the many years of legal battles. However, according to a senior police officer, Volpe arranged through his connections to spend his term just outside Toronto at a minimum-security institution, more like a hotel than a jail, that had excellent food, colour television and the minimum of security. (This was the so-called "country club" to which Harold Ballard was later sent to serve out his time after a fraud conviction.) According to his lawyer, David Humphrey (now a district court judge), "Paul Volpe went to jail with his head held high and a smile on his face." With six months off for good behaviour, Volpe served just under eighteen months of his sentence. This was to be the first and last major prison term in his long criminal career.

CHAPTER SEVEN

"A Sinister Array of Characters"

AFTER EIGHTEEN MONTHS in prison, Paul Volpe was released in late 1969. The situation in Toronto looked good. Finally, both Volpe and Klegerman were out on the street, together for the first time since 1964. Respect for Paul Volpe in the underworld was enhanced after the details of the Angle extortion were fully known. Paul was a big man who could call in senior members of the Magaddino family in Buffalo to support his extortions. He was indeed Mafia, and all that implied. The years from late 1969 until 1978 were the golden period of Paul Volpe's criminal career. He had no serious rivals in Toronto; he had a trusted and brilliant lieutenant in Natie Klegerman; he expanded his power base into areas he had not dreamed of in the early 1960s; and he was able to put together a loose federation of criminals under his command for diverse operations in a number of criminal areas (loan-sharking, illegal gambling, shady diamond deals, land fraud, extortion, and massive involvement in the construction industry) in a number of different locations throughout Ontario, especially in the Toronto-Hamilton and Ottawa areas, and in the United States, mostly in and around Atlantic City and New York City. It was Natie Klegerman who was mainly responsible for Paul Volpe's massive criminal expansion in the 1970s. Klegerman's ingenuity and organizational ability and Volpe's charisma and "respect" on the street made for a formidable criminal combination.

As we have seen, Volpe broke from the traditional Mafia clannishness in his hiring practices. He listened to Klegerman's advice and took talent where it lay. This was regarded as a source of his strength. Other Mafia groups in Toronto and southern Ontario still worked almost entirely within the Italian structure of the old Mafia. Paul Volpe, though he often used more experienced, tougher and less educated Italian muscle for enforcement, constructed with Klegerman's help the first real multicultural mob in Canada, with an Italian mafioso at the helm.

Through his own extensive contacts in the crime world, Klegerman helped Volpe recruit new talent, such as Chuck Yanover, a middle-level enforcer and organizer for the Volpe group; Ian Rosenberg, a lower-level enforcer, quite handy with dynamite; Murray Feldberg, a loan shark; Ron Mooney, a Toronto break-and-enter specialist, who helped set up crooked card games; Sam Shirose, a card specialist who also organized gambling activities for Volpe; David McGoran, the realtor who organized enforcement activities and was convicted of bribing a juror for Paul Volpe during one of his trials for the Dick Angle extortions; Raymond "Squeaker" Greco, a heavy muscle, fence, and drug connection; Joe Moses Levy (or Levey), a fence who helped steal and then recirculate stolen jewellery; Randolph Wheatley, an enforcer brought in to help with construction-industry violence; Ken Armitage, a bodyguard and driver with a criminal record for "false pretences" and keeping a bawdy-house; Tony Iatti, a bodyguard and enforcer; Jimmy Bass, yet another enforcer; and many, many other criminals and rounders who thrived in the Volpe-Klegerman orbit. Klegerman also helped Volpe move into new areas of business such as diamond frauds and business and stock frauds, and helped organize his collections and loan-sharking empire into a more cost-efficient, manageable, business-like unit.

However, it was in the construction industry in Ontario that Paul Volpe really got an edge in 1970. What Paul Volpe did and how this came about is explained in the 770-page report of the Royal Commission into Certain Sectors of the Construction Industry under Judge Harry Waisberg, which was commissioned by the premier of Ontario in the spring of 1973 and finished its work in late 1974. Premier William Davis had been persuaded to set up the royal commission after a series of bombings and shootings rocked the construction industry in 1971–73. These acts of violence had to do with some labour contracts that were being manipulated by certain union officials and company executives who, in turn, had brought in the mob to assist. Also, certain companies, such as one operated by Cesido Romanelli, were trying to prevent other companies, such as Acme Lathing and Gemini Lathing, from merging and becoming more serious rivals. Cesido Romanelli used violence to prevent the merger and recruited Paul Volpe to do the job. As mentioned, Morton Shulman, the NDP member of the Legislature, had made a series of dramatic revelations in the provincial house about mob activity in Ontario, especially in the construction industry. The issue could no longer be avoided, although most senior law-enforcement officials in Ontario, including the attorney general of the time, Allan Lawrence, had publicly denied the existence of a Mafia organization in Ontario. Officially there was no major organized-crime problem in Ontario.

The Waisberg report hit southern Ontario like a bombshell when it was tabled at Queen's Park on December 19, 1974, and it made people dramatically aware of corruption and the role of the mob in the construction industry. The *Globe and Mail* gave the report full front-page coverage, excerpting important sections inside the paper. Many of the mobsters involved, including Paul Volpe, Natale Luppino, and Chuck Yanover, had been star witnesses before the commission, along with prominent figures in the construction industry in Ontario, such as Angelo and Elvio Del Zotto and Marco Muzzo. Union officials, such as Gus Simone of the Lathers' Union, Local 562, were also called to testify in the year and a half of Judge Waisberg's extensive inquiries.

Judge Waisberg began one of his most important chapters by describing the events at a 1971 meeting in the Mona Lisa Restaurant at 2954 Dufferin Street, Toronto, the mob gathering-place of its day. (It was here that Paul Volpe, Jimmy Luppino, Charles Yanover, Remo Commisso, and a host of other mobsters met on a regular basis in the 1960s and early 1970s.) As Judge Waisberg wrote:

The meeting which took place in the Mona Lisa Restaurant in the Spring of 1971 introduced to the lathing and drywall sector of the construction industry a new element. It was at that fateful meeting that Cesido Romanelli and Angelo Del Zotto took steps that resulted in the hiring of escorts. The chapter on violence [an earlier chapter of the Waisberg report dealing with the actual bombings and shootings] *described an attempted telephone call from the restaurant, after which Angelo Del Zotto gave Romanelli the name of a man to contact. According to Simone, Romanelli did in fact make contact. Following that contact, a sinister array of characters was introduced to this sector of the industry.*

The first "sinister character" whom Judge Waisberg named was none other than Natale Luppino of Hamilton, who was hired as an "escort" by Romanelli in May 1971, although he had no previous experience in the construction industry. Natale Luppino, of course, was the brother of Paul Volpe's good friend and colleague Jimmy Luppino of Hamilton, the son of the old don of southern Ontario, Giacomo Luppino, and himself a long-time associate of Paul Volpe. Paul was even godfather to Natale's first son. Natale had been a heavy or enforcer over the years, specializing in extortion and beatings, for which he possessed a long criminal record. Both Angelo Del Zotto, one of the most prominent and successful construction barons in North America, and Romanelli claimed that the Mona Lisa meeting had never taken place, but Judge Waisberg rejected this contention, and found that the evidence tendered by Del Zotto and Romanelli was "contrived".

Natale Luppino quickly made his muscle felt. In Ottawa, the head of the Plasterers' and Cement Masons' Union was Jean-Guy Denis. Romanelli, who was involved in several large construction projects in Ottawa at the time, wanted to have the union in his pocket. Denis was urged to co-operate, first by Romanelli, then by Natale Luppino. He was asked either to set up his own union or to hire certain "employees" of Romanelli's and Luppino's choosing. Denis referred to these potential "employees" as "not the type of people I would want to work with under any circumstances." Denis was offered help in his re-election and a trouble-free union if he co-operated. He refused. Natale Luppino became more insistent – and threatening. "You might not make it home tonight.... Just be careful on your way home, a car might run you down," he told Denis.

At a second meeting Denis was offered a five-cent-an-hour

bribe for every hour worked by his seven to eight hundred men, simply to stay off the job and let someone else police it. Again, Denis refused to capitulate. Then Denis was threatened with broken legs and broken arms. "If I didn't fall within their requirements of what they wanted to do ... Natale Luppino actually made it clear that I might not make it home.... He was trying to establish a monopoly, complete control over the drywall industry, and he felt he was doing well in Montreal. He was doing well in Toronto, but Ottawa was an obstacle that he wanted to get rid of."

Denis had clear and strong ideals of freedom, which he demonstrated by fighting for Canada in the Second World War, and he was not about to give up the freedom he had helped win by handing his union over to the mob. He felt that if he stood up to them, they would ultimately have no alternative but to back down. "I didn't want them to take over the market," said Denis. "I didn't think what they were trying to do was right. I knew that it was against the wish of my membership and I felt that to either accept their offer or run away from them would have been to make them stronger, and I didn't want that. I felt the only way to stop them was to stand up and fight, which is what I did."

But organized crime fought back. On the evening of January 8, 1973, two strong-armed men arrived at Denis's Ottawa house and asked Paul Denis, Jean-Guy's son, for his father. When they were told that Jean-Guy was not home, the two enforcers stormed into the house, savagely striking the sixteen-year-old boy. They kept repeating to the young Paul Denis that his father was to "lay off". As a result of the beating Jean-Guy's son spent a week in the hospital with a concussion, and eventually had to be operated on to correct internal injuries. Jean-Guy Denis was appalled, but even more determined: "This is Canada and everything should be peaceful ... and when I realized these people were organized crime I decided to stand up and fight. And I am not going to suggest that I wasn't scared. I was. But I was more determined to do the right thing than to run away. And I feel that had I decided to fold up, they probably would have picked up the Ottawa market and obtained their monopoly."

Before the intimidation was over, Denis wished he had purchased a remote-control starter for his car in case it was rigged with bombs, but he showed that a courageous man can stand up to the mob. And he won. The mob didn't take over the Ottawa union local, and backed down in face of Denis's refusal to co-operate. Jean-Guy Denis deserves the Order of Canada in recognition of his tremendous courage.

But things were more under control for the mob in Toronto, where Paul Volpe himself was personally on top of the situation. And working with Volpe was Klegerman associate Chuck Yan-over, a well-known Toronto biker associate and criminal, and one of the more interesting of the "sinister characters".

Charles (as he prefers to be called) was born in Belleville, Ont., on September 30, 1945, the son of an upper-middle-class Jewish clothing merchant from Toronto named Ben Yanover and his wife, Eve. Always fascinated with guns as a youth, Yanover mowed lawns all over Belleville to be able to purchase his first gun at the tender age of fourteen. Charles moved to Toronto in his teens, and by the mid-1960s he was operating a motorcycle shop called City Motor Bike on Weston Road in the west end of Toronto. While many have referred to Yanover as "Chuck the Bike", this is a bit of a misnomer, for while Charles knew many bikers through his shop, he never was actually a member of any of the many Toronto-area criminal biker gangs. Through his connections with many of the heavies in the biker gangs, and because of his desire for easy money and adventure, he involved himself in some of their criminal operations and helped supply them with arms that he imported from the United States. Also, he would help the biker gangs unload motorcycles they had stolen by fencing them through his business. In fact, one of Yanover's first convictions, which occurred in January 1971, when he was twenty-five, was for possession of stolen property and a restricted weapon, and it arose out of his work with the biker gangs.

In December 1971, Yanover was released from prison and, through his mentor and friend Nate Klegerman, was introduced to Paul Volpe. Yanover was taken to Volpe's home to swim in his luxurious pool and discuss some criminal projects. Volpe then recruited Yanover to help out as part of his enforcement arm by arranging some shootings and bombings. These, it turned out, were the bombings and shootings set up by Romanelli through Volpe to prevent a merger between Acme Lathing and Gemini Lathing, the two Toronto companies that were his rivals in the lathing business.

Yanover brought with him his heavy muscle in the form of Ian Rosenberg, a close friend and somewhat unstable enforcer, and Jimmy Bass, later charged with the murder of Rosenberg and his girl-friend. Yanover has natural management skills and prefers not to dirty his own hands. He is a gentle persuader, not a heavy-muscle type. He is also, as was Paul Volpe, a natural talent-spotter and organizer, and is quite good at getting other people to do things for him – especially physically nasty things. In his relations with Paul Volpe and Volpe enforcers, Yanover assumed a kind of middle-management position.

Chuck Yanover doesn't really look like a mobster, though he does frequently wear dark glasses and drive a Mercedes-Benz. He is short and muscular with longish hair, which tends to give him the appearance of a 1960s hippie. He is handsome and not at all threatening in appearance, for he doesn't wear a fedora or affect any of the Mafia style of dress popular with certain gangsters in Ontario (Paul Volpe, for example, often used to dress like a character out of *The Godfather*). He is a chameleon, who always had a great ability to mix with both low life in the mob and senior mobsters such as Paul Volpe, as well as with journalists, police, and other members of respectable society. Yanover has the gift of the gab, and is just polished and charming enough to pull off any scam. He is genial and generally quite amiable in manner, without the hard edge one often sees in men who grow up in the tough street world of major Canadian or American cities. He is almost gentle in comparison with most of his associates and colleagues in organized crime. He has modelled himself upon his mentor and sponsor in the criminal world, Nathan Israel Klegerman.

Klegerman took the young Yanover under his wing in 1971 and trained him in the art of the con. He taught Yanover always to deal in cash and to keep no books – that the only accounting system he needed was, in the words of Yanover, "how to move money from one pocket to the other." Klegerman also taught Yanover the art of carefully choosing the victim. This is crucial to successful confidence operations. The victim has to be either weak, naive, or somewhat shady – but without the finesse or resources to retaliate against the con man. Klegerman himself was a master at selecting the right victim, and managed to operate quite successfully in Toronto, New York City, and Europe for over twenty years (with the notable exception of the five-year stint in the pen for fencing stolen jewels). Klegerman taught him, in the words of the master, Phineas T. Barnum, that there is indeed a "sucker born every minute." You just had to know how to spot them.

Charles Yanover is a complex man and a thorough-going rascal. Beneath his ingratiating charm lies a deadly cunning. Not that he is an evil person out to cause gratuitous pain or hurt; it's not that simple. He is what used to be called a rogue in the best sense of this very eighteenth-century term: an endearing villain with whom it is difficult not to empathize just a bit. But his is not a character from an eighteenth-century novel. He is a real, live (and lively) confidence man extraordinaire in our midst.

Yanover thrives on what he calls "walking" people – that is, working out an elaborate scam or scheme, suckering his victim in, and making a "score". Though fascinated with guns and dynamite and a self-proclaimed arms dealer, he thinks of himself as essentially non-violent. However, violence inevitably becomes a part of his elaborate schemes in one way or another. Also, it is important to remember that he began his career with violence, as an enforcer for the Paul Volpe mob, shooting up and dynamiting lathing companies in the Toronto area and booking free-lance enforcers to bring loan-sharking victims into line through extortion.

In his early days with the Volpe mob, with which he was associated for over eight years (from 1971 to 1979), Yanover was known affectionately as "Chuck the Bagel", as he would take a bite out of a bagel and leave it behind as his calling card. It was a novel method of intimidation. One of his jobs for the Volpe organization was collecting loan-shark money from Flite Investments, run by Nate Klegerman and Murray Feldberg, which was at the corner of Spadina and College in the same building Klegerman used for his international fencing operation in 1962.

Two chapters of the final report of the Waisberg commission, issued in November 1974, dealt with the activities of Yanover. Along with the construction violence for which he was partially responsible, he had been the subject of the special joint O.P.P.–Metro Police intelligence investigation, code-named "Project B", that had led to the establishment of the royal commission. Paul Volpe and Charles Yanover were prominently featured, complete with mug shots and surveillance photos (including one with Yanover on his motorcycle, chatting with Nate Klegerman in front of Creeds in downtown Toronto, where Volpe's wife worked), in the chapter on violence in the construction industry and in the chapter called "Other Activities", which deals with the mob incursions into the industry. After painstakingly examining all of the evidence, including Yanover's and Volpe's sworn statements and testimony under oath before the commission, Judge Waisberg concluded that "Yanover's testimony was not credible" and that Yanover was certainly involved in some of the violence, including the shooting up of Acme Lathing on July 19, 1972, and the bombing of Gemini Lathing on July 21, 1972, at the behest of Paul Volpe.

Evidence, including a parking ticket of Paul Volpe's that was found in Yanover's possession, certainly pointed to the conclusion that Volpe and Yanover had planned the violence together. The ticket was issued on June 30, 1972, at Bathurst and Steeles. Yanover denied "ever riding with him" (Volpe), but later admitted he "may have ridden with him." Yanover testified that he was meeting with his lawyer, Allan Mintz, on December 14, 1972, to discuss his defence on a possession-of-a-firearm charge. Klegerman and Volpe were also meeting with the lawyer. Yanover said Klegerman gave him Volpe's ticket and asked him if he would pay it as he was going to the police station anyway (he was on parole and had to report regularly).

Judge Waisberg dismisses this explanation in his final report: "It is more probable, however, that Yanover was with Volpe at the time the summons was issued and it must be more than a coincidence that it was this very area of metropolitan Toronto where the shooting and bombings of Acme and Gemini took place starting July 1972. The explanation is insignificant in that Yanover was involved in a charge of possession of guns and was present at a lawyer's office accompanied by Volpe and Klegerman when this charge was being considered. It would appear, therefore, that Volpe and Klegerman had more than a passing interest in the proceeding."

Understatement was one of Judge Waisberg's strongest suits. He was very careful in his final report to carefully weigh all of the evidence and not to make any major leaps in the conclusions he drew. Moreover, Waisberg was extremely cautious in his wording, offering detailed explanations for his statements. It is because of Judge Waisberg's restraint that Yanover was never charged with perjury before the commission. Waisberg preferred to let the facts speak for themselves, and to show that Volpe and Yanover were lying, rather than to charge them with perjury. "I found Yanover and Kiroff [a Yanover associate and enforcer] to be arrogant and unreliable witnesses," said a frustrated Judge Waisberg in his final report.

In an earlier chapter Waisberg stated: "It is a reasonable inference, therefore, that Yanover participated in the shooting [at Acme]. He was probably hired by those attempting to break up the merger plans of Acme Lathing and Gemini Drywall. The evidence relative to a number of incidents described in this report shows a connection between Yanover and Volpe, and a connection between Volpe and Romanelli. This opens a reasonable inference that Romanelli was somehow connected with this incident." Elsewhere in the report Waisberg explains that Romanelli had brought in Volpe and the mob, the "sinister array of characters", in order to take over the construction industry.

Judge Waisberg never actually said what Paul Volpe's overall plan was. He simply pointed to an arrangement, which he found "sinister", between Paul Volpe and the mob on one side and certain construction companies and union leaders on the other. He pointed at Agostino "Gus" Simone of Bolton, Ontario, the head of Local 562 of the Lathers' Union and the business manager of Local 675 of the United Brotherhood of Carpenters and Joiners, representing the drywall workers, and implied that he took bribes, that he was very friendly with Paul Volpe, and that he was living rather well for his salary (a picture of his luxurious house was included in the final report). According to Judge Waisberg, Simone received cash payments from contractors and was able to buy his lavish $100,000 home on a salary of only $17,000. This was "quite improper", according to Judge Waisberg's final report.

The finger was also pointed at Cesido Romanelli and Angelo Del Zotto for arranging through Paul Volpe to have mob "escorts", Natale Luppino and Domenic Zappia among others, brought into the companies and the industry. Waisberg also strongly suggested that Paul Volpe arranged the bombings and shootings at Acme Lathing and Gemini Lathing in Toronto to prevent a merger, using his enforcers Chuck Yanover, Ian

Rosenberg, Joe Bagnato, Randolph Wheatley, Thomas Kiroff, and others to actually plant the bombs or act as enforcers.

Waisberg also pointed to the improbability of Paul Volpe's statement of assets. As part of his testimony, Volpe was required to file a statement of his assets and net worth. Volpe claimed he was unemployed and had few valuable possessions. By implication, this was supposed to mean that he couldn't possibly be involved in crime, since he had obviously not had big profits. This was the very strategy that Rocco Perri, the King of the Bootleggers in Canada in the 1920s, had used before the Royal Commission on Customs Violations in Ontario in 1927. Volpe claimed in a signed statement, dated June 19, 1973, and delivered to the commission, that his only assets as of December 31, 1971, consisted of "cash in the sum of $55,000, a gun collection worth $2,500, clothing and jewelery valued at $2,000, and cameras and radio equipment valued at $1,000." Volpe's statement of net worth offsets these modest assets with $3,000 owed to a lawyer and $7,500 owed to a relative, leaving his net equity at $50,500. Judge Waisberg concluded this was "a most unusual net worth statement". Waisberg also found it odd that Paul Volpe claimed to have no occupation or bank account. Volpe's luxurious home, at the time, was in his wife's name. Other properties and possessions, including office buildings and huge tracts of land, were in the names of associates, relatives, and friends. Waisberg's questions were understandable. Major mobsters have a habit of not registering valuable possessions in their own names; it certainly helps when Revenue Canada or government commissions are poking around. This was true of Rocco Perri in Hamilton in the 1920s and it is true today.

Finally, Waisberg spent many pages of his report documenting Paul Volpe's organized-crime connections and his importance. He also featured the testimony of Superintendent Routledge, the officer in charge of the RCMP Criminal Intelligence Service, which ran for almost ten pages of the final report. Superintendent Routledge gave a detailed analysis of what organized crime was and who the main players were in Ontario. He named Paul Volpe as a senior member of organized crime here, along with Johnny Papalia, the Luppinos of Hamilton, and others. He showed that Luppino was very well connected with a number of big names in organized crime, including Paul Volpe of Toronto and Paolo Violi of Montreal. Routledge's testimony also pointed out the importance of "family" connections. He mentioned that Volpe was godfather to Nat Luppino's child, and he testified about an important mob wedding in Toronto in June 1972, which had been attended by every major mob leader in Canada, including Paul Volpe, Johnny "Pops", all the Luppinos, Frank Sylvestro (the loan shark and mob boss of Guelph), Vic Cotroni and Paolo Violi of Montreal, and an old, respected mafioso from Italy named Giuseppe Scettecasi. However, Judge Waisberg stopped short of tying this Mafia activity directly in with the activity in the construction industry.

In his final report, Judge Waisberg went only so far as to conclude: "The evidence indicates that it was a deliberate and calculated move that brought Paul Volpe, Natale Luppino, and Joseph Zappia into the construction industry. There is some evidence that involves Yanover, Wheatley, and Kiroff with the acts of violence described earlier. Through Volpe there was a connection between Luppino and [Domenic] Zappia [also an enforcer for Volpe at the time] on the one side and Yanover, Kiroff, and Wheatley [a Yanover associate and biker] on the other side." He further states: "The evidence of Cesido Romanelli, Angelo Del Zotto, and Elvio Del Zotto impressed me as contrived. Romanelli and Angelo Del Zotto denied the Mona Lisa meeting which obviously took place, as supported by Angelo Del Zotto's writing in Simone's notebook. Angelo and Elvio Del Zotto denied any knowledge of the employment of Luppino when the evidence makes it quite clear that he was the constant companion of Romanelli, a Del Zotto partner who was in frequent contact with them. The Mona Lisa meetings and the Luppino hiring are of greater significance in the light of the denials."

Finally, Judge Waisberg concluded with the following statement about the role of organized crime in the construction industry: "Considering all of this evidence, it is a reasonable inference that there existed at that time an association of persons for the purpose of conducting illegal activities."

In other words, Paul Volpe was acting as a fixer for both sides, for the unions and the companies, using conventional organized-crime techniques, including extortion, bombing, threats, and beatings, to keep certain people and certain companies in line. Volpe was successful in his endeavours here to the extent that he was trusted by those he served. By 1974, though, the public and political pressure brought to bear on the situation by MPP Morton Shulman and Judge Waisberg, through his royal commission, made it essential for Paul Volpe and the mob to move more into the background – at least for the moment.

Judge Waisberg felt that the commission had served a valuable purpose: "I am of the opinion that the measures taken succeeded in blocking these activities [of Paul Volpe and his associates and employers] in the sectors of the construction industry under investigation. I suspect that it has been made clear to all, that activities in the construction industry are subject to the same rules of law that govern the community at large."

Notwithstanding the above, Paul Volpe was to keep a hand, albeit discreetly, in the construction industry. Gus Simone, still the head of Local 562, despite all the negative publicity, remained a friend and associate of his, maintaining close ties right until the end. Simone put Volpe associate Pietro Scarcella on the payroll of his union, was one of the last people to see Volpe alive, and even went to Paul Volpe's house after Volpe's body was found to offer his condolences and assistance. (Scarcella, incidentally, was the last person known to have seen Paul Volpe alive on the day of his death.)

In spite of all of the research and investigative efforts of the royal commission, however, very few charges were laid as a result. Howard Morton of the Crown Attorney's Office was responsible for monitoring the daily transcripts of the commission with a view to laying charges. He looked at a wide range of possible charges, including perjury, against Paul Volpe, Chuck Yanover, and others. Finally, though, there were only six charges laid against union and company officials of accepting or giving "secret commissions", a lesser form of bribery, and according to Morton, at least five were convicted. Also, Cesido Romanelli was later charged with perjury separately, with Gus Simone as the chief witness against him. He was acquitted, as Simone's credibility was undermined by the defence counsel, David Humphrey. Simone had co-operated with the commission by giving names and dates of certain "secret commissions".

Morton said, "Paul Volpe's name kept coming up. . . . He helped deals go through for both sides." He gave no explanation of why Paul Volpe and Chuck Yanover, as well as other Volpe enforcers, were never charged, but he did say that he was very "frustrated at the difficulty of bringing charges." He also felt that ultimately a royal commission is counter-productive in the fight against organized crime in that it "interferes with ongoing investigations," ties up police with other duties, and takes away the element of surprise. Said Morton, "It's nice to have organized criminals think the police are everywhere."

Whatever the reasons, the Waisberg commission did not succeed in getting organized crime out of the construction industry, and did little to impede Paul Volpe's power or influence. As late as 1983 there is considerable evidence that he was closely involved with the unions in settling disputes, especially the dispute between the drywall unions and the labourers' union over jurisdiction in the residential housing field. As noted above, Volpe maintained a close relationship with Gus Simone, who in April 1985 was charged along with six others, including Marco Muzzo (who had admitted before the commission that he used bribery with the unions as a tactic to gain advantage for his companies), in a fraud involving workers' welfare funds. The police investigation of this fraud began as a result of Volpe's continued close connection with Simone throughout the 1970s and early 1980s and after a series of fires in 1983 caused $3 million in damage to houses under construction.

Paul Volpe continued dealing with high-ranking union officials and unions, including those outside the construction industry, like the Teamsters-affiliated Launderers' Union in Toronto. He developed a close relationship with the president, Jimmy Hoffa's friend Gil Davis, who later mysteriously disappeared from Toronto after laundering some American Teamsters' pension money through New York City.

Many in law enforcement and on the street think the royal commission even added to Volpe's stature and respect in the criminal world. He was looking more and more like the "Mr. Big" of Ontario organized crime. And his continued involvement in the unions until his death in 1983 is still under serious police investigation.

CHAPTER EIGHT

A Matter of Respect: A Day in the Life of Paul Volpe and "Operation Oblong"

THE GOLDEN PERIOD of Paul Volpe's criminal career was in the mid-1970s. This was the time when he consolidated and expanded his criminal activities and enjoyed the greatest financial prosperity, with the minimum of police and public attention. It is useful therefore to take a look at how his operations worked during this period and how he functioned on a typical day.

Mobsters don't run a normal office. They don't always work from nine to five. They don't have regular bank accounts or daily business lunches at the Courtyard Café or Winston's. But they do have a business to run, an "office" to manage, "employees" to hire, fire, and otherwise discipline, and cash-flow problems. Cash-flow problems are susceptible to creative solutions.

Volpe's day-to-day routine during the 1970s hardly varied. He'd carefully leave an associate or a nephew to watch his north Bayview Avenue home in his absence, then would drive his wife to her office in the morning, usually in a spiffy red Cadillac, which he generally parked in a reserved spot in the ManuLife Centre. It was close to Creeds, the fashionable women's store, where his wife was by now vice-president. Volpe would then spend the day downtown, apparently doing nothing but hanging around restaurants and street corners. The streets and malls of Toronto were his office, his business turf. Here he would operate without fear of police interception of his conversations. He liked the area around College and Yonge streets and the sidewalks outside the College Street YMCA. He frequented the ManuLife Centre both because it was handy to his wife's work and because of the many pay phones on several floors, which he could use to conduct business.

The phone was a precious business tool. Volpe did much of his business on the phone, making deals, summoning his enforcers and collectors, arranging and collecting payments. He did the accounting in his head. Loan-sharking arithmetic was straightforward: every week you collected $6 for every $5 you had out, and the payments were strung out for as long as possible so that the principal was never really paid off and the interest income became quite astronomic. He would also use the phones in the many restaurants he frequented. He made use of downtown restaurants, especially those along Yorkville, on Yonge Street, and on College Street. The Colosseum on Walton Street was a favourite, possibly because of the boyhood associations of the location. Sometimes he'd hold business meetings in the back room of the Colosseum. The police knew this too and had the place bugged.

He'd make calls, move to another restaurant (he especially favoured several in the trendy Yorkville area of the city run by trusted associates), make and take more calls. "He lived on the phone," says one old friend. Sometimes he'd meet runners by pre-arrangement on the sidewalk. These included the front people who actually handled the money – Volpe had hundreds of thousands of dollars of loan-shark money on the street at any one time – enforcers (their number varied, but he usually had around ten on the payroll who would arrange beatings, arsons, and other collection activities), and associates, with whom he cut deals and arranged illegal card games and other gambling and fencing activities. He had around fifty such meetings a day. He could often be seen huddling with an associate. His eyes were always busy, darting around, checking.

Sometimes he'd visit his chief associate, Natie Klegerman, in his dingy office at the corner of College and Spadina or at The Bagel, the small restaurant across the street, which was a hang-out for taxi drivers and locals and where the mistress of one of his front men worked as a waitress. Occasionally he would stop off at a downtown news kiosk to talk to the vendor, one of the many people who handled his loan-sharking money.

Volpe also owned a number of properties around the downtown core, although his ownership was not a matter of record. He could often be seen inspecting the renovations of one of these buildings, such as the old office building at Parliament and King he purchased, renovated, and sold at a tidy profit. Chuck Yanover operated here, ostensibly as building manager, and Volpe would sometimes drop in for a talk. Among other buildings Volpe had an interest in at one time was the home of CITY-TV on Queen Street East. Some of his meetings would involve visitors from the United States, who had business concerning properties he owned in the States. Volpe in his prime made investments in other cities. He was always interested in casinos and bought real estate through front people in New Jersey, particularly in Atlantic City just before the 1978 casino boom.

As we have seen, one of the little difficulties of the gangster business is converting money from illicit to legitimate, an operation known, for obvious reasons, as laundering. Volpe showed some creativity in the laundering business. It was one reason why he was so fond of casinos; they provided a useful way to launder money, as well as a ready source of hapless loan-shark candidates. It is also virtually impossible for tax authorities to judge a casino's legitimate take. Other techniques Volpe used from time to time involved real-estate frauds, both in and around Toronto and in and around Atlantic City, and the use of offshore banks and numbered accounts. At one point, Volpe's people owned a camping ground, and by inflating the number of people using it, they inflated its receipts. It must have been a tranquil place to camp!

As well as these more makeshift techniques, Paul Volpe used land purchases in Toronto and Atlantic City to launder a great deal of his criminal proceeds. In Montreal, Mafia Godfather Vic Cotroni for years had Montreal meat magnate William "Obie" Obront as the chief money-launderer for his family. The Quebec Crime Probe in 1977, in its report *Organized Crime and the World of Business*, showed how Obront laundered over $89 million for the Montreal mob through various business schemes. Cotroni had others as well, such as a well-known Montreal stock promoter. In May 1985, a prominent St. Catharines lawyer, Gary

Hendin, was convicted of laundering over $12 million for three Italian brothers, in an organized-crime family in the Niagara region, who were heavily involved in the marijuana and cocaine trade. Hendin would receive the money in cash in paper bags and convert it to U.S. cash. Then he would deposit it in the organized-crime account in a bank in the Grand Cayman Islands – after taking his seven-per-cent fee (over $1 million). Paul Volpe would have admired the efficiency of this mob laundering operation.

When Paul Volpe went out, he often had a bodyguard with him, even when he went to his dentist. Once, when Volpe was having a tricky root-canal job done, his bodyguard insisted on being in the room to watch the delicate operation; the nurse gently led the guard away. Volpe gave her a $5 bill on his way out.

Sunday was a working day for the Volpe organization. Volpe would move around the city as usual, while his associates and underlings collected money from loan-shark victims and others. One bitterly cold winter morning, Volpe phoned to commiserate with Natie Klegerman; the poor fellow was on the street collecting in the cold. Later on Sundays they would meet at a doughnut shop in the Bathurst Street-Wilson Avenue area to discuss the week's take. He would then often go with his bodyguard to a hotel near the Toronto airport for further meetings with criminal colleagues.

Volpe seldom carried much cash. And, as we have seen, he was hardly ever the owner of record of anything, as most of his legal holdings were in the name of his wife, Lisa Dalholt. Volpe found it convenient to be able to tell investigative bodies truthfully that he had no money. He invariably failed to mention that the majority of his personal assets were legally held by his wife. Even the Volpe home at 30 Manorcrest, near Bayview Avenue, was "sold" in the mid-1970s to Paul Volpe for $2 in return for the cancellation of a debt from gambler and thief Ron Mooney. But it was in Lisa Dalholt's name, not Paul Volpe's.

Volpe had very few interests except thinking of new ways to make money. John Rosen, Volpe's lawyer for several years, says he was a shallow person. "He was materialistic and egocentric and wouldn't give of himself materially or emotionally.... I never had an intelligent conversation with him," recalls Rosen. Others who knew him well confirm this. One old friend says, "He was a coward – oh, I don't mean physically a coward, he would punch somebody out or break their back – but when it came to relationships or something that calls for character, he gave nothing, for he had no character to give."

Volpe, of course, was not an old-style Mafia don or Godfather. But clearly he was a man with a long reach in the criminal world; he was a man who had earned the respect of his peers by a ruthless application of criminal muscle, a talent for organizing, a willingness to break through the closed circles of Italian criminal loyalties, and a thorough understanding of the city in which he operated. Volpe was also a man of considerable charm. He projected a positive, upbeat image to many, even some of those whose job it was to put him behind bars. A veteran police intelligence officer who worked on Volpe for years said he would rather spend time with Volpe than with straight people. "He was a fascinating, intelligent, interesting guy to be with." After years of following Volpe around and listening to his phone conversations on wire-taps and bugs, he admitted he admired the man. "He hardly ever swore, was immaculately dressed, and he talked to the police; he knew it was all a game and was happy as long as we played by the rules. He stopped me once on the street with an affectionate, 'How the hell are you?' He would say, 'If you put me in jail, all the more power to you, but do it legitimately.' He loved the intrigue of the game."

His hobbies were gardening, movies (he particularly liked films where the cops were bad; but he didn't like movies about prostitutes, like *Irma La Douce*), and eating Chinese food. His idea of a good time, says one old friend, "was sitting down with a couple of guys and scheming how they could rob somebody or make some money illegitimately." He rarely indulged in everyday leisure activities. He never went to ball games or to the theatre. He hardly ever swam, even though he had a huge swimming pool and later a private pond at his home. He liked cop shows on television, especially the series *Kojak*. And he took great pride in his property and the way it looked. Even though he had a gardener in twice a week, he would enjoy putting on his old clothes and going out himself to help the gardener till the soil.

He was not a religious man and never went to church unless he was to be godfather to another mobster's son (as he was for the son of Natale Luppino of Hamilton). His religion was status. Said one friend of him, "Volpe always wanted respectability, and he wanted to look successful, so he wore expensive clothes, drove fancy cars [for years he drove the red Cadillac, given to him as a wedding present, as well as a Renegade-type American Motors Jeep and later a BMW equipped with its own telephone], and owned beautiful homes. He wanted to impress you with his life-style."

His relationships with his older brothers were often rocky, as he often took advantage of them, too. Yet he was capable of real generosity, often caring for relatives with domestic troubles. He even gave a home to the child of one of his nephews who was separated from his wife. His own domestic life was a break from Mafia tradition; he married outside his ethnic group (Lisa is Danish) and never had children. He was very protective of his marriage. He made every effort to keep his wife out of the public eye. At the end of a business day, the dutiful husband would pick up his wife at the office and drive her home.

A lot of Paul Volpe's power in the mob in Canada also came from the simple fact that he was a native-born Canadian who spoke excellent English and mixed well in most mob groups as well as in society. He was looked up to by other mobsters, such as Jimmy Luppino and Mike Racco, as a "fixer" and communicator with the straight world.

But even more importantly, Paul Volpe's power in Toronto was based on respect. Volpe's is a complicated case because the respect was based as much on what people said he was as it was on his actual achievements; the fact that he was actually initiated into a Mafia group is less important than the fact that people believed he was Mafia. The image was constantly confused with the reality. It was partly because of the respectful attention he was paid that he was able to affect his easygoing charm. He became a professional nice guy, and his partly submerged reputation as a gangster of repute only added to his charisma among non-criminals. Nevertheless, respect in the world of organized crime is a fragile commodity that needs constant reinforcing through intimidation and the creative use of muscle. Volpe, in his heyday, seldom forgot this primary fact. It is the mob way.

The testimony to Volpe's charm comes from many sources, but he was also capable of great ruthlessness. In the early 1970s, an American organized-crime figure came to Toronto to do business with Volpe. He stayed at the King Edward Hotel, where, in a nice piece of irony, he was robbed of his watch. Volpe summoned the seven hotel-room break-and-enter artists he knew and demanded an accounting. All denied knowing anything about the visiting mobster's watch. But a week later, a small-time operator named Hot Nuts Louie (his sobriquet referred to his business, not his equipment) reported to Volpe that one of the seven had passed the offending timepiece through him. Volpe was furious. He ordered the thief to meet him at the Mona Lisa Restaurant on Eglinton Avenue West (the same mob hang-out where the famous meeting described in the Waisberg report took place), then widely used by Volpe's associates. Volpe met him in the basement. "You lied to me," he said. "Don't ever lie to me again."

He smiled and went upstairs to have dinner with Jimmy Lup-pino of the Luppino Mafia family of Hamilton, while an enforcer used a baseball bat to punish the offender. A normally unsqueam-ish mob associate who witnessed the beating was sick to his stomach. The message was clear to everyone: you don't lie to Paul Volpe. It is a lack of respect that will not be tolerated.

Many people with whom Volpe had considerable contact viewed him as essentially decent. They refused to accept that Paul Volpe was also a ruthless Mafia operative. One influential establishment friend of Volpe's once tried to convince me of Volpe's essential decency and good nature. A couple of young punks had been extorting money from a St. Clair Avenue West storekeeper by saying they were "with the Volpes". Paul Volpe heard about this, visited the store, and told them, "Someone's using my name, and if you're paying them, I'd appreciate it if you'd let me stay in your store when the guy comes in saying he's 'with the Volpes'." One of the young toughs eventually had a nervous interview with Volpe, and the extortion promptly stopped. Volpe's friend thought this proved that, though Volpe was a loan shark and a gambler, he was also a regular guy, "a real teddy bear".

On the other hand, Volpe also exploited people's weaknesses and greed. Once a woman came to him with $20,000 to put out on the street for loan-sharking. She came to Volpe because she wanted to make a lot of money illegally. He took the money and said he would do his best. Many months later, when the woman returned for her profits, Volpe just laughed. "What money?" he asked. He knew that she couldn't go to the police, so he simply ripped her off. Volpe was constantly on the lookout for such easy scores.

One of his great assets was his ability to weigh people's strengths and weaknesses of character, a skill honed on the street. According to his former lawyer John Rosen, "He had an excellent insight into people's personality – their strengths and weaknesses – and knew exactly how far he could go with certain people." One police officer who worked with Volpe says, "He should have been a psychologist.... He understood people." He always got others to do things for him. His favourite expression was "I never stick my ass out." He absorbed ideas. And once he had a hook into someone, he never let go. "Paul had a way," a close associate said. "Once he had an in with you, he would walk into your place like he owned it.... He'd take over, use the phones, put his feet on your desk, everything." Recalls one former associate, "He was a human parasite, and I was the host."

Paul Volpe's lawyer for many years was David Humphrey, now a district court judge. Humphrey says of his former client: "He had a great capacity for charm and good humour and was very likeable, as well as a thoughtful and devoted husband to his wife, Lisa, who is very much a lady, and who, I might add, is squeaky clean.... He was a very bright, intelligent, engaging person who didn't drink, smoke, or chase girls and was very business-like about his affairs." To Humphrey, Volpe was a "many-faceted person who would have been a success in any field of endeavour." And he added playfully, "If he were engaged in criminal activity, I'd imagine he would reach the top."

Volpe *did* reach the top, at least for a while, as one of the most successful major organized-crime leaders in Canada.

One early police operation that targeted Paul Volpe, Natie Klegerman, and their group, and that offers some insight into their loan-shark empire as well as their daily movements, was a joint-forces operation and a massive RCMP intelligence operation dubbed "Operation Oblong" by the Mounties (known to some Mounties as "Operation Awful"). It intercepted many of the Volpe group's phone calls and observed the group members around the clock. Volpe, of course, had been the subject of special attention from the police in the past, through projects such as "Project B" on his union activity. But "Oblong" was especially revealing of how the Volpe organization operated on an everyday basis.

Operation Oblong was aimed at Volpe's and Klegerman's loan-sharking and fencing empire; specifically, it was a massive police investigation into the activities of Flite Investments, long suspected by police of being a cover for Volpe loan-sharking, fencing, and money-laundering operations and related extortion, arson, and vending-machine operations. Arranging the putting out and collection of loan-shark monies was one of the Volpe organization's principal and most lucrative activities, and it was done primarily through Flite Investments.

Flite was nominally run by Volpe associate Murray Feldberg, a burly former taxi-driver and friend of Klegerman who provided the Volpe organization with a convenient cover until his death in 1982. (According to one police source, Feldberg had "a Fred Flintstone, Neanderthal appearance".) The business of Flite Investments was conducted out of the office at College and Spadina, which was protected by surveillance cameras and security locks. Klegerman and Feldberg also met frequently in The Bagel restaurant across the street. The police put over 4,900 man-hours into the Flite investigation in an all-out attempt to make a case against the Volpe organization. They bugged the offices and watched all the major participants: Murray Feldberg, Frank Volpe, Paul Volpe, Natie Klegerman, Ian Rosenberg, Jimmy Bass, Joe Levy (a Volpe-Klegerman fence), and Charles Yanover. Yanover was specifically targeted because he shared the Flite office with Murray Feldberg. Yanover ran a company called Vegas Vending, supplying pinball machines in downtown Toronto, for which Volpe heavy-duty enforcers Ian Rosenberg and Jimmy Bass nominally worked. Vegas Vending was in fact the enforcement arm of the Flite Investments loan-sharking empire.

At one point during Operation Oblong, the police interviewed as many clients of Flite Investments as they could (over two hundred in all) with a view to obtaining evidence that would allow them to bring charges of extortion against members of the Volpe organization. When Volpe and Klegerman found out that the police were interviewing their "clients" they were furious. Klegerman then brought each client in after he was interviewed by the police and re-interviewed him himself with a tape recorder on the desk. The police were able to listen to all this through their bug. He would start by saying, in all the legalese he could muster: "I am Nathan Klegerman. We are in the Judicial County of York on ____ , 19__" and so on. He would ask each client who had been approached by the police if he had any complaints. The client, of course, would reply that he was very happy about getting the loans and that no pressure had been put on him. This was Klegerman's ace in the hole, should the police try to charge extortion. In this way Klegerman protected himself even while carrying on the loan-sharking business. Most of the clients of Flite were hand-picked by Klegerman. They were desperate characters, often somewhat shady themselves, like Volpe break-and-enter artist Ron Mooney. They were only too happy to receive money from the Volpe group, and weren't likely to complain. Klegerman also felt that if he dealt with "shit", as he himself put it, it would make him look better. He would say to police or a jury, "Am I that bad? Look at them." These precautions by the Volpe group made Flite Investments impregnable, in spite of the massive police operation against it.

The only fly in the ointment for Volpe and his boys, as far as Flite Investments was concerned – and the incident that finally gave the police something on Flite – came through the activities of Charles Yanover and some of his enforcers. In 1976, an antique-car dealer named Alexander Veronac, who had helped fix one of Yanover's Mercedeses, approached Yanover for a loan. Veronac was overdrawn at the bank and needed money to finance his antique-car business (he rebuilt Auburns and Cords, sleek 1930s cars with running boards). He borrowed $800 in February 1976, paid back $40 every weekend for 11 weeks (the interest, or "juice"), and later made a lump-sum payment of $600 to Yanover. However, by June 1976, he still owed the original $800, and he was flat broke. At that point, Charles Yanover, accompanied by his two enforcers, Ian Rosenberg and Jimmy Bass, drove to Veronac's house. Veronac hid and Yanover and the two enforcers left. Unbeknownst to them, however, they were under surveillance by Peel Regional Police intelligence.

The next month, Rosenberg and Bass returned to the house to collect the money from Veronac, who was too frightenend to go to the police. After Veronac pleaded that he had no money, they threatened him with a hand-gun and demanded the keys to his car. Veronac told them that the car had a lien against it so it wouldn't be much use to them. This was enough to infuriate the somewhat emotionally unstable Rosenberg, who then assaulted Veronac, punching him in the face. When Veronac fled, the outraged Rosenberg chased him down the street, pummelling him mercilessly as the neighbours watched in terror. The police were called, but Rosenberg and Bass left before the cops arrived on the scene.

However, Veronac had gotten the message. When the police did arrive, he refused to co-operate, and shortly after the beating he went with Yanover to meet Murray Feldberg at The Bagel, where he paid off $600. He still owed Yanover $800, in spite of having paid over $1,100 for the original loan of $800.

Eventually, through persistent police work, Bass, Rosenberg, and Yanover were identified and charged with conspiracy to extort, and at the preliminary hearing on March 11, 1977, a reluctant Veronac courageously fingered Bass in court as one of the enforcers who beat him. Murray Feldberg had not been charged, as his name had not been mentioned by Veronac. Later, when Veronac described to police in his heavy accent another man to whom he had paid money, the staff of Operation Oblong figured it was Feldberg. To make sure, they arranged a line-up for Veronac, standing Feldberg and several police officers under the lights (including, ironically, Jim McIlvenna, the RCMP inspector in charge of the élite new police group, the Special Enforcement Unit, which had taken over Operation Oblong from the RCMP intelligence unit in mid-1977). Veronac identified Feldberg as the man to whom he made the $600 payment, so when the second preliminary hearing took place in September 1977, Feldberg was added as a defendant.

The first chink in the armour of the Flite Investments cover had been made, even though the judge did not accept that Flite Investments was a loan-sharking cover. However, this decision was based on a technicality. Since the Veronac extortion began in February 1976, and Flite Investments was not incorporated until April 1976, the judge would not allow that the extortion was part of the Flite Investments operations. In February 1979, Murray Feldberg was sentenced to twenty-one months, Yanover got eighteen months, and Bass, the most violent of the three remaining defendants, got twelve months for extortion. Yanover had made the mistake of leaving two cars behind at Veronac's house during their June visit: one belonged to Vegas Vending and the other was registered to Flite Investments. Feldberg had also made the mistake of threatening Veronac on the phone (with the police listening in). "Pay or else," Feldberg had yelled at a terrified Veronac. This error demonstrated the wisdom of Klegerman's admonition to Feldberg and Yanover that they should "never yell at a customer, no matter what you say.... A yell sounds like extortion."

Ian Rosenberg, though charged, never faced a trial for his role in the Veronac extortion. It had become apparent to Volpe that something had to be done about Rosenberg. He was too unstable and unreliable an enforcer, and rumour on the street had it that he was informing on his colleagues and co-operating with the police in their investigation. Rosenberg had made a mess out of the Veronac collection by beating him in public, thus drawing police attention. He was a real embarrassment to the Flite organization. Moreover, he drank over forty ounces of whisky on an average day and was totally erratic. The organization feared he would talk – if he hadn't already. So on April 22, 1977, the day after Paul Volpe himself was interviewed by the police about his possible involvement with Flite Investments, Ian Rosenberg and his girl-friend, Joan Lipson, were shot to death in her Forest Hill home.

Police were tipped off that Bass and Yanover had something to do with the killing and arrested Bass. Then they proceeded to Yanover's apartment at 111 Braemar to arrest him as well. Yanover saw the police coming, however, and fled to the house of his parents. The police followed and surrounded the house. With guns drawn, they spoke to Yanover through a bull-horn, demanding that he give himself up on charges of suspicion of committing murder. Yanover sent his parents out to talk with the police. When he was finally taken, Yanover, according to two officers present, cried for over ten minutes while police interrogators tried to question him. A few days later the charges were dropped against Yanover, since there was insufficient evidence to link him to the murder. He also had an airtight alibi: witnesses were willing to swear that they were with him at a restaurant called Peaches on Pears Avenue in Toronto when Rosenberg and Lipson were shot to death. Jimmy Bass was tried and acquitted of the murders in 1978. The murder of Ian Rosenberg and Joan Lipson remains officially unsolved to this day, though it is very likely that the Volpe organization exterminated them.

Operation Oblong put Volpe and his organization on notice that their every movement was being watched by the police. The psychological effect was to make Paul Volpe and Klegerman and their people think the police were everywhere. It's what one policeman refers to as "saturating your target to the point of paranoia." This psychological warfare against the Volpe organization by the police was eventually to prove most effective.

CHAPTER NINE

A New Organization: The Rise of the Siderno Mafia Family

EVEN AS PAUL VOLPE was expanding his operations and solidifying his hold on the Ontario construction industry, another organized-crime group in Toronto was busy making its muscle felt. As we have seen, this group, referred to loosely as "the Siderno Mafia", was originally made up of recent immigrants from southern Calabria, from the towns in and around Siderno Marina in the province of Reggio Calabria in southern Italy. Most of the members of this group, such as the Raccos and the Commissos, came to Canada in the late 1950s and early 1960s.

Michele (Mike) Racco, who ran a bakery shop on the corner of St. Clair and Nairn in Toronto, was for years the pre-eminent leader of the Siderno group, although there have always been many closely allied sub-groups and factions. Because of his extensive ties with key members of the Calabrian "Honoured Society" in Italy (with whom he consulted frequently by long-distance telephone), with prominent members of the Calabrian Mafia in Long Island, Albany, New York City, and Connecticut (whom he frequently visited both in Toronto and in the United States), and with senior Calabrese mafiosi in Montreal, such as Vic Cotroni and Paolo Violi, Mike Racco was the most powerful and the most respected of the Siderno group leaders until his death of a heart attack in 1980. One senior Toronto police intelligence officer maintains that Mike Racco had been the head of a ruling commission of three of the Siderno Mafia groups in Canada. The other main leaders of the Siderno mob were among the pallbearers at Mike Racco's funeral.

In order to understand the mob wars that were to climax in the early 1980s with the deaths of Paul Volpe and Mike Racco's only son, Domenic, it is necessary to take a brief look at the leadership and activities of the Sidernese Mafia in North America.

"Lou", a source inside the Volpe group, and himself a Volpe associate, in a 1978 interview, referred to Volpe's mob as the "old Mafia" as opposed to the newer, nastier hoodlums of the Sidernese Mafia. In the second *Connections* series, broadcast in 1979, "Lou" (wearing a black hood) differentiated between the two mobs from his vantage point:

The old group [Volpe's] *never believes in bombing bakeries or blowing up cars, but these new Italian immigrants coming to Canada, they came here and they brought along with them traces of narcotics, whereas the old group never got involved in narcotics. This new group, we've learned that they are smuggling narcotics into Canada. There have been many arrests if you look in the papers. You see these Italian names and it is none of the old group. The old group are still trying to control Toronto and it is very difficult with the new group sabotaging out at the west end, and the old group does not do that kind of work.*

A senior Toronto police intelligence officer adds that during the late 1960s and early 1970s the new Siderno group was involved in a number of extortions in the Italian community and was having a major internal battle. "There were bombings over territories every Friday night for a while, yet we couldn't convince the brass that the group should be taken seriously." There were killings as well in battles over beverage-company territory and over bakeries owned by rival factions. Two beverage-company officials, Filippo Vendimini and Salvatore "Sammy" Triumbari, the president of Cynar Dry, were shot to death in 1967 and 1969, respectively. Vendimini had owned a shoe store on Bloor Street and worked for Triumbari at Cynar. Both were in one of the Siderno Mafia factions in Toronto and were heavily involved in extortion, arson, counterfeiting, and other Siderno mob rackets.

A top-secret United States government report based on U.S. and Ontario police-intelligence investigations of the Siderno Mafia in the mid-1970s shows how the group was formed and how it operates in North America. Metro Toronto police in the late 1960s had completed a special project on the Sidernese Mafia, code-named "Project E". The Ontario Police Commission then did its own lengthy classified study of the Siderno group in 1972, drawing on some of the findings of Project E. The information in the U.S. document about the Francesco Caccamo papers and the Toronto Mafia comes from earlier reports by Toronto and Ontario police. (Caccamo appealed his eventual conviction on an arms charge all the way to the Supreme Court of Canada, but the courts upheld the conviction and, in doing so, implicitly recognized the validity of the documents known as the "Caccamo Papers". The authorities later tried, unsuccessfully, to deport Caccamo from Canada.) The excerpt below is the first material to be published from this internal U.S. police document.

1) *While effecting the arrest of one Francesco Caccamo for counterfeiting and illegal possession of a revolver, the Ontario Canadian Police uncovered an archaic 27 page document written in the Italian language. This document has been described as an authentic ritual for a secret Italian criminal organization.*

2) *The Ontario police have been gathering information on a seemingly new organized crime group which has emerged as a segment of the Honored Society of Calabria, Italy. After finding the document in Caccamo's home, the Royal Canadian Mounted Police found it necessary to collaborate with Dr. Alberto Sabatino, Chief Commissioner of the Criminal Intelligence Branch, Central National Criminalpol of Rome, Italy, for translating this centuries old composition. This document is filled with references to blood, punishment and violent death. The elaborate wording is of such flowery language it makes little sense to one not versed in idioms of the Italian language. One section describes initiation rites during which a new member takes a "bloody dagger in my hand and a serpent in my mouth" – symbolic vows indicative of his punishment should he fail or betray the society.*

In 1890, New Orleans was rocked by the murder of the Chief of Police, David Hennessy, by Black Hand members, many of whom were later lynched by angry mobs.
(Seymour Fleischman / *Playboy's Illustrated History of Organized Crime*)

Rocco Perri, Canada's "King of the Bootleggers", is seen here at Toronto's Union Station in 1939. Accompanied by R.C.M.P. officers, he is on his way to Windsor to stand trial for allegedly corrupting Canadian Customs officials.
(City of Toronto Archives / Globe and Mail Collection #60416)

Paul Volpe's childhood home on
Walton Street in downtown
Toronto survived unscathed until
the late seventies, despite sur-
rounding development.
(Norfolk Productions)

This picture of the young "mystery
hero", Paul Volpe, appeared on the
front page of the Toronto *Telegram* on November 12, 1952. The
accompanying story lauded Volpe's
"quick-thinking action" in stop-
ping an attack on a hotel detective.
(Canada Wide / *Toronto Sun*)

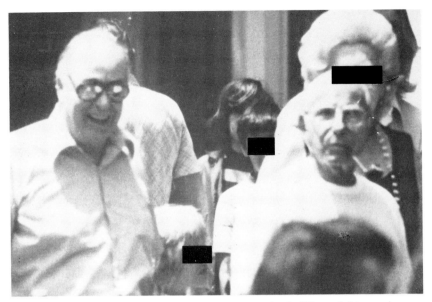

Paul Volpe's criminal mentor, New York City mobster Vito de Filippo (left), a senior lieutenant in New York's Bonanno family, is seen on the streets of New York City with Carmine Galente, boss of the Bonanno family, in this police surveillance photo from the 1970s. Galente was later brutally murdered.

Two of the Luppino brothers of Hamilton, Jimmy (left) and Natale (right), close friends and criminal allies of Paul Volpe, are shown here at the funeral of Eugene Volpe.

The former head of the Montreal Mafia, Paolo Violi, in the mid seventies. He maintained close connections with the major Mafia groups in southern Ontario until his murder in 1978.
(CBC-TV / Norfolk Productions)

The longtime Godfather of the Montreal Mafia, the late Vincenzo "Vic" Cotroni. Paul Volpe went to him in 1961 for his blessing before establishing a Mafia family in Toronto.
(CBC-TV / Norfolk Productions)

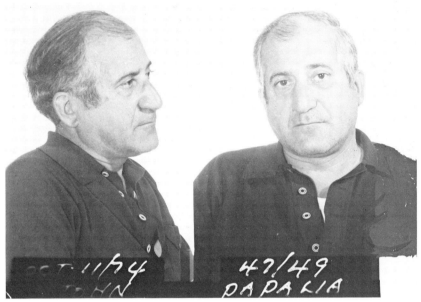

Johnny "Pops" Papalia, who has controlled a leading Hamilton Mafia family since the early fifties. He failed in his attempt to take over Maxie Bluestein's gambling operations in Toronto.

The late Max Bluestein, longtime independent gambling czar in Toronto, fought off attempts by the Mafia to muscle in on his territory in the early sixties.
(*Globe and Mail*)

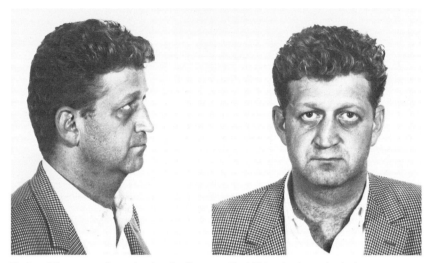

Nathan Klegerman about the time he first met Paul Volpe in the early sixties.

The police mug shot of
Charles "Chuck" Yanover that
appeared in the Waisberg
Commission report.

A police surveillance photo (above) which appeared in the Waisberg Commission report shows Nathan Klegerman, Volpe enforcer Ian Rosenberg (later murdered), and Frank Volpe meeting on the streets of Toronto during the violence in the construction industry.

Acme Lathing (above) after it was shot up in 1974.

(Right) One of the companies bombed during the construction-industry violence of the early seventies.

The late Mike Racco, as seen in *Connections*, was one of the major leaders of the Calabrian Mafia in Ontario.
(CBC-TV / Norfolk Productions)

Mike Racco's only son, the late Domenic Racco, after he was arrested for the shooting of three youths at the Newtonbrook Plaza in 1971.

3) Dr. Sabatino, who has conducted an extensive investigation in this area, has uncovered evidence that concludes that, within the Districts of Reggio, Calabria and Catanzaro and their towns and villages, with the exception of Cosenza, branches of the Honored Society do exist and flourish. This is referred to by Dr. Sabatino as the "Mafia" Calabrese. Although most of the secret Italian criminal organizations were originally designated to be Honored Society, over the years it became popular to refer to the Sicilian segment as "Mafia", the Neopolitan segment as "Camorra" and the Calabrese segment continued to be called "L'Onerata Società" or the "Honored Society".

The following is excerpted from the hitherto top-secret Ontario Police Commission study.

For some time now we have been gathering material here in Ontario relative to what has now emerged as a cell or locale of the Honoured Society of Calabria. The material has been collated and analysed and is now being forwarded to you for information and record purposes. The information is for the most part self-explanatory, but I feel that I should comment briefly on the significance of the Toronto Judge's decision on the trial of Francesco Caccamo.

It was in Caccamo's home that the ritual was found and during the same search some counterfeit currency and an unregistered revolver were also located. Relying heavily on the evidence of an Italian-speaking member of the RCMP and Dr. Alberto Sabatino, Chief Commissioner of the Criminal Intelligence Branch, Central Criminalpol of Rome, Italy, the Judge found:

1) That the Ritual was, in fact, an authentic Ritual for a secret Italian criminal organization.

2) That by virtue of his possession of this Ritual, Francesco Caccamo was a member of the organization.

3) Following this reasoning, the unregistered firearm in Caccamo's home was deemed to be a firearm kept for a purpose dangerous to the public peace.

In our view, these findings by the Court are extremely significant. The decision has been appealed but hopefully it will be upheld [it was] *and in that case will certainly prove to be of value in our fight against organized crime.*

The Siderno Group was so named by us as it first appeared that the major figures were all from Siderno in Reggio, Calabria. We are now discovering that there are members of the Siderno Group from the towns of Gioiosa, Fiumara, Locri, Sinopoli, Grotteria, San Giovino, and San Roberto, all in Calabria. In that location the locales are independent of each other; but, occasionally, when circumstances warrant, are mutually beneficial to each other and unite to form a type of loose confederation, each going its own way when a deal has been completed.

We are reasonably certain that we have locales in Toronto, Ottawa, Montreal, and, perhaps, Hamilton. From the information obtained so far it appears possible that there are locales of the Honoured Society in the Flushing-Corona areas of New York State where large numbers of Calabrese immigrants have settled. Most of them have immigrated to North America since the end of the Second World War. While they do business with Canadian born Italians, up to this point those who are Canadian born do not appear to hold any positions of importance within the group.

We have reliable information from L.C.N. ["La Cosa Nostra" – the FBI official designation of the Mafia in North America] *sources to the effect that the L.C.N. is well aware of the existence and identity of these people and are permitting them to operate and develop within certain limits, and there are frequent contacts by these people and known L.C.N. members. Should the decision be made to unite or amalgamate, and we feel this is probably inevitable, quite a dangerous confederation would result. The sophistication of the L.C.N. and the direct and violent Mafia Calabrese could present a serious challenge to law enforcement.*

During the course of our probe into the structure and the activities of the Siderno Group there have been numerous occasions when contacts have been made with persons in, and from, the U.S.A. Enumerated hereunder are the various U.S. contacts and what scant information we have obtained regarding each contact:

Agostino, Domenic, Queens, New York: Nephew of Michele Racco, one of the leaders of the Siderno Group. Telephone No. is either _____ or _____. This number was found in the possession of Vincenzo Galluzzo, at whose residence a ritual initiation was to take place on 20 March, 1971. Galluzzo is believed to be a member of the Siderno Group of the Honoured Society.

Agostino was in Toronto at Racco's on 26 April, 1971....

A call was made by Domenic Racco, son of Michele Racco, at _____, listed to L and F Pizza, 9120 Corona Avenue, Corona, New York, to Domenic Agostino....

Archino, Frank "Ciccio", Jr., _____ , Colony, New York: Subject called Domenic Racco from _____ and was identified as Frank Archino, Jr. Another call he identified himself as Compare Franco. We have information that there was a Francesco Archina employed in 1969 by Commisso Brothers and Racco Bakery in Toronto. Subsequent directories failed to reflect anyone by this name residing in Toronto. Enquiries by U.S. Immigration indicated that one Frank Archina, a U.S. citizen, _____ , Albany, New York, made an application for his brother Vincenzo and his family in 1969....

And so the detailed report continues in the same manner for fifty pages – listing hundreds of names, dates, telephone numbers and calls, and connections between U.S. and Canadian Mafia Calabrese. American immigration-intelligence documents further connect the Canadian and U.S. members of this group through Racco and others in Toronto. It is reported in these papers that Carlo Archina (also known as Archino), a relative of Frank Archino, Jr., is "the overall Siderno Group head in Italy"; that his brother Frank Archina was charged with murder in Denver, Colorado, in 1954, but was found not guilty by reason of insanity; and that another brother, Gino Archina, lived in Albany, New York, where he became the "leader of the Albany 'locale', Siderno Group."

In 1978, *Connections* co-producer Bill Macadam and I conducted several interviews with a member of the Siderno Mafia group controlled by the Raccos and Commissos, intimately connected with the U.S. Mafia Calabrese. His information substantially corroborated the police intelligence information, the secret Ontario Police Commission study, and the U.S. government report. Code-named "Joe", this informer gave us an inside look at this tough and aggressive new mob group.

We formally interviewed Joe in the late 1970s. We filmed or recorded most of the interviews, during which Joe described the initiation procedures of the Sidernese Mafia and the scope of their activities in Canada and the United States, and outlined their power structure. In two *Connections* programs in March

1979, we used a small portion of the interview, disguising Joe in a red scarf and a hat. Here are some relevant excerpts from the recorded interview with producer Bill Macadam, published for the first time. They offer some first-hand insight into the workings of the Sidernese Mafia and help to substantiate police intelligence and street data.

MACADAM: I want you to tell me about the Siderno group.

JOE: It's a very powerful family and it has branches throughout the United States and Canada. One of the branches that is considered a very powerful branch would be the one in Toronto. In Italy it was at one time operated by Anthony Macri. Now it is operated by Carlo Archino, and he has taken over since the death of Anthony Macri. It's a very powerful organization and it can be very heavy at times.

MACADAM: What happened to Anthony Macri?

JOE: He was machine-gunned to death.

MACADAM: This was in Siderno?

JOE: Yes.

MACADAM: And who was responsible for this?

JOE: Joe Molinaro.

MACADAM: Do you know why he was killed?

JOE: Yes. It was over a dispute at a meeting concerning narcotics.

MACADAM: What was the dispute about?

JOE: Well, other families wanted to import and export narcotics and since he was the Godfather he disagreed. He didn't want no narcotics. There were other families that disagreed and the other families took it from there and decided to take him out.

MACADAM: I heard that he was against kidnapping.

JOE: No.

MACADAM: He wasn't?

JOE: No.

MACADAM: It's being run by who now?

JOE: It's being run by Carlo Archino.

MACADAM: He has got tentacles out in other areas in the United States and in Toronto. Is that right?

JOE: Right.

MACADAM: Can you tell me about the Toronto group?

JOE: Well, it's operated by Domenic Racco now. Formerly operated by his father but now it's operated by him. It's a very, very powerful family, the one in Toronto. It's known as the

Sidernese group which is run by the Archino family.

MACADAM: What are they mainly involved in?

JOE: They're mainly involved in counterfeit money, extortion, narcotics, smuggling aliens into the United States and Canada and now and then an occasional hit.

MACADAM: Where does the Sidernese group have ties and cells?

JOE: They have them in New York City, Albany, N.Y., Chicago, Connecticut, Naples, Florida, and the one in Toronto.

MACADAM: How about the New York City one? Is that fairly strong?

JOE: It's fairly strong but the ties that are there, between Siderno and New York, are very, very secretive.

MACADAM: Who runs the New York group?

JOE: The New York group is run by Giuseppe Costa. And the one in Albany is run by the Archino family....

MACADAM: How much control does the group have in Siderno?

JOE: They have, I would say, one-hundred-per-cent control of Siderno.

MACADAM: How about the police?

JOE: They've got them crying in the corner just like cats are. They've got them tamed.

MACADAM: When you say one-hundred-per-cent control, what way do they control it?

JOE: They control it in every way. If there was to be a shooting in Siderno, the guy would be guaranteed to escape it. He wouldn't be stopped or bothered by the police at all.

MACADAM: Do they control business, too?

JOE: They control restaurants, milk shops, cookie shops. Their biggest industry is milk stores.

MACADAM: I want to ask you, how have they really got such control or such a hold in, for instance, Toronto?

JOE: It's a large group and they have a lot of ties, a lot of connections and they know people....

MACADAM: Where is their power derived from?

JOE: Their power drive is mainly from the business industry.

MACADAM: No, but where does it come from? Where does their power come from? Why do people fear the Sidernese group?

JOE: Just for fear itself. They know what they are capable of doing, what they have done in the past and what they can do.

MACADAM: And what's that?

JOE: They'll kill you.

MACADAM: I want to ask you, when you talk about respect, what do you mean by that?

JOE: Respect means to, something like worship a person. Like, if I know you, you've got connections, you've got good ties, you know people. I respect you for who you are, I come to you if I need a favour. If I'm a nice guy to you, if you like me, if you think I'm a respectable person, then that favour would be done by you.

MACADAM: Respect is rather an important part.

JOE: To this Italian group. To the Sidernese, it's a very important thing.

MACADAM: Is it the most important?

JOE: It's one of the first. It's the first important thing. You must know the meaning of respect and you must know how to respect.

MACADAM: There was a time when some papers were found in Frank Caccamo's house in Toronto, which really showed that there were various rituals involved. Was that true?

JOE: Yes, that was true Mafia document. It contained the names of all the soldiers who participated in the Sidernese group. Who was who and who was the secretaries. Very important people.

MACADAM: Have you ever heard about these rituals? What's involved?

JOE: It just, like I say, it contains the names of the persons involved, rules, regulations and actually where the actual dues that the members donate, when they have their monthly meetings, where they go and the amount of it.

MACADAM: This is a sort of ritual where they are sworn in. They're sworn in to, what is it called? The Honoured Society?

JOE: The Honoured Society, right.

MACADAM: And how does someone get chosen to be sworn into that?

JOE: It's very difficult. It takes a very long time and they go by, say if I have a son, and I'm in the Italian Honoured Society. I'm very respectful, I have never broken a rule or regulation.... Say for example my son is seventeen years old and I think that he is respectful and he's nice enough, I would recommend it and then my son would start going out with a few young people of this age that are already in it. But he won't know who they are. And they will take it from there and see how he acts. How much of a man he is. Then from there it will be taken up at a meeting that he wants [to join], that somebody will sponsor him and take responsibility. Which means, that the person that has been hanging out with him for over a year or two, will give his word that if something happens, if he is arrested or something, he'll keep his word and remain silent. Then he'll be taken to a place where a member has a business or a house or something and he'll be sworn in.

MACADAM: How many people are sworn in?

JOE: In the Toronto group?

MACADAM: Yes.

JOE: I would say there's at least four hundred.

MACADAM: How many in New York?

JOE: In New York there's at least a thousand.

MACADAM: And how about Siderno?

JOE: Oh, in Siderno, I don't know, there would be anywhere from fifteen hundred to two thousand.

MACADAM: Were you ever considered for being sworn in?

JOE: Oh, yes I was.

MACADAM: How was it told to you, that you were being sworn in?

JOE: I was officially sworn in in Canada. I was taken and after participating with that group for two years, I was considered a worthy enough person.

MACADAM: Were you sworn in in someone's house in Canada?

JOE: No, it was in a place of business.

MACADAM: Were a number of other people being sworn in at the same time?

JOE: No, not that night.

MACADAM: How many people would turn up?

JOE: There would be five people, then you would go to a restaurant [the Casa Commisso on Lawrence Avenue West] and usually have a little celebration party and see the members there.

MACADAM: So you would go to a restaurant and the other members are there?

JOE: Right.

MACADAM: Do you know how many would be at the restaurant?

JOE: There would be pretty close to forty or fifty. Just so much not to give away to the police if anybody's watching for anything.

MACADAM: But you wouldn't ... What would it ostensibly be for? The celebration.

JOE: To celebrate the new coming of the new member.

MACADAM: Can you just tell me who was present when you were sworn in?

JOE: There was Paul Barranca. Frank Archino was there. Joe Racco, Domenic's uncle, and Remo Commisso.

MACADAM: And then you went to this?

JOE: Then we went upstairs to this little party.

MACADAM: This was downstairs?

JOE: Yeah.

MACADAM: And when you went there ...

JOE: When I went in there that night, they knew they were going to do it, yeah. But I was just told we were going out for a card game.

MACADAM: Can you describe what happens at the swearing-in?

JOE: What actually happened was that we were taken there and when we got there they told me what was going on, what was going to happen and from then on we started the ceremony.

MACADAM: What do they say?

JOE: Well, it isn't Italian. It would be hard to describe in English. You know, they were sacred. If I were to describe it in English you wouldn't understand them.

MACADAM: Do they mean anything or were they ritualistic words?

JOE: Some have meaning and some are just, no meaning at all to it. And then after that you would break and unfold your arms and you would kiss everybody and the reason that you kissed everybody, that meant that you were officially a member. You would write your name in a book.

MACADAM: What do you mean by break and unfold your arms?

JOE: Well, first you would, before you would go into the group, you would fold your arms and everybody would fold them along with you and then they would give you the official words for the ceremony and after that, they were done, they would unfold their arms which means the ceremony is over. You would kiss everybody, write your name in the book and it's over. That's with the five and then you would go upstairs.

MACADAM: Do they introduce you?

JOE: They introduce you to everybody.

MACADAM: But how do they do it? Do they say, "This is one of us"?

JOE: Yeah, "This is Compare Giani." When they say that, you know.... But they're upstairs as though they're there for a bachelor's party. When you go upstairs, they all know what you're doing downstairs and what happened.

MACADAM: And that usually goes on in the Casa Commisso?

JOE: Well, it did in that case, but I don't know where they do it now.

MACADAM: When do you write your name in the book?

JOE: That would be writing your name in the paper that was found at Frank Caccamo's house.

MACADAM: Was that quite serious when that was found?

JOE: That was a very serious document.

MACADAM: Did that create problems?

JOE: It did at the time, when he was arrested, it did create a lot of problems because it said a lot of people who were involved with Racco and it helped, I guess in a way, it helped the police, the Toronto police, because they didn't know what was going on until they found that document. And that opened up a lot of doors.

When asked about the extent of co-operation between Paul Volpe's "old" Mafia group and this new Mafia group, "Lou", the Volpe associate who was also interviewed on the second *Connections* series in 1979 (the one in the black hood), said that there was co-operation, but it was an "uneasy co-operation because the new group are a little more violent than the old group."

One instance of co-operation involved the police man-hunt for Domenic Racco. In August 1971, Domenic Racco fled Toronto and Canada after shooting three young men at the Newtonbrook Shopping Plaza in North York. Domenic, who was always quick on the draw, had been hassled by the young men one night in July. One of them called Domenic's Sidernese colleague a "wop". Even more than the Sicilian Mafia, the Calabrian Mafia have a complex and rigorous code, which considers such an insult a "debt of honour" that must be severely punished. The debt of honour works both ways, as any favour is to be rewarded. At any rate the incident at the Newtonbrook Plaza was a classic case of an insult demanding a dramatic response from the man of honour. Domenic Racco, armed with a gun, returned to the plaza the following night with two Sidernese soldiers. He found some friends of the youths who had made the original insult and simply shot them. As Siderno family member "Joe" later told it on the *Connections* program of March 27, 1979, "Domenic goes by the 1920s style. He'll just drive by, roll down the window, and shoot you. That's his style. And there are people who like that style. He shot three people just for the respect of his friend. Where his father wouldn't have gone for that." After the shooting, Domenic hid out in Albany, at the home of a Sidernese mafioso colleague.

Old Mike Racco, Domenic's respected father, went to Paul Volpe to consult him about what lawyer to hire and how to handle the situation. Volpe took over from there. He got Dave Humphrey to take on the Racco case, and he arranged with Humphrey for Domenic to come back to face arrest and trial. Humphrey went down to Albany and brought Domenic Racco back on August 25, 1971. Domenic Racco, whose bail was set at $116,000, was back on the street within twenty-four hours of his arrest. He was later sentenced to ten years for the shootings.

Paul Volpe assisted the Raccos out of respect for Mike Racco, and Mike Racco was deeply moved. A Siderno group move against Volpe would not take place while Mike Racco was around. There was a mutual respect there, and Mike Racco would never have authorized the murder of Paul Volpe.

Mike Racco had the respect of Toronto and Italian Mafia chieftains and the power to authorize killings in Toronto. He was responsible for keeping a semblance of order within the various groups from the Siderno area. He also authorized a hit-man exchange program with a similar Calabrian crime group in the United States, based primarily in Albany, N.Y., Stamford, Conn., and New York City. In one case two Canadian gunmen, Giuseppe Tavernese and Antonio Perri, working for Racco and the allied Commisso group under Remo Commisso, are alleged to have been sent to Queens in New York City to murder a member of the Siderno group, Giuseppe Magnolia, who was about to testify against his boss, Vincent Correale, in a counterfeiting case. On June 29, 1978, they are alleged to have shot Magnolia six times as he was getting out of the car in front of his house. Although the blood was gushing from his wounds, he still managed to stumble through the house and into the backyard, where he carelessly tossed his gun under a bush. Magnolia then started to walk towards a hospital, but collapsed in front of his house and woke up to find himself in a hospital bed. Detectives followed the trail of dried blood left by Magnolia and found his gun. Later, after a miraculous recovery, Magnolia ironically found himself charged with possession of an illegal weapon. The two alleged Canadian hit men were never caught.

The hit-man exchange program worked both ways for the Sidernese Mafia. When Domenic Racco wanted someone in Toronto taken care of early in 1976, he arranged the shooting from his jail cell in Collins Bay Penitentiary, where he was serving time for the Newtonbrook Plaza shootings. While in jail, Racco received considerable support from other Mafia leaders across the country. Both Paolo Violi, the leader of the Montreal crime family, and Mike Racco let it be known that Domenic was being groomed for the leadership. Out of respect, many members of Violi's mob and the Siderno group, including prominent associates, visited him in the pen, leaving behind gifts of money. Domenic was also allowed to go out on occasional spins in his Lincoln Continental, which was parked conveniently near the prison.

Racco arranged the shooting through the mails as a follow-up to a visit from two American members of his crime family, George Mickley and Frank Archino from Albany. Archino, the nephew of the Albany Siderno group leader, was also a cousin of Domenic's and a relative of the Carlo Archino who ran the Sidernese group in Italy. The letter to Archino, which was improperly addressed, ended up in the dead-letter office of the London, Ontario, post office. When it was opened by postal authorities, they found a bizarre set of instructions. "Blast the legs," it said, "NO DEATH." Also in the envelope was a map showing an area of Toronto not far from both the Casa Commisso on Lawrence Avenue, the restaurant that was the headquarters of one faction of the Siderno group, and the real-estate office of Tony Commisso, the man who was to be shot. Except for the letter being sent to the wrong address, the plan was precisely detailed, and it was written by Domenic Racco. Says Racco family member "Joe": "Well, he ordered it. If he was out on the streets himself, he would have done it himself. My understanding is that he wanted this man shot because he brought disrespect to his father."

Albany hit man and Siderno family member Frank Archino gave Toronto police a signed statement on July 3, 1976. (Archino had told Mickley they were going up to Toronto for the weekend. In the end Mickley spent four years in Canada – mostly in jail.) Archino was mentioned in the Ontario Police Commission report on the Sidernese Mafia. The following is excerpted from his statement of 1976:

QUESTION: We are in receipt of information that on Monday June 27, 1976, again on Thursday July 1st, 1976, you and one George Leo Mickley visited one Domenic Racco in Collins Bay Penitentiary; what, if anything, do you wish to tell me about the discussion you had with Racco in Collins Bay?

ARCHINO: Well, first we talked about how he was and how his family was, then he asked me that ah, somebody didn't say who was supposed to shoot this guy. Then he asked me if I would do it; to make him happy I said I would, but I told him maybe although he thought I would, but when George and I were alone after the visit, George was scared just as much as I was and so George and I were planning somehow to leave so we wouldn't have to do it, but we were too scared to go back to the States because we had no money to pay for the rented car, so we asked him for some money, he gave us $50.00. George and I really planned to leave, but we didn't have enough money, so we just went along with whatever he said, but between George and I, we've talked about it many times alone in the hotel room, we both were scared and we were just planning on how to get back to the States so we wouldn't have to do it.

QUESTION: You were telling me Racco wanted you to shoot someone, is that correct?

ARCHINO: He asked me to.

QUESTION: Who did Racco ask you to shoot?

ARCHINO: Tony Commisso....

QUESTION: What instructions, if any, did Racco give you concerning the shooting of Commisso?

ARCHINO: He told me to dye my hair, dye my moustache, make an appointment with Commisso and make him show me a house for sale and before he stepped out of the car, he asked me, which I wasn't going to do it, to shoot him three times in the leg. Then he drew a map of where Commisso works and then he told me to drive to the entrance of 401 and George would be waiting there for me. He told me to steal a car just before the shooting and George would be waiting at the 401 in our car. After the shooting I would take the stolen car to the 401, meet George and get in our car and go down to Kingston and just stay there.

QUESTION: I'm showing you a piece of white paper with the following written on it in red ink, Keele St., Lawrence, Casa Commisso, Mautti Real Estate, 401 East Highway and the name Tony Commisso. Who wrote those things on the paper?

ARCHINO: Domenic Anthony Racco.

QUESTION: When was this written?

ARCHINO: The first time I went to Collins Bay, last Monday.

QUESTION: Did Racco tell you where to get a gun to do this shooting?

ARCHINO: No, he asked me if I had one and I told him yes, I told him that Tommy Barrara stole one for me, I told him it was in the tire in the car, I told him it was a .38.

QUESTION: What was his response when you told him you had a .38 revolver?

ARCHINO: He said good, don't kill him, just give it to him in the leg.

Upon the confession of the two American hit men, Domenic Racco was charged with attempted murder. However, when the case came to court, Racco, although still in prison, was able to so intimidate the two hit men that they changed their testimony in the middle of the trial. From the prisoner's dock, Domenic made hand motions and other gestures that indicated to Archino and Mickley the consequences of speaking against him. This was backed up by the presence of known Siderno hit men in the front rows of the courtroom during the trial. Archino and Mickley succumbed and said they were lying about Racco's involvement. Domenic was acquitted, and ironically the two American hit men, who up to this point had co-operated with the police, were charged and convicted of perjury. Says "Joe": "Those two kids [the hit men] were in fear. Of their lives, of their families. Fear plays a very important role because that courtroom was pretty well packed with a lot of Italian people who participate in that Sidernese group. All they had to do was go sit there and be noticeable to Frank Archino and George Mickley. That was it. They were there to terrify these two people."

Joe also described how Domenic Racco ran his operations during his period in jail.

MACADAM: I just want to ask you, about how people run things from jail.

JOE: Well, in Racco's case, from what I hear on the streets, he runs his whole business from the jail that he was in. He gets visitors and gets most of this business through visitors.

MACADAM: This is Domenic Racco?

JOE: Right. He gets phone calls. Mostly though he does most of his business when he's on a day pass. He's mainly concerned in getting a day pass just to get into the city where he's not being watched by any guards from the jail or nobody is on top of him. I'm sure there is Kingston police watching him but he's got a way of calling somebody and talking on that phone in codes where it would be very difficult for the police to break that code into what they're talking about.

MACADAM: Can you give me an example of that?

JOE: Well, I don't know none of his codes. The codes he knows are just between him and the certain party he's dealing with.

MACADAM: But it seems amazing that you can continue to run your operation from jail.

JOE: It's amazing, but he's been doing it.

MACADAM: And he's been doing it effectively. He gives orders ...

JOE: He gives orders, he makes decisions. When something has to be done on our side, nobody does it unless they have his permission.

MACADAM: In a way then, Domenic and Mike Racco are quite happy Domenic's in jail?

JOE: Oh, no. In a way his father is very happy that his son is so high up in the underworld. But in another way he is sad, because you never know who dislikes you. Like there was word out on the street in '74, that people were going to get Racco when he got out of jail and the last I heard, on the street, was in '74, that there were people planning to take care of him when he gets out.

MACADAM: Why?

JOE: Well, for one thing, mainly they were afraid of him. He's such a powerful person at his age. He has a lot of connections. A man to run an organization such as this from sitting in jail, you can just imagine how he can run it when he's outside. There are so many things to be done. And there are just people that are afraid of him and the only way to do things without his permission and not be afraid and not look over your shoulder is to get him out of the way. But I don't know if that still stands. That was in 1974.

In jail, Domenic took to body-building, and built himself up from a thin, wasted youth to a solidly muscled, well-built young man. He was proud of his new body and paid a lot of attention to his appearance when he got out of jail in 1978. (So that he might avoid unwanted media attention, the prison let him out after midnight, and he just slipped into his waiting Lincoln Continental and drove to Toronto.) He dressed well, wearing the latest Italian tapered clothes to show off his body, and he was always neatly groomed. He was classically good-looking, tall, dark, and handsome. His personality, however, was erratic, and he would often fly off the handle unexpectedly. This irrational quality frightened people. Yet he was capable of being charming and even friendly to those he cared for. He had a boyishness about his appearance for which he overcompensated by excessive aggression. His chronic abuse of cocaine exaggerated this trait and made him both feared and vulnerable to attack after his father's death. But Domenic's real power came from that of his father, Mike Racco, who was one of the most respected men in the Mafia in southern Ontario.

The power of Mike Racco is seen clearly in a confidential government report that details the continual representations to penitentiary and parole officers in the middle 1970s to have Domenic Racco released from jail. The report also notes the efforts of former Liberal cabinet minister and current MP for Davenport riding in Toronto, Charles Caccia. Among others, Caccia contacted members of the penitentiary service and the minister of justice at the behest of Mike Racco to have Domenic Racco released early from his long prison sentence for the shooting at the Newtonbrook Shopping Plaza. After Caccia's representations on behalf of the Raccos were revealed by the first *Connec-*

tions series in June of 1977, Charles Caccia tabled in the House of Commons his correspondence regarding Domenic Racco, stating that he was merely acting on behalf of a constituent and that he had no idea that the Racco family was involved in organized crime. Caccia said he wrote five letters to former solicitor general Warren Allmand, from October 1973 to July 1975, at the behest of Racco's parents and his priest to try to help obtain early parole because "the young man was suffering rapid deterioration in prison in the presence of hardened criminals". Caccia further requested that Domenic Racco be released so that he could work in his father's bakery, returning to the prison at night or on the weekends. In addition, he had asked Allmand to "take a personal interest in Domenic."

The Penitentiary Service, needless to say, found Caccia's numerous requests "unreasonable". Caccia himself has stated that he stopped trying to get Domenic paroled after Domenic was charged with arranging, from his jail cell, to have someone crippled.

During the actual trial of Domenic Racco, a well-known Toronto lawyer had also been approached numerous times by Paul Volpe, the Luppinos, Mike Racco, and many other prominent organized-crime figures to make sure that Domenic Racco "walked". At all costs, these powerful mafiosi in Toronto did not want Domenic Racco to go to jail for very long. Of course, they were not successful, but their constant representations on Racco's behalf indicated the scope of the power of the Raccos.

As "Joe" mentioned, fear is the source of the power of the Racco-Commisso Siderno group. People in the community know what they have done in the past and what they are capable of doing. They know that they would kill if need be, and that keeps people in line. The murders in the beverage industry in the late 1960s can be directly traced to the Siderno group. In another murder case in the late 1970s, a young man who had just emigrated from Italy to Toronto was killed by the Commisso group for an act of disrespect to a Siderno family relative in Italy. All these murders remain officially unsolved as the police have been unable to gather enough supportable evidence to lay charges. Members of the Siderno Mafia believe fiercely in the code of silence (omertà) and rarely co-operate with the police.

But the Racco family and the Commissos were not the only serious members of the Siderno group in Toronto. Cosimo Stalteri is another leader within the Calabrese Mafia in Toronto. He is wanted in Italy for killing a man at a toy store in an outdoor market many years ago. Stalteri, like most members of the Sidernese Mafia, has little respect for human life. He was in a gift store in Siderno with his son when the child accidentally broke one of the glass toys on display. The owner was outraged, and protested. A fight ensued between Stalteri and the owner, and the owner died after receiving multiple punches to the head. Stalteri fled to Canada, where he has established himself as one of the five most prominent leaders of the Siderno family in Toronto. The extradition treaty between Italy and Canada was written in the nineteenth century, before the Mafia was active in Canada. Manslaughter isn't covered. Neither is organized crime.

Stalteri was one of the six pallbearers at the funeral of Mike Racco (some of the others were leaders of the Sidernese cells in Toronto, including Rocco Zito and Remo Commisso). Paul Volpe didn't go to the funeral, but sent a bouquet of flowers as a mark of his respect for old Mike Racco. With Mike Racco gone, a new era had begun, and younger people attempted to ascend to the pre-eminent positions in the Mafia in Toronto.

CHAPTER TEN

Paul Volpe, TV Star

A S THE SIDERNO GROUP members were consolidating their position and asserting themselves in North America in the middle 1970s, Paul Volpe was at the height of his power and influence in the mob in Ontario. But the middle to late 1970s brought some set-backs for Volpe, not the least being unwanted and unnecessary media and police attention.

On a very warm Good Friday afternoon – April 18, 1975, to be exact – Paul Volpe had a fateful meeting that was to change his life dramatically. He was to have lunch with Bill Macadam, one of the producers of the celebrated *Connections* television series on organized crime, which ran on the national CBC network as two series of programs, the first in 1977 (on June 12 and 13) and the second in 1979 (on March 26, 27, and 28). Macadam wanted to discuss to what extent Volpe was involved in organized crime in Ontario. As the research director and associate producer of the series, I had helped arrange the meeting, for we had targeted Volpe early on in our research as one of the major organized-crime figures in Canada.

The meeting was just a part of the intensive research into mob life in Canada that lasted for over two years, from late 1974 to early 1977. (The project was code-named "Commerce" at the time to keep away prying CBC eyes, since it was thought "Commerce" sounded sufficiently innocuous.) Macadam had met with Dave Humphrey, the distinguished criminal lawyer and Volpe's long-time counsel, to discuss Paul Volpe and organized crime in general. Humphrey, as counsel to Volpe, was on a long list I had prepared of people with some knowledge of organized crime or associated with organized crime whom I thought we ought to interview as part of the early research. Humphrey was cordial, taking the position that organized crime did not really exist. "The existence of organized crime," Humphrey told Macadam, "is like that of unicorns – everyone talks about them but no one has ever seen one." Surprisingly, Humphrey then offered to help set up a meeting with Volpe so that Macadam could dispel once and for all the myth that Volpe was a mobster.

Macadam spoke to Volpe on the telephone later that week, after Humphrey had briefed Volpe. Macadam said he was researching organized crime in Canada for a television program for the CBC. When Volpe asked why Macadam was phoning him, Macadam replied that he had been told that Volpe was one of "the biggest men in organized crime." Volpe denied this by stating that he was simply a "businessman". He didn't even know what organized crime was. Macadam replied that this was great news, and that since Volpe was just a businessman, they ought to have a business lunch to discuss the allegations made against him. Volpe was cornered and had to agree to the luncheon. They agreed to meet outside Dave Humphrey's office on Good Friday and have lunch. While Volpe had his own preferences as to restaurants in the area, they were all closed for the holiday, so Volpe had to agree to Macadam's suggestion of dining at the Courtyard Café. "He obviously would have been more comfortable on his own turf," says Macadam.

Macadam was nonplussed. While we of the *Connections* team had been researching organized crime since November 1974, hitherto we had confined our research to libraries and meetings with police, lawyers, and other journalists. We really weren't prepared to meet with an actual mobster. Macadam phoned me at home that evening and asked me to prepare a rush profile of Paul Volpe and his criminal activities so he would know what to ask him the next day. I immediately pulled together all that we had on Volpe to date, such as his involvement in the construction industry in Ontario and the names of his criminal friends and godchildren and so on. I wrote all of this on a cardboard shirt-stuffer from the laundry (I was out of typing paper and didn't feel like going to the office). I stapled a mug shot of Volpe, torn out of the Waisberg commission report, to the briefing material, so that Macadam would be able to identify him on the street.

It turned out that Macadam didn't need the photo. Volpe stood out like a sore thumb on the trendy street near the Courtyard Café. He was dressed in classic grade-B Hollywood Mafia style: fedora hat, cream-coloured shirt with a white tie, and a white raincoat belted tightly. Macadam went right over and said hello to Volpe, who was surprised that he had been recognized. He didn't seem to realize that he was dressed in a stereotypical Mafia outfit.

But Volpe was not the only one playing games. Macadam, in turn, had to pretend complete ignorance about organized crime. One of the many poses a journalist must assume is that of a naive, even fumbling investigator. It helps draw people out. Anyone who has seen *Columbo* on television knows how it is done. Macadam is a master at this. Once they sat down at the restaurant, Macadam began the questioning by going through the list of facts and naively asking Volpe for verification or for more details. To his amazement, Volpe over the next hour and a half did answer most of the questions and even added significant details that the team knew nothing about, such as the fact that Vito de Filippo of the Bonanno family was "his partner" in a casino in Haiti. Macadam, of course, pretended not to understand the significance of the information and just went right on with the shopping list. Volpe sipped on his Campari, told Macadam to lower his voice once or twice, but went along with the game, finding Macadam harmless and easy enough to fool.

After lunch Macadam suggested that Volpe take him on a walk through the Italian section of the city. If Volpe were indeed just a businessman, Macadam reasoned, no one would pay any attention to him. Once again Volpe was cornered and agreed to the unorthodox proposal.

They drove in Volpe's flashy red Cadillac to the Italian area at St. Clair Avenue West and walked up and down the street. Nobody said hello, even though they walked right by Mike Racco's bakery on Nairn Avenue. Volpe felt he had convinced Macadam that he was not a mafioso, and the two parted on very friendly terms.

Thus began a relationship that was to prove Volpe's undoing.

Over the next two years there were many other meetings between Volpe and Macadam. Volpe thought he had succeeded in proving to Macadam that he was not a criminal. The *Connections* team, however, had already determined that Volpe was an important mobster and intended to devote at least one section of the *Connections* program to him, if he could somehow be persuaded to do an interview. Volpe himself, ironically, provided the excuse the team needed to film him.

One day two cable television repairmen arrived at the Volpe estate. Paul Volpe's wife, Lisa, turned them away, suspecting that they were not legit. When she called the cable company and found out they hadn't sent anyone out, she informed Volpe, who searched the grounds the next day and found a bug by the pool. (Since Volpe hardly used the pool, this bug was not likely to have been very effective – except, of course, for picking up the conversations of visitors.) It didn't take much for Volpe to deduce that the two cable repairmen were in fact Mounties, using the repairman disguise to place the listening device. They could have snuck in at night, but Volpe had some pretty nasty watch-dogs, and the estate was well protected against unauthorized entries. But they obviously had made it back to plant the device.

Enraged by the discovery, Paul called his media "friend" Bill Macadam. "The RCMP," he roared, "have more powers than God! You have got to expose them!" Volpe arranged to have dinner with Macadam and Klegerman in one of his favourite Italian restaurants in Yorkville, owned by a cousin, to go over the RCMP bugging. After another visit by Macadam to Volpe's residence, and long telephone negotiations, Volpe tentatively agreed to Macadam's suggestion that he come out to his house with a crew and film an interview about RCMP surveillance and the individual's right to privacy. Volpe was so sure that Macadam thought he was clean that, after further consideration, he finally agreed to the filming suggestion. Though astute, Paul Volpe was not infallible when it came to judging people.

Fortunately, before the day of the scheduled interview, the *Connections* team got a full briefing from the Mounties, who had assigned to the team a very knowledgeable liaison officer from the intelligence division, who had worked on Volpe in numerous operations over many years. Macadam wore a body-pack tape recorder as back-up to the soundman's tape machine and to record between-interview and post-interview chatter. This often turns out to be quite revealing, especially with someone as talkative, in unguarded moments, as Paul Volpe.

When Macadam and cameraman Francis Granger arrived at Volpe's home, Paul was about to take a late-afternoon nap. Macadam apologized for being a bit late, mumbling something about the traffic. Granger, a tall, gruff, mustachioed Yugoslav with a bit of an accent, tried to ingratiate himself with Volpe by saying, in reaction to the somewhat ominous reception they got from the two aggressive-looking German shepherds, that he, too, was a "dog nut". Volpe rather curtly replied that while one of the dogs was "Okay", Granger was "not to touch this one," pointing at a rather ferocious-looking dog named Caesar, who has been known to bite more than one of Paul's guests when least expected. These were, after all, guard dogs trained to attack intruders (such as RCMP teams planting bugs).

Ironically, the official tape recorder was defective, so no sound could be recorded by Granger, who was used to unusual and dangerous shoots on the project by this time. He had nearly been killed earlier when filming surreptitiously outside an old don's house in Hamilton. One of the don's men deliberately backed his car up behind the surveillance van in which Granger was working, leaving his engine running so that the cameraman was overcome by the fumes from the exhaust. Luckily, *Connections* co-producer Martyn Burke checked the van and found Granger before it was too late.

Unexpectedly, Paul's nephew Anthony was also present. Macadam and Granger were jittery about this because a month earlier in Vancouver, Granger had filmed an interview between Anthony and Martyn Burke. Anthony Volpe was the manager of the Lou Myles store in Vancouver, and the team had claimed that it was, in fact, doing a program on people who had left Toronto for the west coast. This was a tense moment for Macadam, as he did not want Paul Volpe alerted to the fact that they were doing a number on him. Granger, however, thinking quickly, took the initiative by remarking on what a coincidence it was that he would meet the same person on two different projects. Volpe was suspicious, and stopped talking to Macadam to give his full attention to the Granger-Anthony situation. Paul Volpe and Macadam then cross-examined Granger and Anthony on how they knew each other. Granger was convincing. "What a small world," he said. The ruse worked, and Paul and Anthony shrugged it off as merely a coincidence.

Macadam suggested that they get down to work and take a look at the bugging device. Everything was quite cool since both Volpe and Macadam felt they had things firmly under control. Volpe dramatically produced the tiny bugging device and offered to show Macadam how it worked by attaching it to his own tape recorder. "This is the mike – there's a pin in it," Volpe explained. "This is buried in the ground.... Let me show you how it works, Bill.... It's frozen to the ground and only this tiny mike sticks out."

Clearly Volpe was fascinated with the technology of surveillance. This explains why he collected wire-tap and bugging gadgetry, even though possession of such equipment was made illegal in the wire-tap bill of 1974. In a nice piece of irony, Volpe was later, in 1978, charged with illegal possession of such equipment after a raid on his house. He went to jail for several months, although he claimed at the time that he kept the illegal equipment only to monitor the movements of his ducks.

Volpe then showed Macadam where the bug was planted, by the phone jack near the pool. The wire was still on the ground leading to Finch Avenue. ("There is probably over a hundred dollars in wire here ... it's a special wire," Volpe marvelled, clearly impressed.) Paul then showed Macadam the hole cut in the fence to plant the bug and speculated that "they were probably going to kill the dog ... hit him with something because he was barking down here." Since the cable-repairmen device had not worked, the RCMP were forced to do a surreptitious break-in to plant the bugging device, according to Volpe. (One does wonder how the surveillance-planting team deals with such contingencies as a watch-dog attack. Like postmen they must have a routine all worked out for dealing with attacking dogs.)

After seeing everything, Macadam decided to film Paul Volpe holding the wires as if he were just discovering them. Volpe re-enacted his following of the wire and his discovery of the actual bug for the camera. He was quite a ham when the camera was rolling, dressed in his captain's hat and enjoying every moment of this show-business performance. He especially relished it since it would undoubtedly cause much consternation for the RCMP when it was aired, and it gave him a special pleasure to embarrass the Mounties, whom he felt were unfair and even racist.

Throughout all of this, Macadam's hidden Nagra SN tape recorder was recording several hours of their conversation. This is what finally nailed Volpe on the *Connections* program, which was broadcast in June 1977. While chatting with Macadam in his own kitchen, Volpe slipped. In talking about police informers, he told Macadam icily that informers deserved to be killed. Everything else in the section entitled "Portrait of a Mobster" that was the least bit incriminating about Volpe came from interview subjects, who included an RCMP officer and an informer in a red hood code-named "Fred", or from the voice-over of the *Connections* announcer. But in his unguarded chatter with Macadam in the kitchen, Volpe provided a unique glimpse into the mind of a mobster – all clearly preserved on tape.

Here is a sampling of his comments:

Deep down they hate all ethnics ... and if they see an ethnic family that is doing good, they're jealous of it and say, "How come he's got it and I haven't?" ... Who the hell would be a policeman in the first place? Who would take a job as a policeman? ... They're ninety per cent drunks anyway.

It is very characteristic of the criminal mind to feel an outsider to an established order that is intrinsically hostile. It allows the criminal to see his crime career as a natural reaction to racism and unfairness in society. It is the kind of rationalization that is heard from a lot of criminals: that society is hypocritical and even worse than the criminals. "At least in the street we have real values and men are men, and there is honour among thieves," one professional mob hit man told me.

Attacking the RCMP was one of Volpe's favourite sports. Later, after the filming, when Macadam and Paul were alone in the kitchen, Volpe again tried to explain his feelings of helplessness. This is Paul Volpe, victim of police harassment:

VOLPE: Bill, you have no idea what powers the RCMP have.... They've got more powers than God.... God doesn't have the power they have.... They come into this house anytime they want ... smash the house and walk right out.... One day it is gonna come out in Canada.... I honestly believe, Bill, in my heart, that they went so far as to kill people. It has only just come out with the CIA that they are capable of doing it, and I don't put it past the RCMP to do the same thing.

MACADAM: In what way?

VOLPE: They shoot people.... Why they are so disturbed with me, Bill, is that I take no shit from them. I won't bow down to them, and that's the only reason why they would love to strangle me. They would just like to come in the house, but I don't run away from them.... That might be my bad habit. Ever since I was a kid, I've never run away from anybody, I don't care who he is ... he can be ten feet tall, I'll fight with him and that's my upbringing, I can't help it. And because they come in with a uniform on that doesn't frighten me, I don't give a shit for their uniform.... If you think the German Gestapo were bad the RCMP is worse.... I'll tell you right now ... believe me, when I tell ya, Bill, I hope if I die, you'll say Paul is right.

Hoping to stop this tirade and get on to something a little less monotonous than Volpe's paranoia about the police, Macadam asked him how long he thought "he had been harassed." Volpe's reply revealed a classic persecution complex:

Since I was sixteen years old.... During the war they used to come to our house because we were Italians.... When Musso-lini declared war they used to come to our house ... we used to be bootleggers.... My mother had to take pieces of wood for the stove and break it up into smaller pieces ... and they used to come by and say to her, "Where are your sons? Why don't they go into the army?" ... Ninety per cent of the police are of the Waspy type ... and hate all ethnics.

The battle lines were clearly drawn for Paul Volpe. It was "us" – the small but real people – against "them", the police, representing a fascist, hypocritical, racist society. Later in the conversation Volpe expanded on this theme to cover politicians:

Police! They mention organized crime, well why don't they mention about the politicians stealing a lot of money and looking to get more money? ... Why is it that's organized crime and not the politicians? ... They are the biggest crooks in the world.

Volpe got so caught up in his argument that he told Macadam that the RCMP would try to kill him and then pretend it was an accident:

I'm looking to protect myself.... I've had one of them [police] *tell me they would shoot me up the lane, and I put a shotgun in my car and said "Anytime you want ... I'll meet you in the field if you want." I'm looking to protect myself.... Dave Humphrey will tell ya that I put a shotgun in my car, and he sent a letter to the Attorney General stating that I'm carrying a shotgun for a certain policeman.... I'm not going to go up some lane and have some guy take a shot at me and say, "Oh, I made a mistake."*

Having failed abysmally in getting Volpe off the subject of police, Macadam decided to indulge him, and asked him why the police thought he was a criminal. Volpe then went into a discussion of unsavoury police techniques, which included planting evidence and using fourteen-year-old informers. It was at this point that Volpe stated, somewhat gratuitously, that all informers deserved to be killed. This cold-blooded assessment did Volpe considerable damage when it was played back on the air in *Connections* on June 12, 1977. Volpe appeared just after a courageous informer in a red hood, code-named "Fred", himself a mob associate, detailed the criminal activities of Volpe and his associates.

How are you going to find out? You have to surmise it. I mean it is common sense.... They have stool pigeons all over the world ... and the minute a stool pigeon gets killed ... someone kills him, which to me is rightly so, you gotta kill them, you gotta get them out of the way. Anybody that is an informer, he's only looking to hurt people.... They are no good to them only when they can use them.... That was proven when a fourteen, fifteen-year-old kid here – they were using him as an informer, his father got all excited and everything else.... This is not too long ago. They tried to deny it. I mean, ya see, it's alright for them to deny something, Bill, because they don't have to answer to anybody.... I don't know how to explain it ...

They once came down to the house here, the Mounties and searched this house. And I told them, I said, "Don't anybody make a move in this house until my wife gets out.... Stay exactly where you are, because you are not going to plant no shit in this house." ... They have to plant something. So they come back three days later and say you're under arrest.... How the hell can I deny it, Bill, if they find something ... I won't even smoke a marijuana cigarette.... I don't want them around me because they make me out to be the biggest importer in the world.... Bill, I'm telling you, the biggest bullshitters in the world are the RCMP, and I'll tell them right to their face, I don't care.

After all this, Volpe went on to say that only the RCMP used such tactics, that "the Ontario Provincial Police don't go around using those tactics, only the Mounties." Provincial chauvinism? Selective paranoia? Or to use Volpe's own expression, "bullshit"? Actually Volpe at the time was favourably inclined to the provincial police because an OPP intelligence officer who worked on Volpe had made friends with him, or so Volpe thought.

There were other highlights of this secretly recorded interview with Volpe (running to seventy typed pages in all) that helped create such a stir when broadcast.

On his good character and lifestyle:

Bill, I don't care if there's a bug in the house here.... I've got nothing to hide.... I'm not ashamed of anything I do.... I'm not a pimp.... I'm respectful with my wife.... I'll take care of her.... I'll walk around with holes in my shoes if I have to for my wife.... And they [the police] are not going to put me in the same category as themselves.... I don't molest any young girls. I don't go and look to beat up girls and go out and booze.... I don't do none of that stuff, and I don't hit my wife across the face – I've never touched my wife, and I guess that bothers them [the police].

On the possibility of going to jail and how he would handle the police:

Jail doesn't scare me.... They are not going to scare me by saying they'll send me to jail, 'cause I'll tell them in plain English to go and fuck yourself.... I'll be honest with ya ... they will never come and put a hand on me, Bill, because I swear to you I'll rip something off their body ... their nose or ear ... I'll take something off them.

And finally, a comment that was not used in *Connections* but is certainly relevant now. In this statement Volpe again reveals his overwhelming need for personal security in light of the greed of some of his possible rivals in the mob. As Macadam was about to film the bugging device of a table in the house, Volpe stopped him sharply with, "Don't film in the house. I don't want to show anybody the inside of the house because they have big eyes."

Macadam left after several hours, still on very friendly terms with Volpe. Paul did not realize he had been taken, not until a year later, on Sunday evening, June 12, 1977, the day the first *Connections* program aired with the section on Volpe called "Portrait of a Mobster".

On the morning of the broadcast Paul Volpe called Macadam, after seeing some promotional material, and demanded to know if he and his wife were in the show. He made it quite plain to Macadam that if his wife were included – a fact that Macadam would neither confirm nor deny – Macadam's health might suffer (or I should say, he asked pointed questions about Macadam's health, to which Macadam cheerfully responded that he felt "great"). But it was characteristic of Volpe that he was more concerned about his wife than himself, and he knew from the promos – which featured an informer in a red hood talking about the four Mafia-style families in Toronto – that he had to be named and that Macadam had probably set him up during the filming at his house. (He had no idea at this point, however, about the secret tape-recording. Before the first series of *Connections*, hidden tape interviews were almost never used for public-affairs programming.)

There were other things in the program that angered Volpe. The informer from the Volpe organization, "Fred", gave details of the organization and operations of the group. At one point in the section on Volpe, Volpe's clandestinely taped statement about the necessity of killing off stool pigeons is heard over a visual of "Fred" in his red hood. Earlier in the same program, but in another section entitled the "Toronto-Buffalo Connection", "Fred" had named Paul Volpe as one of the heads of the four controlling families in Toronto.

On the morning after the broadcast of "Portrait of a Mobster", a furious Paul Volpe rang Natie Klegerman. Volpe went on and on about his anger over his wife being mentioned (though she was never shown and all that was said about her was that she was a senior officer at Creeds), for above all he always wanted to protect his Lisa from media attention. After venting his anger about that and about the general tenor of the program, which he found personally offensive, he asked Natie what he thought the effect of the program would be. Klegerman at once put Volpe in a better frame of mind by pointing out that "at least you won't have to worry about collecting [loan-shark] debts for a while." This was very true. The television exposure did add to Volpe's credibility as a major and ruthless gangster, and victims were indeed more likely to pay up when asked. When Natie was trying to be intimidating he would say, "Pay up or you owe us nothing," which was a gentle way of threatening the person's life.

Volpe was so angry at being stung by the "dumb" Macadam that police, listening to the wire-tap on Volpe's phone, felt Macadam should leave town for a few days after the program was aired so that Volpe could cool down. Macadam, however, stayed in town and nothing happened.

One of Paul's enforcers, Raymond "Squeaker" Greco, watched the show from his room in the Carriage House Hotel on Jarvis Street, where he was nominally an employee of his cousin John Franciotti, the owner. He was also furious. After the show he stormed out of his room shouting, "Those bastards, those bastards" to anyone in the corridors who cared to listen. However, since at the time one of the main gay bars in Toronto was located in the hotel, and the music was blaring as usual, not too many people heard "Squeaker" curse the *Connections* team.

It is easy to understand the annoyance of Volpe, Greco, and the others in the criminal underworld who were featured in the programs. Klegerman was correct about the short-term advantage in collection activities, which probably led to the temporary lay-off of enforcers such as "Squeaker". But, more importantly, massive publicity brings more heat from the police, and that is the last thing these people ever want.

There was, of course, a tremendous public reaction to the first programs of the *Connections* series, a reaction that directly affected Paul Volpe's routine. There were headlines in all the papers across the country about the programs and their contents. Serious questions about organized crime were raised on radio talk-shows in Toronto, and the attorney general of Ontario, Roy McMurtry, said he would take a closer look at organized crime in Ontario and would order a royal commission if necessary. Editorials lauded the show and lambasted mob leaders such as Volpe. After a meeting with the attorney general, the leaders of the organized-crime units of the three police forces in Toronto (the OPP, the Metro Toronto police, and the RCMP) had an unprecedented press conference on the subject of the Mafia. Inspector Gordon Lennox, head of the Metropolitan Toronto police intelligence unit, verified that several Mafia families were operating in Toronto and Ontario. As Inspector Lennox was about to name names, he was sharply silenced by one of his senior colleagues. This, in itself, was front-page news in the *Globe and Mail*.

The Hamilton *Spectator* featured a front-page interview with then Chief Superintendent (now Deputy Chief) Keith Farraway of the Hamilton police department, which confirmed the existence of at least three mob families operating in the Hamilton area. The leader of the Opposition, Joe Clark (currently the minister for external affairs), called for a royal commission into organized crime at the federal level, as did former prime minister John Diefenbaker. A Toronto stockbroker said his firm was taking a closer look at a few of its clients with "dubious reputations" in the new light of the *Connections* programs. A Toronto insurance executive re-opened investigations on some contracts involving criminal figures. "A program like the CBC production really hit home," he said, adding that he was concerned "about the minuscule percentage of our business that may be in the bad-apple category." People even sent back their credit cards and refused to do business with organized-crime-related firms mentioned in the programs. A popular Toronto radio talk-show devoted a whole three-hour program to public reaction to the shows, and to what could be done about the problem by members of the public. The *Financial Post* reported that construction-company executives in Ontario were taking another look at their subcontractors, union representatives, and suppliers, many of whom had direct ties with Paul Volpe.

In short, the programs put a lot of heat on Paul Volpe and his associates. They lay low for the weeks immediately following the broadcast on June 12 and 13, 1977. Clearly the *Connections* team had made a fool out of Paul Volpe for all the world to see. His candid remarks to Macadam (severely edited to about three or four minutes) made "Portrait of a Mobster" live and literally brought the voice of the mob into people's living rooms. This scam against Volpe was the beginning of his television career and was only to be exceeded by the sting the *Connections* team ran against him in the second series of programs, broadcast two years later under the title "The Casino Connection".

Perhaps one of the most important results of the *Connections* programs was something that was under way even before they aired. In anticipation of the programs, which the RCMP and the other police forces knew about long before the broadcasts, the RCMP set up, in late January 1977, a top-priority task force in co-operation with the OPP and the Metro Toronto police. It became operational in April 1977, just two months before the series aired, and was called the Special Enforcement Unit (SEU). It targeted the leaders of organized crime in Ontario – with a special initial emphasis on Paul Volpe and his associates.

CHAPTER ELEVEN

Another New Organization: The Special Enforcement Unit

THE ESTABLISHMENT of the Combined Forces Special Enforcement Unit, a permanent joint-forces operation run by the RCMP with the participation of the Ontario Provincial Police and the Metropolitan Toronto Police Force, dramatically changed the lives of Paul Volpe, Nathan Klegerman, Chuck Yanover, and Remo, Cosimo, and Michele Commisso, to name but a few in the mob who received their special attention.

The SEU was to become the longest-running and most successful joint-forces operation in the history of Ontario policing. It was set up in January 1977, as a result of the success of the Quebec Crime Probe and in anticipation of the June broadcast of the *Connections* series. Harold Adamson, then the chief of the Metro Toronto police, who along with RCMP Assistant Commissioner Henry Tadeson provided original impetus within the police for setting up the unit, told an early meeting of SEU officers in June that their mandate was simply "to have good investigations which put major organized-crime people in jail." This blunt directive was a result of public pressure for an offensive against organized crime in Canada that was fuelled by the revelations of the Quebec Crime Probe and the CBC-TV series. There was a general feeling that something very innovative and imaginative had to be done to attack the growing power of the mob, and that the old system of utilizing police intelligence units, though it did effectively identify the targets, was not proving a very effective way of wiping out organized crime. The problem was jurisdictional and financial. It was also one of emphasis.

In the past the most effective cases against the mob resulted from a concentrated effort involving the three major forces in Ontario in a joint-forces operation for which money and manpower were plentiful. An example of this was the 1975–76 joint-forces operation (with Montreal police co-operation as well) that resulted in charges and convictions against three major Mafia leaders who were attempting an elaborate extortion in Ontario. They were Johnny "Pops" Papalia, Vic Cotroni, the Godfather of the Montreal Mafia, and Paolo Violi, the acting boss of the Montreal Mafia. Another very early joint-forces operation had been mounted in the late 1960s by the three forces and was aimed at charging members of the new Sidernese Mafia in Toronto. Yet another early joint-forces, pre-SEU success was the so-called "Granny fraud" case of 1976, which involved members of the mob in Ontario and the United States posing as police officers and bank inspectors to steal the life savings of elderly women.

One person outside the police who was in a unique position to see the special value of these joint-forces police operations was Howard Morton, the Crown attorney who had worked with the Mounties on the "Granny fraud" as well as other organized-crime cases. Howard Morton got his first real taste of organized crime in 1973 when he was working as a junior Crown attorney in senior Crown attorney Clay Powell's office. In March of that year, as mentioned earlier, he was assigned the task of analysing daily transcripts of testimony gathered by Judge Harry Waisberg for the Ontario Royal Commission into Certain Sectors of the Construction Industry (prominently featuring Paul Volpe, Chuck Yanover, Nate Klegerman, Gus Simone, and a host of other Volpe associates) with a view to laying charges (for example, for fraud or perjury) against some of the participants. Later, in 1975, he was assigned to the "Granny fraud" case, which involved Hamilton mob and American organized-crime figures. The conspirators used a blue box on the telephone (a device that allowed them to control the victims' telephone lines during the scam) and posed as police officers investigating a corrupt bank teller. The pre-selected elderly victim would be phoned and asked to go to the bank, withdraw a certain amount of money (usually several thousand dollars), and give the money – which was marked – to the "investigating officer" outside the bank. It was to be used as evidence against the allegedly crooked bank teller.

Over a thousand hours of wire-tapped calls were recorded in this major joint-forces investigation, which involved criminals from Hamilton, Ottawa, and New England, including Fred Gabourie of the Hamilton mob, led by Johnny "Pops". At one point in the investigation, Fred Gabourie met Paul Volpe at the CNE to discuss some business. The meeting was observed by police surveillance, though not recorded. No evidence was gathered that implicated Volpe further in this particular scam. The "Granny fraud" case was the first major successful wire-tap case conducted after the 1974 wire-tap legislation was enacted.

In 1976, Howard Morton had several meetings with Attorney General Roy McMurtry about the possibility of the Crown Attorney's Office working on special cases with the police. Morton pushed the Attorney General to set up a special joint-forces unit to deal with the growing organized-crime problem. Before McMurtry, previous attorneys general and solicitors general in Ontario had downplayed the problem of the Mafia, and some, such as Allan Lawrence in the early 1970s, even denied that the Mafia existed in Ontario. According to Morton, these meetings in 1976 with McMurtry led directly to the establishment of a permanent liaison between the Crown's office and organized-crime police investigators, which in turn led, in January 1977, to the establishment of the SEU. The three forces signed a formal, written agreement with the Office of the Attorney General after a lengthy meeting on January 25, 1977. Howard Morton, who was the director of the criminal law branch of the Crown Attorney's Office, was appointed the senior Crown consultant to the new, élite police group, a position that he still proudly holds.

Under the terms of the joint-forces agreement, the RCMP were to provide the premises, the phones, the stenographers, and one-third of the manpower; the OPP and Metro police were to provide an equal number of people as well as cars. The unit was to be under the command of a senior RCMP officer with some experience in the organized-crime area. Though the number of police involved was allowed to vary, according to the case work-load (up to sixty cops have worked at one time for the unit), the basic unit was to consist of seven experienced investigative officers from each force. Inspector James McIlvenna, who had worked on many organized-crime cases (including the Papalia-Cotroni-Violi extortion case) with the élite commercial crime unit of the RCMP, was selected as the commander of the unit, a position he was to hold from 1977 until he was transferred to head the RCMP drug unit in mid-1984. Known affectionately to his underlings as "the Bear" because of his teddy-bearish appearance (though he was known to range from teddy bear to grizzly bear in the same day, depending on the circumstances), McIlvenna put together a crack team of investigators, mostly from the intelligence units of the three forces. "The Bear" is a cop's cop: on his desk, instead of a name plate, is a plate that says, "Every story has three sides – yours, mine, and the facts." He is a no-nonsense, let's-get-'em officer. And it is McIlvenna's vision, shaped in part by input and direction from Crown attorneys Clay Powell and Howard Morton, that has been the basis for the operating methods of the SEU.

The SEU had developed after many years of police reluctance to take the mob seriously. In the 1920s there were the Ontario Temperance Act officers, who policed the bootleg industry, but they did not deal at all with organized crime as a phenomenon. It wasn't until the 1960s that a serious police interest in organized crime developed, and police intelligence units on organized crime were set up.

Normally, the intelligence units of the Metro Toronto police, the RCMP, and the OPP are concerned primarily with gathering information about criminals and occasionally with finding out about the crimes before they happen or learning something about them after they have occurred. But intelligence units have never been as geared to making cases as they have been to gathering intelligence about the criminals – their movements, associates, and activities. The RCMP criminal intelligence unit was particularly good in keeping up-to-date intelligence files on all the major criminal figures. But the problem was that the force got so caught up in the process of gathering information that there weren't many actual cases made against organized criminals.

In some cases intelligence was gathered simply as an end in itself. Jimmy Breslin satirizes this kind of information-gathering as what he humorously calls "Italian geography", in his 1969 comic novel about Brooklyn mobster Joey Gallo, entitled, appropriately enough, *The Gang That Couldn't Shoot Straight*:

Italian geography ... is a practice of such as the F.B.I., various police intelligence units, and newspaper and magazine writers. Italian geography is the keeping of huge amounts of information on gangsters, the price they pay for clothes, the restaurants in which they eat, the names of all relatives out to the fifth cousins, their home addresses, and their visible daily movements. All this information is neatly filed and continually added to. It is never used for anything, and the gangster goes on until death.

There is no denying the importance of knowing where Paul Volpe had lunch, what people he was meeting with, and what his daily movements were. These are crucial facts – but not as ends in themselves.

To avoid the Breslin-type critique, the RCMP in Ontario decided that in addition to having an excellent intelligence capability, they needed to have an élite group of the best cops on organized crime from all three forces, focussing on specific criminals and criminal actions and slowly building cases that would hold – with a view to laying charges as soon as possible. And the more charges and cases the better.

Police intelligence in Ontario, which consisted of the combined resources of the RCMP (with its National Crime Intelligence Centre in Ottawa), the Ontario Provincial Police, the Metropolitan Toronto Police Force, and the Ontario Police Commission, to say nothing of the Hamilton-Wentworth Police, the Ottawa Police Department, and other local bodies, together already possessed more than enough information on who were the major, middle-rank, and minor figures in organized crime in Ontario. Essentially, police intelligence knew who many of the players were, how and with whom they operated, where they went, who were acting as their fronts, and so on. What was missing was action – making a charge and ensuring that the case was airtight. To do this required vast resources in manpower, time, and money. It also required incredible determination and patience, and flexibility. In addition it required the ability to be able to make a quick deal with informers and criminals who wished to co-operate in exchange for either money or immunity. The SEU provided all of this and more.

When the SEU was established, so was a unique set-up between the police and the Crown Attorney's Office, directly linked to the Attorney General himself, that allowed for considerable latitude in granting immunity to informers and criminals who wanted to break with their crime families. There had never been in Canada anything like the Witness Protection Program in the United States, which provided the mob defector with a new identity, police protection, immunity from prosecution when necessary, and financial support. The Witness Protection Program in the United States was started in the 1960s as a joint endeavour of the FBI, the U.S. Attorneys' Offices throughout the United States, the Federal Marshal's office, the federal organized-crime strike forces in the various regions, and other offspring of the U.S. Department of Justice.

One of the first criminals afforded protection under the U.S. Witness Protection Program was Paddy Calabrese, the former Buffalo mafioso who was to be used for several of the *Connections* stings, including one against Paul Volpe. Paddy's story was made into a James Caan film, *Hide in Plain Sight*, which focusses on one of the many inadequacies of the program, namely its failure to sort out the ramifications in the personal lives of those involved with the witness. In this case, the ex-husband of Paddy's wife lost contact with his children because Paddy and his family (including his stepchildren) were given new names and hidden away by the government. Also, the Witness Protection Program tends to drop people after they have testified in trials, and all too frequently the "protected" person ends up going back into crime – or, in some rare instances, is actually killed by the mob. All in all the Witness Protection Program has been quite successful in the United States, although over the last decade it has become slightly unwieldy. Some 15,000 informers have gone through the program across the United States since it has been in effect.

The SEU has had the luxury of profiting from the U.S. experience and has fine-tuned its program to 1970s and '80s Canadian requirements. Under the Ontario plan, far fewer law enforcement agencies were involved, and the police were given a direct line to the Attorney General.

Naturally enough, one of SEU's first major targets in organized crime in Ontario was Paul Volpe. Volpe, of course, had been the subject of special attention from the police and special projects in the past, such as "Project B" on his union activity, a joint-forces operation, and the massive RCMP intelligence operation dubbed "Operation Oblong", which intercepted many of Volpe's and Klegerman's phones and watched them around the clock.

Some of the many operations that involved Paul Volpe in the early days of SEU were "Operation Overlord", "Operation Top Hat", and an expanded version of the RCMP's "Operation Oblong", which, as we have seen, targeted Volpe's and Klegerman's loan-sharking empire. Operation Overlord specifically targeted Paul Volpe for prosecution for being a crime boss. Operation Top Hat concentrated on Paul Volpe's illegal gambling operations. One of the Top Hat successes was to be the busting of the Bathurst Street Bridge Club in 1979, which was a front for Paul Volpe and Sam Shirose's poker and craps games. Shirose was the manager, and the "club" stayed open from eleven at night until eight in the morning on Tuesdays, Saturdays, and Sundays. Volpe and Shirose were found guilty and fined $8,000 and $10,000 respectively for keeping a common gaming-house. Another successful Top Hat operation was the bust of a Volpe card game at Sylvia Bungaro's Rosedale home in 1978.

The SEU is still in its early stages here in Ontario. The Cecil Kirby case in late 1980 (looked at in depth in later chapters) marked the first major breakthrough and challenge. Had the SEU not been in place in November 1980 when Kirby made his call to the RCMP offering to act as an informer, it is entirely likely that the information simply would have been filed away in some intelligence file, Kirby would have become a poorly paid informer, and the Commissos would still be operating in the streets of Toronto, planning extortions, murders, and bombings. The SEU was able to come up with a package for Kirby that included immunity from prosecution for past crimes, a financial settlement, and protection, in exchange not only for his testimony in court on a host of charges, including contract killings involving more than fourteen criminals, but also for his co-operation as a body-packed double agent, operating under SEU control within the Commisso crime family. So the SEU in this case, at least, went considerably farther with more efficiency than is usually the case under the cumbersome Witness Protection Program in the United States, though the program in the U.S. has used witnesses operationally. There was the 1977 case of mobster Chuck Carlo, who walked into the FBI and offered to co-operate in operations against the Magaddino crime family in Buffalo. Carlo was set up in a phoney, FBI-controlled fencing operation. Everything was video-taped, and as a result, many Buffalo mobsters were arrested, as well as several political leaders. Similar FBI scams that have been run with protected witnesses have come under some attack in the United States since the Abscam cases and the John DeLorean acquittal in 1984. There are some in Ontario who now charge that similar excesses are occurring in Ontario with the SEU.

Certainly the SEU is not without its critics. Long-time criminal lawyer Earl Levy – who has defended Natie Klegerman, Chuck Yanover, and other organized-crime figures and who knew Paul Volpe – and his law partner, Louis Silver, point to one case in particular that they feel demonstrated the use of poor SEU techniques. These techniques included the pre-targeting of the suspects (or what the judge called "trial by ambush") and the use of an informer who had been given immunity.

A Toronto diamond merchant and sometime diamond smuggler named Maurice Zahler had been arrested by the police for a possible fraud against Peoples Jewellers in Toronto on a diamond deal. Zahler, who was originally from the secretive world of Antwerp diamond dealers, was arrested by Metro Toronto police and charged with fraud. However, knowing of the intense police interest in Paul Volpe and his associates, Zahler, who had been involved with Klegerman and the Volpes in various diamond transactions over the years, offered to give the police evidence that would implicate a "Mr. Volpe" in an illegal diamond swindle if they would drop charges against him. As it turned out, he meant Frank Volpe (Paul's older brother), not Paul. The Zahler case was then given to the SEU, Zahler was thoroughly debriefed on his activities with the Volpes and Klegerman, and in 1979 charges against Zahler on the original alleged fraud were dropped. Instead, Zahler's information led to thirteen charges, which were later broken up into two sets of charges against the Volpe groups, with Klegerman as the common element.

In one set of charges, Paul Volpe, Nathan Klegerman, and Morris Cooper, a Volpe-Klegerman associate, were charged with defrauding Maurice Zahler and his company, Zahler Diamond Company, of $450,000 worth of diamonds between August 1972 and December 1975.

In a second set of charges, Frank Volpe, Nathan Klegerman, and Murray Manny Feldberg (whom Klegerman and Paul Volpe used to front Flite Investments) were accused of defrauding Mabrodiam Diamond Importers and Mark Davidovitz of $580,000 worth of diamonds between September 1976 and March 1978. Davidovitz, in this case, had agreed to co-operate with the SEU and testify against his former associates.

A third set of charges involving diamond frauds were brought against Paul Volpe, Nathan Klegerman, Morris Cooper, Ian Rosenberg, and Charles Yanover, but they were dropped before coming to trial. It is worth taking a brief look at this third case, for it shows how organized crime can work effectively, even when caught.

The case was based on the testimony of a Klegerman associate from a previous diamond swindle who had agreed to inform, and on evidence gathered with body-packs. In this fraud, Klegerman, with Volpe's help, put up the right credentials to obtain with a very small deposit a consignment of diamonds worth $1.5 million from a New York City wholesaler. Klegerman took the diamonds back to Toronto to dispose of them, with no intention of paying the New York City merchants the balance. The diamond merchants hired detectives to check Klegerman out further, and when they found out about his organized-crime connections, they called in the OPP and the RCMP. The merchants then body-packed themselves for some of their meetings with Volpe and Klegerman in Toronto.

Eventually charges were laid for fraud, as Klegerman and Volpe had never paid, but the merchants were not keen to press the affair. Their checking of Klegerman's associates had led them to names in New York City and Toronto that made them extremely nervous. The merchants, as is their wont, struck a deal, got their diamonds back, and withdrew charges. Volpe and Klegerman's connections in this case paid off. It was a measure of Volpe's influence that he could intimidate the New York diamond trade. But this case had nothing to do with the later Zahler cases, which actually went to court in 1981.

All these cases involved the Volpe group taking consignments of diamonds through Nathan Klegerman with little or no down payment and ripping off the owners of the original diamonds by not paying for them. These deals involved complex transactions, verbal understandings (which were always open to interpretation when Klegerman was involved), and "memorandums" of agreement. Cleverly, Klegerman also made secret tape-recordings of certain meetings with some of these diamond dealers, in case there were future problems. Klegerman was that devious and that methodical in his shady dealings, especially in the netherworld of the diamond trade. After his 1963 arrest and its consequences, Klegerman had decided not to take too many chances, and if he did, he was determined to protect himself – to "cover his ass".

As a result of Klegerman's defensive activity, the complexity of the business dealings, and the general unreliability of the chief witnesses against them, the Volpe group won every one of the major diamond cases brought by the SEU that went to court. Earl Levy, the lawyer for Klegerman, says the Volpe group won because it was shown that the SEU informers – Davidovitz, Zahler, and George Tichy (an SEU informant and a Bay Street jeweller who had had business dealings involving diamonds with Klegerman and Frank Volpe) – were offered some sort of deal in exchange for their testimony against the Volpe group. The Crown denies this, stating that the cases were lost because the diamond trade is such a netherworld of borderline transactions that it is very difficult for anyone outside of it to separate legal from illegal deals. Or as one Crown attorney, Jeff Casey, simply and eloquently put it, "A jury found them not guilty as charged." A police source who worked on one of the cases says that it was lost because by the time it got to court, two years after the charges were laid, the witness's actual testimony was "a watered-down version" of what he had originally said and didn't have the same impact it had when he first spoke with the SEU. Time changes many things, including some people's memories.

Turning to another example of alleged SEU incompetence or failure, lawyer Earl Levy points to the later 1982 Korean case against Yanover and Klegerman. (Examined in detail in a later chapter, it involved an alleged plot to assassinate the president of South Korea; Yanover had offered his services to the RCMP as a double agent, for a price.) Levy, who acted for Yanover and Klegerman in the matter, feels it was a bit of a frame-up by the SEU. Levy quotes the opinion expressed by the trial judge during earlier diamond cases, in which he found that the SEU engaged in "trial by ambush". There is, of course, some truth to this, in that the SEU's mandate is to make cases against major organized criminals at all costs. It is one way to break organized crime. Silver goes farther than Levy and compares the situation to the DeLorean scam in the United States, where the object was to "get" DeLorean one way or the other, by hook or by crook. Louis Silver says it is "iniquitous for the SEU to have as their raison d'être having someone charged or convicted simply because he is who he is." He says that "vast amounts of money are wasted following people around," and that the whole "pernicious SEU operation avoids their having a public inquiry" into organized crime. The fact that the SEU also often makes deals with other bad guys in order to have charges laid against their own special targets further exasperates both Silver and Levy.

The civil libertarians certainly have a point. But then the SEU is not trying to be fair. The police forces have spent many years identifying the leaders of organized crime in Ontario and deciding who are to be the targets for special attention. It takes a lot of time and money to make a firm case against any major organized criminal, for the criminal spends a lot of money and time insulating himself from direct involvement in the illegal activity itself. Those who are targeted are among the more prominent and sophisticated of the organized criminals, who represent a clear and present danger to society and who are continually carrying on operations that are against the law. To take them out of society requires a concerted police effort against them, and the SEU certainly provides the means for accomplishing this end. It has been shown that it is not enough for police to know the daily movements of organized criminals (which is what police intelligence officers do); they must have the hard facts to make a case against them and to put them behind bars for as long as possible. This is the SEU's sole purpose.

Of course there have been errors in judgment and blind alleys over the eight years of SEU operations. One former SEU officer I interviewed felt that the SEU often throws a lot of money into a project and "gets very little." Operation Oblong, this officer maintains, "could be considered an SEU failure, considering the amount of time, money, and manpower expended to make one case [the Veronac case], which didn't immediately knock out Flite Investments as a going concern." Still, as noted earlier, this operation did put Klegerman, Paul Volpe, Yanover, Feldberg, and company on notice that their every movement was being watched and that the police would get them if they made one false step – which, of course, was inevitable. It is a kind of psychological warfare, which, in the end, the police have to win, given the financial and human resources that the SEU provides. And in the case of Flite Investments and Vegas Vending, it was eventually successful, as the convictions in the Veronac case put the companies out of business by 1979, three years after the original extortion against Veronac took place.

According to SEU veterans, the philosophy of the SEU has been to saturate the targets, running investigations around the clock, with physical and electronic surveillance of their homes, offices, and meeting-places, including restaurants that they frequent (for example, they bugged and watched the Colosseum Restaurant at Walton and Yonge streets for years because the Volpes used to meet people there regularly) and other businesses they visit on a regular basis. This, of course, requires a great deal of manpower and financial resources, and it means that not too many of the top organized-crime leaders can be targeted at the same time. The SEU also makes use of immunity deals and ad hoc witness-protection programs to coax organized-crime soldiers or small-time operators to inform on or work against people who are targeted. "The point," says one SEU veteran, "is to know the pre-targeted individual better than they know themselves, and put them on notice that they are being watched ... to saturate them from the investigative point of view." According to Inspector James McIlvenna, who was the head of the SEU for its first seven years, "the philosophy of SEU is to keep the battle against organized crime going on a number of fronts, and eventually make headway.... From 1977 to 1983 the Combined Forces Special Enforcement Unit made seizures totalling over $11 million and laid over 1,100 charges with very few acquittals, and the cost of this was minimal." McIlvenna is particularly infuriated by Silver's charge that "vast amounts of money are spent on SEU investigations." "What vast amounts of money?" an enraged McIlvenna retorts. "This is one of the cheapest units in existence in the province, and anyone charged [has] committed a crime and is duly convicted." McIlvenna feels that investigating organized crime "is like circling the wagons.... You look for the major people and if they are insulated you target his key people and charge them, and break down the whole system and cut off the financial resources of the Mr. Big."

As for the charge that the witnesses the SEU sometimes uses are criminals themselves who have made a deal, McIlvenna has an answer. "We can't put a guy up to lie," he states, adding wryly, "even with my ethics." It is inevitable that the SEU uses people who are tainted themselves, because, as McIlvenna points out, "organized crime preys on people who cannot usually complain or are criminals themselves." This is one of the overriding reasons that it is so difficult for police to penetrate organized crime, because the mob picks its victims so carefully. In an address to a convention of Crown attorneys in 1981, McIlvenna summed up the problems of using the type of witnesses that the SEU has to use to convict mob leaders:

No prosecutor will like the usual organized-crime victim as a witness. This victim is usually heavily in debt, possesses weak characteristics, and in fact is probably a criminal himself. At the very least he is a liar and a cheat. But this along with corruption and negligence is why organized crime flourishes. An organized-crime victim usually does not complain. He cannot, because he is dirty himself or he is afraid of the consequences.... It is certainly difficult for us to like these victims, let alone use them as witness complainants, and organized crime knows this.

McIlvenna also told the Crown attorneys the best way to win the battle against organized crime. It was a unusual statement for an RCMP inspector to make, and it nicely sums up what the SEU is all about:

The truth is that in organized-crime investigation and prosecuton, Crown attorneys have to think like policemen and policemen have to think like lawyers ... but a rare investigator is the one who can gain the trust of a witness, develop and document a thorough investigation, and assist the Crown until the final appeal is heard. Policemen are told in training, "Your job is done when you make the arrest," but in organized-crime cases this is only the beginning. The job has not been done until the accused has gone to jail.

Crown attorney Howard Morton agrees, and is very proud of his achievement in helping to set up the SEU and of its accomplishments over the years. He clutches a huge computer log and rattles off the number of SEU cases – over 1,100 individuals charged to date, confirming Inspector McIlvenna's head count. When you examine the particulars a little more carefully, however, it becomes apparent that of these 1,100 cases, very few are major crimes of major organized criminals.

Still, the SEU has successfully prosecuted a number of the leaders and soldiers of organized crime in Ontario. Among others, it has put Paul Volpe, Remo and Cosimo Commisso, and Chuck Yanover before the courts and in jail on a number of charges ranging from minor offences such as illegal gambling activities (Operation Top Hat) and illegal possession of wire-tap equipment to such major offences as extortion (Operation Oblong) and conspiracy to commit murder. And, most significantly, the SEU has succeeded in putting organized-crime leaders in Ontario on notice that their every move *may* be under police scrutiny.

Under such intense pressure by the police at home, some Canadian organized-crime leaders, like Paul Volpe, began to look for a more favourable climate outside of Canada for some major operations.

CHAPTER TWELVE

The Day of the Condor: The Atlantic City Connection Exposed

THE VOTERS OF ATLANTIC CITY, N.J., approved legalized gambling casinos for their city in a referendum in November 1976. New Jersey has always been perceived by the public as a mob state. It is. Some state senators, assemblymen, and mayors of major New Jersey cities have been convicted of accepting bribes or working with organized crime over the years. Indeed some of these high-ranking public officials have been members of the Mafia themselves. While certainly not a member of the Mafia, Harrison Williams, a United States Senator from New Jersey, was jailed for corruption and expelled from the Senate. Tony "Pro" Provenzano, a senior vice-president of the Teamsters Union, Local 560 – the largest local in the United States, and one located in New Jersey – is a senior lieutenant in the Gambino crime family and is now in jail for a mob murder. His brother, Salvatore "Pro", also a mobster, runs Teamsters Local 560 in Tony's absence. New Jersey has long been a very corrupt state with an extremely serious Mafia and organized-crime problem.

This is the kind of environment that welcomed legalized casino gambling in the city famous the world over as the home of Monopoly (and where real-life Monopoly is played for keeps). By the 1970s the glory of its heyday in the '20s, '30s, and '40s, when it was a major resort town on the east coast of the United

States, had faded, and the famous boardwalk was in quite a state of decline. Casino gambling, it was said, would restore some of the glitter. There was some initial concern about a moral decline being encouraged by legalized gambling and the risk of criminal elements becoming attracted to the revitalized city. When the referendum was passed, New Jersey assemblyman Steven Perskie put things in perspective in this assessment: "This town will rise on gambling, but it will be a family town, just like it has always been, with taste.... We may be selling a piece of our soul, but we're putting a high price on it." It seems that material values in New Jersey inspire even men of the cloth in this somewhat decadent place. During the official ceremonies for the passage of the bill allowing casino gambling in Atlantic City in June 1977 (the same month that the first *Connections* series aired in Canada), a New Jersey priest invoked God's help in his prayer for the casino spirit: "Give us Thy Grace, O God, to always put the value of human life above the value of the dollar, lest the blessing of casino gambling become a curse."

Well, this was New Jersey, and the fact that human life was even publicly considered more important than money was noteworthy. Shortly after this inspiring invocation, the governor of New Jersey, Brendan Byrne, issued the following warning to the mob: "Organized crime is not welcome in Atlantic City," he shouted to the crowd. "And I warn them, keep your filthy hands out of Atlantic City, keep the hell out of our state."

Assemblyman Perskie may have been correct when he said, "This is a family town." Unfortunately for the well-intentioned governor, it is a Mafia "family" town, and "the filthy hands of organized crime" were and still are well entrenched throughout the city and state. Certainly the arrival of casino gambling hasn't discouraged or disillusioned the mob, though there has been quite a mob war going on in Philadelphia and southern New Jersey over who will control this Las Vegas of the east. After legalized gambling came in, "organized crime began flocking to Atlantic City like a bee to honey," according to Colonel Clinton Pagano, the head of the New Jersey State Police. And so they did, even from Canada, as Colonel Pagano and his police were to find out.

The Angelo Bruno Mafia family of nearby Philadelphia had controlled mob operations and the rackets in Atlantic City and southern New Jersey since the early 1950s. But when gambling was legalized in 1977, the leaders of the Mafia in the United States, the so-called "ruling commission", which was made up of the leading dons in the country, decided that henceforth Atlantic City was to be treated as an "open city" by the Mafia. It was not just the preserve of Angelo Bruno and his family. Paul Volpe and his associates were among those who decided to buy and sell land in Atlantic City to cash in on the casino land boom. Before actually buying any land in New Jersey, in late 1977 and early 1978, Volpe had several meetings both in Toronto and in New Jersey with top New Jersey-area crime bosses who allowed the move into Atlantic City. Volpe's meetings were with top Bruno lieutenants and Gambino family members, some of whom came to Toronto to discuss Atlantic City, and with whom Volpe felt he must clear his financial move onto their turf, even though the city was technically "open". It was the politic thing to do, and Volpe has always been the supreme diplomat in his dealings with other Mafia leaders and groups.

Initially, Paul Volpe and his associates set out to launder money – even to make legitimate money – through Atlantic City by simply buying and selling land. (This in itself triggered police interest, underworld intrigues, and gossip about the moves, and finally media attention and major police and grand-jury investigations.) Volpe was certainly onto a winner in funnelling money from Toronto and Montreal into Atlantic City on behalf of a number of legal and illegal interests, not the least of which was his own Toronto mob. Moreover, non-mob people were interested in speculating on the land, and there was a lot of greed that Volpe could exploit to his own advantage (which, of course, was another of his talents). Even his own enforcer, Chuck Yanover, not generally an investor in real estate, bought some land there through Volpe. Other Toronto and Montreal people got into the land deals. Angelo Pucci, Volpe's cousin and associate; Toronto lawyer John Cocomile; Meyer Feldman, another Toronto lawyer, who frequently represented Toronto mobsters Domenic Racco and Remo Commisso of the Siderno group in legal matters; David Mahoney, a Montreal and Atlantic City businessman; Antonio Montemarano, a Toronto-area businessman; Gus Boem, a Toronto-area real-estate man and accountant; and a host of others from the Toronto and Montreal areas poured millions into (and in many cases out of) Atlantic City.

A Volpe real-estate associate in Atlantic City later revealed in the *Connections* program one of the major reasons for mob interest in the land in and around Atlantic City. "My Toronto connections feel that by 1990 we'll have sawdust casinos, which is what they are really waiting for." "Sawdust casinos" are not the elaborate and scrupulously monitored major casino houses, such as Resorts International, that now operate in Atlantic City, but the unadorned slot-machine parlours and card-game centres that operate on the fringe of gambling areas like Atlantic City with the minimum of media and police attention. Volpe could have brought in Sammy Shirose from Toronto and set up a mini-International Casino, just like the old days.

This was Paul Volpe's dream – to one day have his own casino again – and this time, conveniently, right in the States. In the meantime Volpe and Pucci and their associates contented themselves with making money on Atlantic City land deals. This involved nothing more than raising capital in Canada and putting out minimum down payments on huge chunks of speculative land, then reselling them later at a nice profit. These Atlantic City land deals had the added bonus of not even being illegal.

Here are some of the transactions involving the Volpe-Pucci group, some of which later came under police, media, or grand-jury scrutiny.

From June 1978 until May 1979, $4.75 million of real-estate investments can be traced directly to the Volpe-Pucci group. These involved a $3-million, 17.9-acre tract of land in Brigantine, N.J., a suburb of Atlantic City, which was to be used for a ninety-duplex housing development. The purchaser, for Pucci, was Lauder Hill Development Corporation, listed in Toronto as a corporate entity under the Pucci Enterprises umbrella and incorporated in New Jersey in August 1978 by Pucci's Toronto accountant Augusto Boem. (Boem also shared a rented house with Pucci near Atlantic City, next door to the home of his Atlantic City real-estate agent.) One of the sellers of the land was no less than the mayor of Brigantine, the Hon. John A. Rogge. When Mayor Rogge later learned of Boem's and Pucci's connections with Paul Volpe, he made the following statement to the *New York Times*: "This is my town, and I don't want the Mafia here."

Other purchases in the Atlantic City area – some purchased through Pucci's New Jersey companies, First Dimension Realty and Topland Holdings, and some through Durham Square Realty

Limited, an Ontario firm that lists Paul Volpe as president and Lisa Dalholt, his wife, as secretary/treasurer – included the following: 1715–17 Atlantic Avenue, Atlantic City, purchased for $125,000 on June 30, 1978; 815–17–19 Arctic Avenue, purchased for $65,280 on June 30, 1978; Verona Avenue, Egg Harbor Township, New Jersey, land tract purchased by Pucci for $155,000; Tilton Road, Egg Harbor Township, land purchased for $373,000 by Pucci on November 15, 1978; 115 Vermont Avenue (like the cheap light-blue properties in Monopoly, these were cheap in real life, too), $16,640 for a half-interest; 14–20 North Maine Avenue, for $425,000; and on February 2, 1979, two parcels containing fifty-five tracts of land, purchased through David Mahoney of Absecom, an Atlantic City restaurant manager whose address is listed as 111 Queen Street East, Toronto, the headquarters of Pucci Enterprises (the tracts later sold for $589,000).

Another Maine Avenue property was sold in August 1979 by Angelo Pucci and Paul Volpe with Toronto lawyers John Cocomile and Meyer Feldman for over $1 million. Another property bought at a sheriff's sale by the Volpe-Pucci group, in partnership with lawyers Cocomile and Feldman, was the Uncle Dicks property in Egg Harbor Township and sixty-two properties in the Inlet section of Atlantic City. Topland Holdings (Pucci) owned thirty-five per cent, Durham Square (Paul Volpe) thirty-five per cent, and John Cocomile and Meyer Feldman owned fifteen per cent each. Twenty-eight of the sixty-two Inlet properties were sold, and thirty-four properties were still owned by Pucci as of April 1983. In another property, Cocomile and Feldman put up $135,000, while Paul Volpe and Angelo Pucci put up $172,000.

Not content with legal land deals, Paul Volpe got involved with a little illegal skimming from some of his investors – as some of them were later to find out.

John Cocomile invested about $200,000 in Atlantic City in 1979 after he was approached by Paul Volpe. Volpe, through his company Durham Realty, would put up down payments on certain properties and then sell the properties to someone else, while also jacking up the price and pocketing the profit. When Cocomile found out about Volpe's duplicity, he became an informant for the Special Enforcement Unit, obtained a Certificate of Lis Pendens issued by the New Jersey courts, and registered it against the properties to effectively prevent Volpe and his associates from selling the remaining properties they owned in New Jersey. When John Cocomile arrived at RCMP headquarters with his tale of woe in 1979, he was told by one of the officers that while it appeared that he was a victim in this case, "you are bound to get fleas when you go to bed with a dog." This police officer, fortunately, is still with the SEU. Cocomile has since died. A police operation was begun, and Cocomile was accorded police protection on at least one of his trips down to Atlantic City by way of Philadelphia. Police surveillance began to pick up meetings of Cocomile and Feldman with Paul Volpe, Angelo Pucci, and Volpe underling Pietro Scarcella at Cocomile's and Feldman's offices.

Another Toronto developer who was closely associated with Gus Boem in investments in Atlantic City was Anthony Montemarano, president of Baycrest Consolidated Holdings of Toronto. Baycrest formed Harbor View Holdings Company in New Jersey in June 1978 in order to develop the multi-million-dollar Harbor View Villas on a ten-acre tract sold by a Frank Drake of Brigantine to Baycrest. Baycrest also purchased 1,100 acres of land in Hamilton Township, near Brigantine, for $3.9 million, for a $150-million, 4,200-unit housing project, according to a *New York Times* report of May 1979. Bernard S. Abramoff, president of Jerome Realty Company of New Jersey, who served as the real-estate broker for most of the Pucci purchases, told the *Times*: "Mr. Pucci introduced me to Mr. Montemarano, and he took me to Drake." A partner of Abramoff is one Martin Blatt, a lawyer connected with organized crime, who was suspended from the practice of law by the New Jersey Supreme Court for two years in 1974 for falsifying records in relation to an investigation of corruption in Atlantic City.

Meanwhile, in September 1977, even as Paul Volpe held his initial meetings with the New Jersey mob and potential Toronto investors, the *Connections* team was once again going into action, although neither Paul Volpe nor members of the team believed it was conceivable that there would be a follow-up series on the Mafia. Public demand was so great that the CBC had insisted that a second series be prepared that would include areas of organized crime that there had not been time to explore in the first series. The new series was to be two years in the making.

It was clear from the start that the new series was going

to have to be even more explosive than the first one – both to attract viewers and to justify the huge expense of doing another series of exhaustive documentaries. The first series broke new ground merely by identifying and showing the leaders of the Mafia in Canada. They were seen walking the streets of our cities, openly conducting their activities. The sophisticated surveillance techniques that were used to do this had rarely been used on television before. These included night-lens filming, hidden-microphone and hidden-camera interviews, and set-ups in which the subject to be filmed was led into a situation where he would unknowingly be photographed. For the second series to have any impact, the team decided that it had to go much farther, actually infiltrating mob groups and televising the mobsters in action. They themselves could, in their own words and actions, explain or show sophisticated organized-crime operations, such as the laundering of money. Naturally, considering how important he was in the mob and how well the team knew him by this point, Paul Volpe was chosen as one of the first targets for an elaborate scam operation. The scam was to involve both the infiltration of Volpe's group by one of the people on the team and the filming of Volpe and his associates meeting with and talking to the infiltrator, gangster to gangster.

To do this, Pasquale Calabrese, known affectionately as "Paddy", was added to the team. Paddy had had a reasonably distinguished career as a soldier in the Magaddino crime family of Buffalo. His uncle had been a don, and Paddy once robbed Buffalo City Hall in broad daylight for the mob. It was said that this was the only time City Hall had been robbed from the outside.

Paddy, as mentioned earlier, had been the first mafioso in the United States to go on the Witness Protection Program, which got under way in the late 1960s. The program, as we have seen, provided a new identity and police protection for organized criminals who wished to defect and testify against their former colleagues and bosses. The idea was to get at the leaders of organized crime through the testimony and co-operation of underlings such as Paddy. Paddy's defection from the "Arm" (as the mob in Buffalo was called) resulted directly in the successful prosecution of the top members of the Mafia in Buffalo, including the feared and untouchable boss of the Magaddino family, Frederico Randaccio, and his lieutenant,

Pasquale Natarelli (whom Volpe had used as "Mr. Palmer" in his extortion of Dick Angle). After his testimony against the mob, Paddy was resettled on the west coast and given a new name and identity.

However, after defecting and testifying at many sensational trials, Paddy, who always liked to live close to danger, got bored. Finally he convinced the police to let him infiltrate various criminal groups across North America, including those in Alaska, California, and Vancouver, B.C. In Vancouver Paddy worked for the Co-ordinated Law Enforcement Unit (CLEU) in an elaborate operation in which he pretended to be an American mobster interested in working with the Vancouver mob on certain criminal activities of mutual interest. Paddy's work for CLEU was very productive, both for intelligence on the Vancouver Mafia family of Joe Gentile and his associates (which Paddy easily infiltrated) and for successful prosecutions against the leading members of the Vancouver mob and the Commissos, their connection in Toronto.

Paddy is fearless. As a Mafia soldier he was daring and original, and as a police agent he was imaginative and courageous. Paddy always liked to push an operation to its limits, frequently risking his life to get to the heart of the matter. On the CLEU operation against the Vancouver mob there were several objectives. One was simply to gather as much intelligence as possible from the inside about the Gentile family set-up and their political connections. Another objective was to actually nail some senior Vancouver and Toronto mobsters, as well as their political and judicial connections, on as serious a charge as possible. The police decided to settle for arrests on an elaborate counterfeit-money operation involving the Vancouver mob, the Commisso family of Toronto, and the western U.S. mob.

Paddy, on the other hand, wanted to hold out to get top-echelon mobsters on more serious charges, such as a heroin deal he knew was going through. He also wanted to wait in order to ensnare other senior members of the mob in Vancouver who were about to fall for the drug scheme. The police were determined to go ahead on the counterfeit operation, but Paddy did everything he could to stop them, including contacting the *Connections* team in the middle of the sensitive operation, and revealing what was going on and how he felt the police were about to blow the case. He was obviously using us as leverage against the police to put pressure on them so that he could complete the operation in as professional and complete a manner as possible – from his point of view. While the police went ahead anyway on the counterfeit-money arrests (thus blowing the rest of the operations, in Paddy's opinion), Paddy decided to do an interview with *Connections* (the first series) on the other aspects of the operation, including the political connections and the heroin deal. We included his material and his interview in the programs. This is Paddy's way. He isn't the type to give up.

Paddy has guts. Once, when I was visiting him in his office in a western state, Paddy and I could see a woman being mugged on the street. Without batting an eyelash, Paddy rushed down and subdued the mugger and held him for the police. He came back to the meeting with a painful, bruised hand, but he was proud of what he had done.

And so we of the *Connections* team went to Paddy to concoct a plan for infiltrating the Volpe organization. Intelligence sources and informers on the street had alerted the team to Paul Volpe's involvement in the purchase of land in and around Atlantic City through a number of front people there and in Toronto. The team knew who the major front people were, but really didn't see how this information could be made into a visually sensational television experience. Paddy rose to the challenge and devised an elaborate scam operation, which we would film and tape throughout. In consultation with Paddy, *Connections* co-producer Martyn Burke, who also thrived on dangerous, challenging assignments, co-producer Bill Macadam, and I decided to have Paddy pose as a front man for some Mafia money that was coming out of Italy and needed laundering in North America. The money was to move through Toronto sources to Atlantic City. The idea was somehow to get Volpe's organization involved.

Martyn Burke came up with a plan. He and the soundwoman would pose as "Mr. and Mrs. Ed Burton", potential buyers in Atlantic City, and would look at a house with one of Volpe's Atlantic City real-estate connections. This would open the door. Then Burke would raise the topic of laundering money, mentioning that he had a friend who represented tainted interests in Italy. It was hoped that things would develop from there. Amazingly, Bonnie Rae Off, one of the Volpe group's Atlantic City real-estate connections, fell for the story, and within days

Paddy was phoning her for an appointment in Toronto with herself and "her Canadians".

The *Connections* team flew Paddy out to Los Angeles so that he could make his call from the luxurious Beverly Hills Hotel in order to further impress the Volpe group (this was in the days when the CBC current-affairs documentaries were a priority and were given money to work with). Paddy was to use the phoney name of "Frank Angelo" and the team had thoroughly briefed him on Volpe and his associates as well as on the Atlantic City real-estate agent. The team even printed up "Frank Angelo" business cards with addresses in Rome and Toronto and installed a special red phone in the Toronto CBC office of *Connections*, which was to be Frank Angelo's "Toronto office". Paddy's first call to Bonnie Rae Off went smoothly. He talked of their "mutual interests" and suggested that he get together with her in Toronto because "it is a better place to meet because of your people there." Off readily agreed, and a date was set. One thing that soon became clear about her was that she was greedy and not very clever. Later, during her third meeting with "Ed Burton", she was to give the game away. Speaking directly into Burke's hidden mike she would tell him: "We move money from Italy through Toronto very well, and they've established a bank in Toronto through which they move it." She would go on to say that she was quite used to handling dirty money and that "we front it in such a way that it is clean." She fell for the *Connections* sting hook, line, and sinker.

Finally the day of the first big meeting in Toronto arrived. The *Connections* team decided to arrange the meeting by the pool at the Hampton Court Hotel on Jarvis Street (just across the street from the main CBC studios), because all the rooms looked out onto the pool area, making it very easy to film from any room. The team took several rooms, just to be safe, and decided to film with two cameras in case of problems – and also to provide several camera angles to help in the editing later on. Through a ruse, the team managed to get three ideal rooms (one on the third floor and two on the second) for filming. The entire *Connections* office, including secretaries and researchers, was involved in this set-up, moving in masses of equipment, holding certain tables by the pool so the correct camera angles could be set up, and briefing Paddy and arming him with a suitable cover story and the right credentials, which included an arms catalogue and phoney stock certificates from some notoriously disreputable Caribbean banks. It was essential that Paddy look, or appear (and sound), as "Mafia" as possible, which really wasn't too difficult considering his background and experience. Paddy knew all the right body language and street terms and had just the right look to carry it off.

The meeting was supposed to be with Bonnie Rae Off and Volpe's cousin, Angelo Pucci, one of "her Canadians". Pucci had started out as a waiter at the bar of the Park Plaza Hotel and had done quite well in real estate through his company, Pucci Enterprises, owning office buildings and warehouses in the Queen Street East and King Street East area of downtown Toronto. His main commercial building space was at the corner of King and Parliament. Supervising the renovations for Angelo Pucci on a daily basis for some months was none other than Paul Volpe. (Paul Volpe and his brothers were filmed by *Connections* leaving 111 Queen Street East.) Another part of the Pucci real-estate empire was in North Bay, Ont., which is also the place that he has been known to claim as a source of financing. Pucci had become landlord to a number of legitimate Toronto enterprises, including small businesses, graphic artists, theatrical agencies, and one of Toronto's television stations – CITY-TV. (Paul Volpe was later to be charged along with Pucci in a fraud relating to the CITY-TV building.)

There is no question that Pucci had been a close business associate of Paul Volpe's, and that some of his land in Atlantic City was purchased for Volpe. Mob sources close to Pucci and Volpe confirmed this. *Connections* knew therefore that he was representing Volpe's interest now in his meeting with "Frank Angelo".

On August 20, 1978, the day of the meeting, all the concealed television cameras were in place at the Hampton Court Hotel. Just before the scheduled meeting, however, Bonnie Rae Off called to say that Angelo Pucci couldn't make it after all. Neither could she make it up from Atlantic City. For a while the team thought Pucci suspected something, but in the end, the meeting was re-scheduled for two o'clock the next day at the same spot.

At the appointed hour Paddy waited anxiously at the prese-lected table. Finally Pucci arrived, but, to the shock of Paddy and the entire *Connections* team, he had brought Paul Volpe with him instead of Bonnie Rae Off. An excited Martyn Burke, listening in on a radio-mike pick-up, immediately phoned Macadam and me while we were interviewing a Volpe mob associate at Macadam's house. Burke was worried about Paddy's security, but it was decided not to abort the operation, even though with Volpe present it became more dangerous. The team decided that Paddy had the chutzpah to pull it off. The entire meeting was recorded and filmed by the surveillance cameras and microphones. Paddy remained cool as Volpe began a process of interrogation.

VOLPE: I don't believe this. You came three thousand miles for this conversation?

PADDY: We got some money...

VOLPE: Great ... How much money are we talking about?

PADDY: How much money? Oh, five or six.

VOLPE: Hundred million?

PADDY: No, just a million.

VOLPE: Because we talk with people with two or three hundred million from Italy that want to invest.

Volpe was clearly lying as much as Paddy was. Thinking quickly, Paddy then told Volpe that there was no use talking to him, because he had only a paltry five or six million to invest. His bluff called, Volpe retreated from his interrogation for the moment so that negotiations could continue.

VOLPE: No. I mean because it doesn't make any sense here, five or six million.... It's no problem to take it out of Italy; if someone wants to stick their ass out they can take it out ... if it's in American dollars.

PADDY: It's coming out of there ... but we need an easier outlet.... This is why I came.

VOLPE: I'll give you the easiest outlet in the world, send it to me.

Volpe was clearly interested. Though he was still suspicious of Paddy and suspected a set-up, he was too greedy to let it all go by. He changed his tack and decided to question "Frank Angelo" on his credentials. Paddy had said he had an uncle in New York City who "knew people", which is street language for saying he was "connected", a mafioso or a close associate.

VOLPE: What does your uncle do there?
PADDY: He was in the garbage business in New York.

The waste disposal industry has long been dominated by organized crime in New York City, which is why Paddy chose this occupation for his "uncle". A recent book by two American professors, criminologist Alan Block and sociologist Frank Scarpitti, entitled *Poisoning for Profit: The Mafia and Toxic Waste in America*, outlines the long-time Mafia control of garbage collection in the northeast United States.

VOLPE: He's your uncle through ...?
PADDY: My mother's side.
VOLPE: Does your father... uncle, know anybody in New York?
PADDY: You talking about people?
VOLPE: Yeah.
PADDY: Yeah, he knows somebody.

Still persistently checking, Volpe demands to know a name he can check Angelo out with.

PADDY: All right, you want me to have him call you?
VOLPE: No, no, not me. I don't even want to talk to him....
I can send someone down to New York to find out about you.

Here Volpe nicely illustrated to the television audience the process of insulation, which is so vital to an effective mob leader. He certainly did not want a New York City mobster calling him on his phone about this.

Having stated in no uncertain terms that he would check out Angelo's references, Volpe relaxed and referred to Pucci (who had been sent to check with Bonnie Rae Off about Angelo), stating that Pucci was "the best guy in the world. I'm his partner. Best guy in the world for real estate." Volpe decided to proceed with caution. He boasted, "We're dealing with the biggest construction guys almost in Canada here...." But Volpe still had to validate the appropriateness of Angelo's credentials, flimsy as they were: "You hit the right thing, the garbage business, whoever you are, couldn't be any stronger, the garbage business." Paddy, pretending hurt, asked, "You think I'm lying to you?"

Volpe responded in a slow, cool fashion, "No, I don't think you're lying."

Meanwhile, Pucci returned. He explained how he and Volpe had been purchasing land in Atlantic City and how much money they were making: "I'll tell you there's not a better place in North America in my opinion right now . . . it's tops." And Volpe concluded that if Angelo wanted to get the money out of Italy, he'd find a way, "by hook or by crook, I'll get it out. . . . It's a natural thing." And so the meeting ended, with Volpe adding one more warning to Angelo, for emphasis: "Well, Frank, I'm going to be honest with you. I'm going to find out about you. I'm going to get someone to reach your uncle."

The meeting ended with a general agreement to meet the next day, once Volpe had had a chance to check Frank Angelo's credentials.

Though the team was ecstatic about how much of the film material linked Volpe to Atlantic City real-estate deals, it was decided that it was too dangerous to allow Paddy to have another meeting. So the next day "Angelo" phoned Pucci, claimed pressing business elsewhere, and walked out of the lives of Angelo Pucci and Paul Volpe. Operations terminated, the team got Paddy out of the country that very day.

When "The Casino Connection" aired on March 27, 1979, it was dramatic television. The team had succeeded in presenting dramatically a mob activity that is difficult to explain, let alone to show. And the television audience was party to a mob meeting from the inside. Volpe had been taken to the cleaners, and in front of millions of viewers across Canada.

For Volpe the fall-out from the broadcast was profound. All the newspapers and other media in Canada, including radio and television, covered the story, and the *New York Times* ran a feature article on the *Connections* sting, followed later by a front-page exposé of their own on Volpe and Pucci. On March 29, 1979, the front-page headlines of the Philadelphia *Bulletin* reported: "TV Show Links Mob Money, Atlantic City." The cat was out of the bag. The governor of New Jersey, Brendan Byrne, who had been seen on the program making his firm statement that "organized crime was not welcome in Atlantic City" and that the mob should "keep their filthy hands" out of the state, got on the phone and ordered Colonel Clinton Pagano, the head of the state police, to target the Volpe-Pucci group and "do something" to try to keep them out. Soon after this, a New Jersey grand jury began sitting to investigate the complex land deals of Paul Volpe and his associates. Volpe now had to publicly declare his interest in certain properties. Suddenly Paul Volpe appeared in the paperwork filed with the state government, first as "vice-president" and later as "president" of Durham Square Limited, the real-estate firm in Toronto ostensibly run by Pucci that was buying property in Atlantic City. Volpe's assets miraculously rose from the $55,000 he declared before the Waisberg commission to over $5 million, and for the first time Paul Volpe was obliged to pay considerable taxes. *Connections* had quite an effect.

But this was only the beginning, as the police in New Jersey moved against the Volpe group in a massive way as a result of the program's impact. It was part of a joint state police and New Jersey justice department investigation that targeted Volpe and his associates as well as other organized-crime leaders involved in any way in the Atlantic City area. Colonel Pagano met with Major Bob Winters, a senior New Jersey State Police official, and together they evolved a strategy that was to prove successful and every bit as thought-out as anything the SEU did in Canada.

Major Winters explained the evolution of "Operation Condor", which was the code name of this major police response to the problem:

Initially organized crime entered into various land deals and speculation in and around Atlantic City with the idea of legitimate transactions. They could have made money simply by buying and selling. However you cannot change the spots of a leopard. We knew that sooner or later they [organized crime] would see the opportunity to cut corners and make easy money, and they would take it. We thought that if we investigated all of the deals of the organized crime people and their associates that we would find some illegitimate activity. For this reason we constantly reviewed the land speculation around and in Atlantic City, keeping charts. Names and deals leapt out at us, and we followed up with investigations until we found something wrong.

Winters's boss, Colonel Pagano, has called the operation against Volpe and his associates a partial success: "Our Volpe investigation was a unique situation, and we interrupted a lot of the Volpe activity."

In a confidential report for the New Jersey State Police, a state investigator working on Operation Condor reported that "$200,000 of income in 1979 and 1980 could be attributed to Volpe through testimony and documents provided by Gus Boem and Angelo Pucci." Boem was subpoenaed to testify before the grand jury and said that he met Pucci and Volpe "through their wives" and that he and Pucci later "offered Paul Volpe a twenty-per-cent partnership." Pucci testified that "he was trying to sever all ties with Paul Volpe, even though he is my cousin."

Not long after the *Connections* program on Atlantic City and the follow-up features in the New Jersey press and on the front pages of the *New York Times*, things really got hot in southern New Jersey. Angelo Bruno, the old-school Sicilian-born don who had ruled the area for over twenty-five years, was brutally murdered. His death marked the beginning of a mob dispute over the lucrative territory that was to last for some time. Many key Bruno lieutenants and allies, as well as Bruno rivals, were also killed in the ensuing mob war. The fall-out from this battle for control later caused serious problems for Paul Volpe and may have led to his own murder.

Still, even with the Philadelphia-New Jersey mob wars, the legal problems with Operation Condor, and lawsuits brought by some of his investors (such as the one undertaken by lawyer John Cocomile), Atlantic City was very profitable for a long time for Volpe and his circle. No wonder Angelo Pucci boasted to "Frank Angelo" in *Connections* about his Atlantic City land deals.

But Volpe didn't realize at first the total impact that the *Connections* revelations were to have on his life and business, especially in Atlantic City. In New Jersey, there were troublesome police and grand-jury investigations. In Canada, the police accelerated their efforts against him. More importantly, Volpe lost a lot of face on the street, by the way he was publicly exposed by a television team. Simply by allowing himself to be filmed and recorded, Volpe lost some crucial respect in mob circles in Canada – and in the mob, respect is everything.

Paul Volpe came to rue the day he first met *Connections* co-producer Bill Macadam and became a television star in a series of programs. The Special Enforcement Unit's operations against Paul Volpe intensified, this time with American police joining in a major way. From 1977 until his death in 1983 Volpe was constantly before the courts on one charge or another, charges which included diamond fraud, illegal possession of wire-tap equipment, land fraud, and illegal gambling activities.

At the very time Volpe was desperately trying to appear more respectable, with his lavish homes complete with tennis courts and swimming pools, he was receiving more and more negative publicity. He was already, according to *Connections* co-producer Bill Macadam, living "like a man under siege", even before the new *Connections* shows. Now he became almost reclusive.

But as Volpe was to find out, the worst was yet to come. The media and law enforcement were not his only enemies. Volpe was also rapidly losing the respect he had spent years building up with other mob leaders in Canada and the United States. He was becoming a threat to the underworld through his high profile, and the underworld has its own way of dealing with such matters, as Paolo Violi found out in 1978 when he was gunned down by a rival gang leader's hit men.

CHAPTER THIRTEEN

The Commisso Crime Family: Canada's Murder Inc.

A S VOLPE UNDERWENT humiliation at the hands of the media and the police in the late 1970s, one of the most successful criminals of the Siderno group in Ontario, Rocco (Remo) Commisso, was watching Volpe's decline with great interest. Commisso was poised for his own move against Paul Volpe, which would come in time as Volpe's power eroded even more.

Clearly Remo Commisso had come a long way since 1961 when, at the age of fifteen, he arrived in Canada from Calabria with his two brothers and his mother. His older brother Cosimo was twenty-three, and his younger brother Michele was only thirteen at the time. Their father, Girolomo Commisso, had been a don in the Siderno area in Italy until he was gunned down in a Mafia feud in the late 1940s. (As is frequent in Mafia vendettas in Italy, no one was ever arrested for the murder of Girolomo Commisso.)

In Remo Commisso's youth, his uncles started the well-known Commisso/Racco Bakery in Toronto, which they later sold to some distant cousins. (When Remo was arrested in Vancouver in 1978 for a heroin deal, the owner of the Commisso/Racco Bakery in Toronto, who had never been involved in any criminal activity himself, helped out with the bail as a sign of respect and good will.)

By the late 1970s, Remo Commisso had set up an organization, a sub-group within the Sidernese Mafia, which rivalled the best of the Sicilian Mafia structures existing in the United States and which was, in terms of pure muscle and audacity, one of the most powerful Mafia groups in Canada. Remo Commisso and his older brother Cosimo controlled a criminal organization that imported and distributed heroin with the Vancouver mob and the Calabrian Mafia in Italy, fenced stolen goods across North America, printed and distributed counterfeit money throughout Canada and the United States, ran a vast extortion network in Ontario, arranged insurance and land frauds in the Toronto area, and engaged in contract killings and contract-enforcement work across Canada and the United States – the whole gamut of violent criminal activities one usually associates with the Mafia.

Remo Commisso has always kept up close ties with the old country, specifically with the Mafia in Calabria, and has even operated in Calabria since his Canadianization. As recently as 1972, Remo returned personally to Calabria on a hit mission to help some of his allies in the Siderno area of southern Calabria in a battle for territory and the "honour" of the family (though he fled Italy after his car was fired upon). He also arranged a shooting in Calabria in the early 1980s. Remo Commisso has always believed in the old country and the old values, the Mafia the way it used to be: violent, lean, cutthroat, and vindictive.

He has always believed also in the concept of the vendetta, so popular in Sicily and southern Calabria for centuries. Remo Commisso has a memory like an elephant. Nothing is ever forgotten, especially if it has to do with revenge or the honour of the family. He is rather Jacobean in his thirst for revenge. Although his father, Girolomo Commisso, was killed in the late 1940s, it was only recently, in 1982, that Remo arranged his final acts of revenge in a little town in Calabria when he had the sons of his father's 1940s rival murdered. Remo has that long a reach and memory. A breach of honour or respect, even if it happened thirty-five years ago, must be avenged.

Remo Commisso has also been adept at maintaining close connections with the movers and shakers in the criminal world in Canada. He has always mixed with the best – has always been "well connected", as they say on the street. Wire-tap evidence at the Quebec Crime Probe in 1976 made it clear that Remo was also a key Toronto operative for the crime boss of Montreal at the time, Paolo Violi. Whenever Violi was planning an operation in the Toronto area, he would have his people contact Remo Commisso, his man in Toronto.

Significantly, Remo was present as an honoured guest at the biggest Mafia wedding in Canada: the 1972 union between the Luppino family of Hamilton and the Commisso family of Toronto. The guest list at the wedding was a veritable Who's Who of the Mafia of the time. Paul Volpe was there, as were his good friend Jimmy Luppino, Jimmy's brother Natale, and their father, old Don Giacomo Luppino. Volpe had maintained his ties with the Luppinos, and was godfather to Natale's son. (Being a godfather to a mobster's child is very important in the Mafia world – it speaks volumes on a person's "connections" and how much "respect" he commands. While Natale Luppino has always been a rather low-level enforcer type, Paul Volpe became godfather to his son as a mark of respect to his brother Jimmy, a mob leader, and to his father Giacomo, one of the most respected Mafia dons in southern Ontario.) Other prominent Mafia figures at the wedding included Johnny "Pops" Papalia of Hamilton, Pietro Sciarra of Montreal (later murdered after testifying before the Quebec Crime Probe as he was coming out of the Italian version of the film *The Godfather*), Frank Sylvestro of Guelph (a former lieutenant in Rocco Perri's bootlegging empire in the 1930s who later established his own loan-sharking and gambling fiefdom in Guelph and Toronto), Paolo Violi of Montreal, Rocco Scopelliti of Toronto (a Siderno family member in drugs), and finally, the most respected figure in the Canadian Mafia, old Vic Cotroni, the long-time Godfather of the Montreal Mafia.

Remo has also been quite close to west coast mobsters. In 1976 he got involved in a counterfeit-money plot that included Carlo Gallo of Vancouver and Franco Magisano, a mafioso from Washington State. In 1977 Commisso also arranged some heroin deals with Vancouver crime leader Joe Romano (who was originally from Syracuse, N.Y., and who was a close friend of Angelo Branca, at the time a senior justice on the British Columbia Court of Appeal), before Romano was kicked out of Canada as an undesirable after serving time for an extortion conviction.

Remo Commisso has also kept close contacts with fellow Calabrian Mafia members in the United States. In fact he participated with them in a hit-man exchange program set up by Mike Racco and the U.S. affiliates of their group in New

York State and Connecticut. It was Remo who arranged the shooting of Giuseppe Magnolia in Long Island in 1978, using two Toronto hit men, as well as a later attempted murder in Stamford, Conn., on behalf of a local Mafia leader allied to Commisso. In exchange, American Calabrian Mafia leaders have sent hit men up to Toronto to take care of a few people. The attempted shooting by Frank Archino, set up for Domenic Racco in the mid-1970s, is just one example.

Remo Commisso is a somewhat sophisticated person, though by no means as suave as was Paul Volpe. He dresses nattily, often wearing silk scarves around his neck. He pays attention to his appearance and looks after his hair and clothes. And he knows his own mind and position. He made a deliberate decision not to marry, though he has a girl-friend, because of the uncertainties that have always been inherent in his criminal life-style. Remo can be likeable, and according to one of his friends, is well-read and "educated". (In Kingston Penitentiary he once worked in the prison library.) He commands a lot of respect from other criminals by the manner in which he carries himself, and by the seriousness of his intentions. His long-time lawyer, Edward Greenspan, has said that Remo "is very business-like and not a problem client" who tries to second-guess his lawyer. Remo's English is quite good for an Italian-born mafioso (certainly a lot better than that of his older brother Cosimo, who has a much stronger accent and tends to talk through his nose). He is looked on as a leader of the family by the Commisso family itself, and he knows how to insulate himself from direct involvement a lot better than many other leaders in the Siderno criminal groups. He used to frequent places like Rooney's, a trendy bar in Toronto, and always went to the right weddings and funerals. Remo Commisso has been the Commisso family public-relations man with other mob groups.

But Remo has another side. He is quite jealous, with a nasty temper. One-time lawyer for the Commissos Meyer Feldman (who, as we have seen, bought some land in Atlantic City with Paul Volpe and has dealt as a lawyer with underworld characters in Canada for three decades) says that in his "twenty-three years of dealing with these guys ... *the* one that I really, really had an uneasy feeling about was this Remo.... I never had a doubt that this Remo would put you away if he wanted to ... but

I never had this feeling about Paul [Volpe].... Remo had this scar down his face.... He just looked and acted the part." Other lawyers and crime reporters have had the same feeling about Remo Commisso. A senior cop who worked on Remo Commisso says he is "a vicious, vicious bastard and a real killer." Remo Commisso is the type of person who somehow conveys "mob" merely by his demeanour. Just his look instils fear. He always has been, as they say in underworld parlance, a "serious man". And he has always preferred to avoid publicity at all costs.

The *Connections* team found this out in 1976 when we tried to get an interview with Remo. Co-producer Martyn Burke parked a surveillance van with cameraman Francis Granger inside near Remo's headquarters, the Casa Commisso Banquet Hall on Lawrence Avenue West in Toronto. Burke then stopped Remo as he was about to enter. The plan was to stop him long enough for Granger to get good footage of him for use in the *Connections* series.

The following dialogue was captured on the hidden tape recorder Burke was wearing:

BURKE: Excuse me. Remo? Are you Remo? I am looking for Mr. Commisso, is that you?
COMMISSO: What do you want? Come inside.

Remo Commisso didn't ask, he *ordered* Martyn Burke to enter the Casa Commisso. Burke later recalled that "his eyes just turned to stone.... I've never seen anything like it. He just emanated violence."

BURKE: No ... I'd just as soon talk to you out here rather than...
COMMISSO: Inside!

One of Martyn Burke's special talents is his ability to keep the target subject talking and in camera range long enough for the cameraman in the surveillance van to get adequate footage. Burke is absolutely ingenious in doing this, at times forcing even the most paranoid of crooks or spies to stop and open up. He knows how to catch people off guard and take advantage of it.

So when Remo Commisso ordered him "inside" the Casa

Commisso, Burke just blithely ignored the request and carried on talking, saying anything to keep the target in sight of the camera.

> BURKE: I'm from the Canadian Broadcasting Corporation...
> COMMISSO: Yeah?
> BURKE: ... and I'm told that you're Mr. Rocco Commisso. Is that your name?
> COMMISSO: I am Rocco Commisso. What do you want? ["Remo" is his nickname and Rocco is his given name.]

Burke had to keep this inane dialogue going a bit longer without actually going inside the Casa Commisso.

> BURKE: Oh ... we were doing something ... and we were told to talk to someone named Remo Commisso. Is that you?
> COMMISSO: [angrily] Come inside. I don't wanna have to talk out here. Come inside!

Commisso then entered the darkened banquet hall, leaving Burke no choice but to follow him in. The room was filled with many ominous-looking heavies and enforcers, who seemed to be having a meeting. Later Burke recalled, "It was like a scene out of a Caravaggio painting, all shadows with beams of sunlight coming into the dark room ... like a scene from *The Godfather* ... incredible faces staring out from a twelve-foot conference table in a boardroom-like setting."

> BURKE: I'd rather not talk in here.... If we could just...
> COMMISSO: Well, I've got nothing to hide.
> BURKE: Well, okay, our producers were trying to find a man by the name of Remo Commisso, and I was wondering whether that was you. Is it you?
> COMMISSO: Who gives you the right to go around and look for the name Commisso? Producer, no producer.... I don't give a fuck for your producer or anything.

At this point Commisso was shouting at Burke and looming over him menacingly. Burke, after all, was very much in Commisso's own territory, and he found it rather claustrophobic. Since there was no longer any real reason to stay inside, Burke decided to get out of this clearly dangerous situation as quickly as possible, and since he probably had enough footage of Remo Commisso (taken while they were chatting at the doorway), he wanted to remove the cameraman and the surveillance van.

Unfortunately, he couldn't go directly over to the truck, as Commisso and his men were watching him intently as he retreated. If he had walked over to the van, its cover would have been blown, and he and the cameraman would have been in even more danger from these clearly unpleasant characters. Burke walked off and then ran to a pay phone a few blocks away to notify the *Connections* office that there was a problem and that he might need some support to extricate the van and the cameraman. Burke sounded very out of breath and harassed when he called. Thinking he was in serious danger, I phoned Inspector Gordon Lennox, then the officer in charge of Metro Toronto police intelligence, and asked him to send a car out immediately to assist Burke and the cameraman.

Meanwhile, Bill Macadam, the co-producer, jumped into his car and rushed down to the Casa Commisso at ninety or a hundred miles per hour, going through every red light on the way. He was deliberately breaking the law, both to get to Burke quickly and on the off chance that he might be stopped by the police for speeding and could prevail upon them to lend assistance in his rescue mission. Burke, however, had been able to flag down a police car before Macadam arrived on the scene with additional police support, so that the cover was not blown by the police assistance. Then, covered by the police and Macadam, who had arrived and parked near a police car a block away, Burke was able to move the surveillance van out of the Casa Commisso parking lot without incident. Everyone was safe, and in spite of the drama caused by Remo Commisso's threatening and aggressive stance, the team had enough footage of him for the *Connections* program.

The *Connections* team finally did succeed in getting an interview with Remo Commisso by using a body-pack. Macadam arrived at the Casa Commisso after Burke's aborted visit for a conversation with Remo. At first Remo was his natural hostile self, an attitude compounded by the fact that Commisso at first thought Macadam was veteran *Globe and Mail* crime reporter Peter Moon, whom he hated because of some exposés Moon had written about Commisso and the Siderno Mafia. Remo hit

Macadam across the face with a newspaper, thinking that at last he was punishing Peter Moon. But once Macadam established his identity, Commisso talked with him for some time. This was all wonderful, but after Macadam left he found out that the body-pack tape recorder had malfunctioned. Nothing of this sole successful interview with Remo Commisso had been recorded.

The funny thing about mobsters, even killers such as Remo Commisso, is that although they can be a real terror, they can also be terribly afraid of the power of the media. On one occasion during the filming of the second series of *Connections*, I was trying to get footage of Remo Commisso and a hit man walking out of the main courthouse in downtown Toronto. With a cameraman, I openly approached Commisso, who was flanked by the hit man and another mob enforcer. To my surprise, Commisso and his friends panicked when they saw they were being followed with a camera, and rather than assault us or otherwise intimidate us, they actually fled. They went out one door, and when we followed they entered another. This continued for the next few minutes. It was like a Marx Brothers comedy, yet these were vicious Mafia killers that we were chasing in and out doors and around the block. Remo simply did not want to be filmed with these people on this particular day. The camera was a more potent weapon than a gun, and Remo Commisso remained an elusive target for us.

Even while Paul Volpe continued his expansion and the scope of his activities in the early and middle 1970s, it was the Commissos who had established themselves as the prime criminal muscle in the city. After the death of Mike Racco (from natural causes in 1980), the most serious, structured, and respected group within the Siderno Mafia in Toronto was to be that run by Remo Commisso. Remo established his pre-eminent position through a combination of ruthlessness and "connections" – in the United States, Hamilton, Montreal, Toronto, and, most significantly, in the old country itself.

There were very few areas of criminal activity where the paths of the Commissos and the Volpe organization crossed. The Commissos have always been involved in things like drugs, counterfeit money, the smuggling of aliens, heavy-duty extortion contracts, and murder. Paul Volpe always avoided drugs as an activity, was never involved in counterfeit money or alien smuggling, and got involved in murder only as a form of internal discipline, if at all. He certainly never took on hit contracts as the Commissos have consistently done. The activities of the Paul Volpe organization were much more sophisticated and cerebral, though Volpe did indulge in everyday enforcement work and extortion when necessary. The Commissos, in turn, did try the sophisticated land deal, but on a much cruder level than anything Volpe's group achieved. Gambling was an area in which both organizations operated, but in very different areas of the city and under very different conditions.

When the Commissos got involved in land deals they concentrated on hidden titles, a money-laundering operation to hide the source of profits made from drugs and contract murders. In one documented case, Remo and Cosimo were in secret partnership with Alberto Bentivogli in owning a Toronto restaurant, as well as twenty-three acres in Richmond Hill and land in Burlington. In another case in which Remo Commisso was ultimately charged, but not convicted, he allegedly used mortgage broker Carmen Molinaro, who was eventually convicted on five counts of forgery, and of uttering, in an elaborate mortgage-fraud case brought by the Special Enforcement Unit. The loans officer in the bank involved was a woman who was pressured into co-operating with the crooked mortgage-loan scheme.

While Paul Volpe and his group did its fair share of extortions, the Volpe group and the Commissos operated with different values. Basically, the "new Mafia" of the Commissos, Raccos, and other Siderno-area criminals are involved in areas such as drugs and heavy violence and murder, where the Volpe organization or the "old Mafia" in the city of Toronto fear to tread (or rather refuse to tread). This is an important distinction. The "old Mafia" of Paul Volpe had some standards and a regard for human life. The new group has no standards and no regard for human life. Ultimately, this would become apparent to all in the underworld in Toronto, and Paul Volpe was easily taken out. In the law of the organized-crime jungle, might is often right.

Between 1977 and 1981, while Paul Volpe was busy investing money in land in Toronto and Atlantic City and becoming a television star, the Commissos were up to some very nasty projects. These included heavy-duty extortions and collections, bombings, arsons, insurance frauds, brutal conspiracies to kill, and cold-blooded murder. These crimes are a matter of public record, an extremely unusual occurrence in the world of "omertà" in the Mafia, but only because of the defection from the Commisso ranks of one of their top hit men, the well-mannered and soft-spoken enforcer Cecil Kirby, who was himself a willing participant in the crimes and was later to play a major role in the drama unfolding around Paul Volpe.

Some of the hard facts of the more interesting crimes planned by the Commissos and executed by Kirby make enlightening reading. Remo and Cosimo Commisso were to plead guilty to all these crimes on April 13, 1984, in courtroom 42 at the old City Hall in Toronto in front of Judge Arthur Meen. The Commissos admitted their responsibility for sixteen brutal crimes in all.

- In the fall of 1976 Kirby was asked to blow up a truck or car of a salesman for Appia Beverages, in Toronto, a beverage company that was in fierce competition with another beverage company that had Siderno family involvement. In the late 1960s and early 1970s there had been a series of bombings and killings in the beverage industry in Toronto, a result of an internal fight with the Sidernese Mafia. As we have seen, in 1967, Salvatore "Sammy" Triumbari, the president of Cynar Dry Limited, a bottler of Italian soft drinks, was shot to death as he left his home in the Toronto suburb of Downsview. Two years later, a close friend of Triumbari's who had worked for him at Cynar, Filippo Vendimini, was shot and killed as he entered his shoe store at 1086 Bloor Street West in Toronto. Both men were murdered as part of the earlier power struggle within the Calabrian mob. (After Triumbari's gangland execution, Alderman Joseph Piccininni of Toronto denounced the use of the word "Mafia" in the Toronto media at the time. "There is no organized crime among Italians of Toronto.... The word is just used as a gimmick.") The Commissos were thus continuing the 1960s feud by arranging the bombing of Antonio Pinheiro's car. Pinheiro was a truck driver and salesman for Appia Beverages. At eleven at night on October 23, 1976, Pinheiro's car exploded in his driveway. Kirby received a mere $1,000 for this bombing, which was just a small part of the much larger battle between the Commisso associates and their rivals.

- In November 1976, Kirby was told by the Commissos to threaten a man in the construction industry with a bomb in order to motivate him to pay a certain drywalling bill. If successful in the operation, Kirby was promised $10,000. Accompanied by Cosimo Commisso, Kirby watched his target at 225 Wildcat Road in Downsview (his office) and at his home in the Kingcross Estates in King City, Ont. (not far from Volpe's new house). On November 11, 1976, Kirby left a stick of dynamite in the mailbox at 12 Blueberry Lane, the home of A. Pozzebona of Pozzebona Construction. Then, posing as "Mr. Murphy", Kirby called Pozzebona's secretary and told her there was a message for Pozzebona in his mailbox. He phoned back later to say that Mr. Pozzebona had better pay his plastering bill or the next time his car would be bombed. The message was received, but Kirby was paid a measly $500 from the Commissos for his extortion work, and not the full amount he had been promised. Apparently the intimidation had not been enough for the victim in this case to pay up.

- In late December 1976, Cecil Kirby was asked to appear at the Casa Commisso Banquet Hall to meet with Cosimo Commisso. Kirby was hired, for $10,000, to kill one Dennis Mason, who was to testify as a Crown witness against a Commisso ally in an upcoming trial. Commisso gave Kirby the address of the pizza parlour where he said Mason worked. Kirby ordered a pizza and waited outside the delivery spot to shoot Mason when he arrived with the pizza. Kirby was foiled, however, when another employee delivered this particular order. On December 26, 1976, Kirby was given five sticks of dynamite by the Commissos. He attached them to an electric blasting cap on the top of the heater vent in Mason's car. At ten-thirty that evening Mason got into the car and turned on the ignition. Fortunately for Mason, the dynamite Kirby used was defective and the explosion was considerably diminished. Kirby was furious at being given useless dynamite. He was a professional, and this was no way for a hit man to operate. Mason sustained injuries to his right leg and a hearing impairment as a result of the blast.

Ironically, it later emerged that Cosimo Commisso had given Kirby incorrect data (as well as faulty dynamite), because the Dennis Mason who was blown up was the wrong Dennis Mason. This person had absolutely nothing to do with the case – or with any kind of criminal activity. A very religious family man, who lived with his mother, he was a totally innocent victim. He is alive today merely because of the faulty dynamite. The real Dennis Mason went unscathed. As the Crown later pointed out, trying to eliminate a witness "represented the ultimate act of lawlessness.... Our society exists because we, as citizens, put our trust in the courts.... No other crime could strike as powerful a blow at the administration of justice." That is, if the right Dennis Mason had been killed. No member of society is safe from such random use of brute force.

- In early May 1977, Kirby was called to the Casa Commisso and contracted to bomb the Wah Kew Chop Suey House at 111 Elizabeth Street in the Chinatown district of Toronto, for a fee of $14,000. The owner of the restaurant, a local gambling organizer named Sunny Lem, was being extorted by the Commissos, and they wanted to frighten him. Kirby was instructed to do as much damage to the property as possible, and to do the bombing at six in the morning, when no one was around. Pretending to use the washroom in the restaurant while waiting for a take-out dinner, Kirby planted a powerful explosive with a timer. It went off prematurely at four, after Kirby had phoned to make sure no one was still there. Kirby maintains to this day that he never meant to kill anyone at the restaurant, and that he tried to warn them. He just assumed nobody was there at that hour. However, people work late at Chinese restaurants, and there were two people on the premises. The restaurant's cook, Chong Yin Quan, was killed, and Sunny Lem, who was the target of the attack, escaped with only a broken arm. The distraught and frightened widow of the cook, on the advice of her attorney, was eventually to decide to sue Cecil Kirby for the burial costs in the death of her husband after a 1981 front-page story in the *Globe and Mail* revealed that Kirby was responsible for the bombing. The city of Toronto ultimately picked up the tab for the funeral, and the widow's action has quietly disappeared, though Remo and Cosimo Commisso have pleaded guilty to hiring Kirby to do the bombing. Again, a totally innocent person with no known connection to organized crime was a victim of the mob. Who says that mobsters only kill each other? Is anyone really safe if this activity is allowed to continue?

- On February 13, 1978, Remo Commisso called Kirby to the Casa Commisso. He was offered $2,000 to bomb the house of a construction worker named Ben Freedman at 41 Shenstone Road, in north Toronto. Freedman owed a lot of money to other contractors at the time, and the Commissos were hired to put pressure on him to pay up. Kirby put an explosive in Freedman's car, which exploded at eleven that evening, causing extensive damage to the automobile. Freedman got the message.

- In May 1978, Kirby was instructed by the Commissos to extort money from Max Zentner of Montreal, a developer who owed money to a Commisso associate. Kirby was also engaged to extort Zentner's partner, John Ryan of Hamilton, Ont. Throughout the summer of 1978 Kirby made threatening calls to Ryan, his staff, and his children, as well as doing damage to his property. On August 1, 1978, Kirby blew up Ryan's car in his driveway. He received $3,000 for his services. It is not known whether Zentner paid up, but he certainly got the message.

- In early 1978, the Commissos hired Kirby to blow up an apartment building at 1400 Dixie Road in Mississauga that was owned by two brothers, Jerry and Roman Humeniuk. They owed some money to certain electrical contractors associated with the Commissos. On March 13, 1978, Kirby set off a bomb that damaged an underground lobby near the parking lot in the building. To cap things off, on April 15, 1978, Kirby placed a stick of dynamite on the front lawn of Dr. Roman Humeniuk at 313 Pinegrove Road in Oakville, Ont. It exploded at half past midnight. No one was injured. Then on July 19, 1978, Kirby placed another bomb at 1400 Dixie Road, causing another explosion at the apartment building. Finally, between July 31 and August 9, 1978, Kirby made threatening phone calls to residents of 1400 Dixie Road. On March 20, 1979, he called Dr. Humeniuk, demanded $196,000, and advised Humeniuk that his family would be killed if the amount was not paid. The Commissos paid Kirby $3,000 for all his trouble in this operation, so presumably the Humeniuks paid the Commissos something.

- On July 5, 1978, Kirby was asked by Remo and Cosimo to burn down the Avala Tavern on Eglinton Avenue West in Toronto. Remo gave Kirby a key to the back door so he could arrange the fire without any trouble. Kirby used the key later that night and poured fuel oil on a couch and set it ablaze. Unfortunately for Kirby, very little damage was done, as the Toronto Fire Department promptly put out the fire. Later, another arsonist was called, and he burned the building down. The second arsonist was convicted of arson, though apparently neither the Commissos nor Kirby were involved in the subsequent arson.

- In August 1978, Cosimo Commisso and Kirby were driven by a third person to Niagara Falls, Ont., and met with the owner of a restaurant called Vaccaro's Italian Gardens, who wanted his place blown up so that he could collect the insurance. Kirby was offered $10,000 for the job, but he disapproved of the plan because too many people might have been killed. The job was then given to another arsonist, who eventually destroyed the restaurant.

- Again in 1978, Kirby was hired by the Commissos to extort money from Frank Mauro, who owned Cook-O-Matic. Kirby beat up the person who he thought was the owner of the company, but he was mistaken; it was Peter Antonucci, then a warehouse manager for Cook-O-Matic. Having made this mistake, Kirby was not paid.

- On June 26, 1979, Cosimo Commisso met with Kirby at a fitness centre on Jane Street in Toronto where Kirby was working out. Commisso asked Kirby to torch a house in Bradford, Ont., that was owned by a close friend named Pietro Crupi. He was told to burn it down when the tenant was not home. Michele Commisso later explained that Crupi had tried to evict the woman tenant but wasn't successful. Kirby then went inside the house and set fire to a couch on the main floor, causing $17,000 damage to the house. Kirby was paid only $200 because the owner complained that the damage was not extensive enough.

- In August 1979, Kirby was asked by Cosimo to burn down a hotel in Acton, Ont., on behalf of the owner, for yet another insurance fraud. Kirby asked for $10,000 for the job, but he was never contacted again to commit the arson. Apparently the owner got a better deal elsewhere. The hotel was torched later, killing one person, and the owner was subsequently convicted of murder.

- In April or May of 1980 Kirby was told by the Commissos that they wanted a man in Montreal killed on behalf of the man's "partner", who would realize a profit at the victim's death. Cosimo offered $20,000 to $25,000 for this murder. In late July, Kirby flew to Montreal and met with Cosimo at the Bonaventure Hotel. Cosimo was already in place, having driven from Toronto. Kirby and Cosimo then did some surveillance of the intended victim's home and business addresses. At this point Kirby found out that the target was none other than Irving Kott, the famous stock promoter and manipulator fictionalized in the novel *The Midas Touch* by Ivan Shaffer. He was also a well-known associate of the Cotroni family in Montreal. This was quite a heavy target for the likes of the Commissos to take on. As Kirby and Cosimo were watching Kott's residence, Kott emerged, driving his 1978 Mercedes right past them. Cosimo remarked to Kirby that he would have killed him right then and there if he had had his gun with him. Cosimo Commisso was that impulsive and cold-blooded: Human life meant nothing to him. Later Cosimo stressed the importance and urgency of this killing.

Kirby returned to Toronto, constructed an elaborate bomb, and picked up a .22-calibre hand-gun. Then he drove from Toronto to Montreal and staked out Kott's house once again. At one point Kirby was about to shoot Kott through his front picture window when he was observed by a passer-by.

He left town immediately. Kott had had yet another close call. Back in Toronto, Kirby met with Cosimo and told him what had happened. Commisso was upset when Kirby reported his abortive attempt, and two weeks later Kirby returned to Montreal. This time he tried to plant a bomb in Kott's car, but he was unable to find it. Again he returned to Toronto unsuccessful. Finally, on August 28, 1978, he once again drove to Montreal. He telephoned Kott's office at eight in the morning and found that Kott was there. He then went to the underground parking lot at 5425 rue Casgrain and found Kott's car. He placed a bomb with a trigger mechanism beside the muffler pipe and right under the driver's seat. A little after five that evening, two men associated with Kott were walking through the garage. They noticed two wires hanging from the car and stopped to check it. At that moment the bomb went off, hurling both men into the air. They were sent to hospital, but were not too seriously injured, though the car was a total write-off. The day after the explosion, Kirby, back in Toronto, told Cosimo that he had bombed Kott's car. Three weeks later Cosimo Commisso came to Kirby's house and told him that the wrong people were injured, but gave Kirby $3,000 for his services anyway. Irving Kott was very lucky. Kirby later said he felt badly about the two innocent victims, one of whom had his hearing permanently impaired.

- Certainly the most ludicrous and frightening of the series of bombings was this one. Cosimo had dined at a restaurant called Napoleon's at 79 Grenville Street in Toronto, and was insulted by one of the restaurant employees. In retaliation, he ordered Kirby to blow up the restaurant (just a block away from the Ontario Police Commission and the main morgue in Toronto) as a sign of his "displeasure". During the early-evening hours of May 4, 1980, Kirby phoned the restaurant but got no answer. Then he placed a bomb made up of two sticks of dynamite, a battery, and a timer on the window ledge on the east side of the restaurant. At quarter past nine the bomb went off, prematurely, injuring three women who were sitting inside the restaurant. Napoleon's was substantially damaged and never reopened. Kirby received $1,000 from the Commissos for this petty act of revenge. By conventional standards, blowing up a restaurant for bad service is certainly an over-reaction.

- In July 1980, Kirby was asked by the Commissos to bomb the house of Maury Kalen on behalf of Cotroni family associate Willie Obront (the Montreal meat magnate, then hiding out from Quebec authorities in Florida), in connection with a debt of $100,000 that Kalen allegedly owed to Obront. Kirby placed a stick of dynamite equipped with a detonating device at Kalen's home at 123 Heath Street West in Toronto. No one was hurt. Fortunately for Kalen, he had moved from that address, and Kirby declined to continue the job because he felt the security at the new Kalen residence was too difficult to penetrate. Kirby was paid $2,000 for this, even though he blew up the wrong house (or rather, the right house at the wrong time).

- The final Commisso-Kirby operation in this particular series of brutal mob crimes was to take place between August and October of 1980, when Kirby was asked to break either the arms or the legs of Alphonso Gallucci, of Gallucci Construction, because he owed $54,000 to a Commisso associate and was in a dispute with York Lathing and Lincoln Iron Works regarding contract costs. In this operation Kirby, having learned from some of his past experiences with the Commissos, asked to be paid up front – whether the extortion was eventually successful or not. Cosimo offered Kirby a percentage of the take, and Kirby tentatively agreed, but finally he changed his mind and declined the offer because of the lack of up-front money. Cosimo persisted in trying to recruit Kirby for the assault, but Kirby remained firm and didn't do it.

In summarizing the Crown case against the Commissos in a Toronto courtroom on April 13, 1984, after the Commissos pleaded guilty to all charges, Crown attorney Murray Segal made an impassioned plea to Judge Arthur Meen on behalf of all citizens of Ontario. His words sum up so well the case society has against organized crime that they deserve to be quoted at some length:

May it please Your Honour, there is no need to elaborate at length on the facts. They speak for themselves. They portray organized crime practiced by an underworld family engaged as brokers of extortion, violence and death. You have before you some of the most serious crimes found under our law: counselling murder, planting bombs, causing injury and death, extortion, arson and the like.... The accused terrorized the community. They commissioned killings, beatings, threats and property damage all over Ontario and beyond.

The convictions in these cases, coupled with the facts on which they are based, clearly demonstrate that organized crime exists in Ontario. Organized crime, taking this case as an example, reaches out to the construction industry, the bottling industry, to the business world, to the administration of justice, and to innocent victims and their families.

Beyond that, imagine the sense of evil that would prompt someone to blow up a restaurant because they did not like the service, or to oblige a friend by committing an arson to get rid of an unwanted tenant, or to kill a witness in a prospective prosecution.

To say that some of the accused's attempts did not succeed, with respect, does not ensure the credit of the accused. It is no credit to them at all that persons who they set out to kill, such as Mr. Mason or Mr. Kott, did not meet the same tragedy that befell Mr. Quan.... Every time a bomb was set, the public and the police were put at grave risk.

Your Honour, a case like this one strikes at the heart of the average citizen.... One has to imagine the terror and anxiety caused by these random bombings, these extortions, threats to family members, including children.

Segal then explained the use of Cecil Kirby as an informant, granted immunity for his former crimes in return for his co-operation and testimony:

Were it possible to prosecute high-ranking members of the underworld without the use of informants, it would be done. But it is often impossible to obtain legally admissible evidence against sophisticated criminals without the use of informants. It must be understood that the informant in this case was not the person who gave the orders to kill, to burn, to threaten, and the like. Cosimo and Remo Commisso gave the orders and stood to gain the most from such crimes. The use of informants has ensured that those who stood to gain the most, will lose the most.

The Crown had negotiated the guilty pleas for a lesser sentence to ensure "the removal of these dangerous offenders from society for a long, long time." A long-drawn-out trial could have resulted in the Commissos getting off scot-free.

It is somewhat amusing to consider the arguments brought forth by the lawyer for the Commissos, Louis Silver, as he attempted to mitigate the offences for which his clients were charged:

I am advised, for some considerable time he [Remo Commisso] took an interest in his church, he being a Catholic. I am advised that he was most generous with that church, as well as other charitable requests that may have been made upon him from time to time.

Another mitigating factor, Silver pointed out, was that Cosimo Commisso, with members of the Commisso family, "originated the concept of the chocolate Easter egg, very popular amongst the Italian people, and marketed that for a number of years, really as an adjunct of their bakery business." Chocolate Easter eggs and money to the Catholic Church! The judge, needless to say, was unimpressed by these so-called redeeming qualities and gave the Commissos the stiffest sentence he could under the terms of the negotiated guilty plea – eight years for Cosimo and six for Remo.

Of course the Commissos were successfully prosecuted for these brutal crimes only because of the defection of one of their hit men, Cecil Kirby, from their ranks. While the crimes were being planned and implemented by the Commissos and Cecil Kirby, between the spring of 1976 and the fall of 1980, Cecil Kirby was a professional enforcer and free-lance hit man working for the criminal world. But dramatically, in November 1980, Kirby offered his services to the RCMP as an informer and agent. And it was while he was under RCMP control in early 1981 that he undertook his most interesting contract-murder assignments for the Commissos – the contracts to murder a mob moll in Connecticut and to assassinate Paul Volpe in Toronto.

CHAPTER FOURTEEN

The Gentleman Hit Man and a Killing in Connecticut

O NE WARM MAY AFTERNOON in 1983, Cecil Kirby phoned me at my CBC office. At the time I was working as an investigative reporter and associate producer for CBC-TV's flagship current-affairs program, *the fifth estate*. I had been trying to get in touch with Kirby for some months before his phone call, for a *fifth estate* exposé on the police use of informers. But Kirby had been an elusive quarry, even though I had received messages through his lawyer. Finally, on the morning of May 17, 1983, long after I had given up trying to reach him, Kirby phoned me at my office and dramatically said he wished to meet with me within the hour at the parking lot of Casa Loma. I immediately accepted the invitation, even though it threw off my entire day's plan, including afternoon tea with the daughter of former Soviet spy Igor Gouzenko. Meeting with Kirby, whatever the circumstances, was an offer I could not refuse.

Kirby had called me because he had just seen a recent episode of *the fifth estate* that had featured a fascinating interview with a suave Montreal hit man named Donald Lavoie. In effect, Kirby wanted to say that he would be even better television than Lavoie, who, he had to admit, was quite gripping and candid in his descriptions of what went through his mind as he killed people. The meeting had to take place an hour after his call, because he needed time to shake his police protection. This was a meeting he wanted to have without the RCMP watching or listening in.

At first glance Cecil Kirby looked like anything but a hit man and enforcer for the mob. A short, mustachioed, impish-looking man in his mid-thirties, he had long, curly red hair and appeared innocent, boyish, and shy. Soon, however, I became aware of the cold, hard look in the eyes, and the muscled torso, and I began to see that this man was capable of inflicting damage.

As Kirby insisted, we met in the parking lot at Casa Loma and then walked around to the back area for privacy. Kirby related his career of breaking bodies and arranging bombings in a disarmingly casual way. It was eerie. He was soft-spoken, gentle, and calm, yet the story he had to tell was certainly engrossing as he described beatings, bombings, and attempted killings for the mob, and a cast of characters that would make even Mario Puzo blush.

Shortly after this first meeting with Kirby, which lasted several hours, I wrote an excited memo to my boss, veteran journalist Ron Haggart, the senior producer of *the fifth estate*, detailing the journalistic coup:

I had a lengthy meeting with Cecil Kirby, hit man and bomber for the Commisso family. A truly fascinating raconteur. He called me because of my previous inquiries and our recent piece on Lavoie. Believe it or not, Kirby is even cooler and more casual than Lavoie in describing murders and bombings.... He rattled off facts and figures: 14 bombings for Remo and Cosimo Commisso, contracts on mob figures including Paul Volpe (Domenic Racco put up some of the money for this as well as Remo Commisso).... One of his victims survived because he was given defective dynamite which simply sent up a smoke cloud ... very disappointing for Cecil! Lots of fascinating, inside stories of the mob.... Certainly a treasure chest! The main problem is that CK wants money.... I offered to help him get a U.S. writer (Tom Renner in New York City, an old friend who ghosted Vinnie Teresa's books), hoping that he would then do our show for nothing. We are to talk again.... I shall stay with this. It could be quite an item!

Indeed, it was "quite an item" when an exclusive interview with Kirby was aired nationally on *the fifth estate* on March 6, 1984 (except for the Toronto area, which was blacked out at the request of the Crown attorney; the show was aired there on April 25, 1984). Across the country it created quite a stir. But who was this man who maimed and killed people for the mob?

Cecil Kirby came from a lower-middle-class family in a small town north of Toronto. He was always a street kid, and at eighteen, for excitement, he joined Satan's Choice, a criminal bike gang then allied to the notorious Hell's Angels. He enjoyed the element of danger, and he thrived on the easy money gained through brute intimidation. He did drive a truck for a living for a while, and even ran a gym and fitness club. But that was real work. During his six years in Satan's Choice he underwent a slow process of brutalization. He established a reputation for violence and, as he himself now says, for "getting into all kinds of trouble." Kirby is naturally intelligent, but like so many characters in the underworld, he was attracted by the easy money (which is tax-free) and the glamour of organized crime.

In the spring of 1976, when he was twenty-five, an old, well-connected biker friend introduced him to Cosimo Commisso, a mobster with whom he was associated. At this point Kirby took up full-time enforcement work. Cosimo hired Kirby to carry out a car bombing, and as we have seen, his work was satisfactory, since he would work for the Commissos for five years after this first bombing, committing, according to his own estimates, well over a hundred serious, indictable offences in the service of the mob. In a good year he made $75,000 tax-free for breaking arms and legs and blowing up the occasional house or car. The pay was not bad, and the job certainly was not boring.

But what does Kirby say of his work? In his *fifth estate* interview, Kirby was extremely frank with the show's co-host, Bob McKeown:

McKEOWN: How did you get away with it?
KIRBY: It was easy for me to do. I had no conscience at all at the time.... I didn't feel guilty about nothing.... When I hit anybody, they never saw me coming, and never even so much as got a look at my face. I hit them fast, you know, and hard enough that they wouldn't remember what I looked like.
McKEOWN: Where would you do it?
KIRBY: I usually picked my own ground. After following these people around for a few days, I would pick my own ground.

An underground garage, in the dark of the night, you know. Always a dark time specifically. Let the dark work for you, hide your features and your face.

McKEOWN: Would you know how badly you hurt them?

KIRBY: Oh, I could tell sometimes. Hitting them you could hear the bones cracking.

McKEOWN: If you had to break someone's legs, how would you do it?

KIRBY: Most of the time I carried a blackjack that was powerful enough to break somebody's legs.

McKEOWN: When you hurt people, how did you respond?

KIRBY: I had no reponse at all. I had no emotion at all about it.

But Kirby's life had changed dramatically three years before the nationally televised show was broadcast. It changed when he decided to inform or, as Kirby himself would say, to "rat on" his former colleagues and friends. This about-face was an act of desperate self-defence.

Kirby knew, better than most, that many hit men for the mob are eventually killed themselves, because of inside knowledge of serious crimes, including murders. Kirby decided that he just "knew too much", and decided to offer his services to the RCMP as an informer and undercover agent to "take out" the Commissos – before they took him out to protect themselves. It was just a question of time, he felt, and he figured he'd better strike first.

So in November 1980, Kirby, out of the blue, rang up the intelligence unit of the RCMP in Toronto. He spoke with an incredulous Corporal Mark Murphy of the National Crime Intelligence Unit, who happened to take the call. Recalls Kirby, "I couldn't identify myself at the time. I just said to him if you would like to talk to me about some people involved in organized crime and a few unsolved murders, will you meet me in half an hour?" A sceptical Murphy eventually agreed to a meeting, which took place at Casa Loma later that day. Kirby told his incredible story. The meeting, which lasted about half an hour, "put butterflies in his [Corporal Murphy's] stomach," according to Kirby. Murphy still needed to be convinced that Kirby really wanted to help the police against the mob. Murphy and Kirby then met regularly once a week for a few months so they could get to know and trust each other.

This cosy situation changed suddenly in February 1981, after Cosimo Commisso offered Kirby a contract to kill a woman in Connecticut. This was to be his first real undercover operation for the RCMP, the first of two "hits" he undertook while under Mountie control.

Vince Melia, fifty-five, a Sidernese mobster close to Mike Racco who had become one of the leaders of the Calabrese mob in Connecticut, contracted out to his Canadian counterparts to have his brother's troublesome girl-friend killed. Vince Melia was no stranger either to Toronto or to the police both in Canada and the United States. Melia had lived in Toronto for several years before moving to Connecticut. The following entry under Vince Melia's name appears in a U.S. Immigration intelligence report on the Siderno mob:

Melia, Vincenzo: born 29 April 1929, 32 Wakemore Street, Darien, Connecticut. During a conversation between Michele Racco, Toronto, Ontario and Domenic Torrente of Montreal, Quebec, it appeared that Torrente was having problems with Melia, and he wished Michele Racco to intercede in the difference. Racco, in a later conversation with Melia discussed the differences noted above. Melia stated that he told someone (probably Torrente) that Racco was to decide. A third discussion took place between Michele Racco and Joe Marterisano (phonetic), who informed Racco that he had received a call from Melia and was told to call Racco to be brought up to date on things.

Clearly Melia was well connected and a force to be reckoned with on the international mob stage.

So when Vince Melia contacted his ally Cosimo Commisso and asked him to send a hit man down to Stamford, Conn., to kill a hairdresser named Helen Nafpliotis, Cosimo Commisso named a price and readily agreed to provide a Canadian hit man. This was part of the hit-man exchange program between Canada and the States. Nafpliotis was having a messy affair with Vince's brother Nick, whose wife was in a jealous rage over the thirty-two-year-old, bleached-blonde hairdresser, and had already on one occasion gone after Helen with a hockey stick. More importantly, Helen had been an eyewitness to a Melia shooting. She had to go.

Cosimo Commisso first approached Cecil Kirby with the

lucrative contract near the end of January 1981. Commisso offered Kirby $18,000 (American) for the killing, and a bonus of several thousand more for disposing of the body. Kirby asked Commisso why an American hit man couldn't do the job, and Commisso explained that "it was a family matter," and they didn't want any outsiders to know about it.

On February 5, Kirby told Corporal Murphy of the approach, and Murphy advised Kirby to take the contract. The RCMP and the FBI would mount a special operation to sting both the Commissos and the Melias.

On February 16, in the late morning, Kirby met with Cosimo Commisso at the Casa Commisso on Lawrence Avenue West. Kirby asked Cosimo if the contract to kill the girl in Connecticut was still available, and when Commisso said it was, Kirby offered to do the killing. This delighted Commisso, but he told Kirby that they wouldn't discuss the murder until they met with another man, a New Yorker who was "one of the family", at the Howard Johnson's near the airport in Toronto. In New York, this other man would provide all the necessary information, plus a gun, a car, and "whatever else was needed". This meeting was just a preliminary one, to introduce Kirby to his New York connection for the murder. Commisso told Kirby that the job was to be done forty miles outside New York City and that he would be receiving his expenses before he left Canada. Cosimo Commisso added that he would receive $5,000 when he got down to the States, and the rest of the money would be paid a month later when he returned from Connecticut.

After this dramatic meeting, Kirby left the Casa Commisso and immediately phoned Corporal Murphy. He arranged to meet with Murphy at Casa Loma (this is obviously one of Kirby's favourite haunts for clandestine meetings, though an informer should not be a creature of habit). The next day, Tuesday, February 17, Kirby agreed to co-operate with the police on this operation.

After his meeting with Murphy at Casa Loma, Kirby, now an RCMP undercover agent, went out to the Howard Johnson's, where he met Commisso and his American contact in the lobby. He was introduced to Antonio Romeo.* Romeo and Commisso

---

*Antonio Romeo also pops up in American intelligence reports. This is from the U.S. Immigration Department's report on the Calabrian Mafia: "Romeo, Antonio, _____ , Norwalk, Connecticut. A telephone contact of Fred Melia. Also a telephone contact of Antonio Spoleti of Hamilton, Ontario, who has no criminal record. However, Spoleti has telephone contact with Paolo Violi of Montreal, Quebec, a member of the L.C.N. family of Vic Cotroni."

talked a lot in Italian, and Kirby was told to meet with Romeo the next day at the Marriott Hotel in Stamford, Conn., where Romeo would introduce him to someone called "Vince". In the presence of Romeo, Commisso told Kirby that Vince would give Kirby a gun and the keys to the girl's apartment. Kirby was told to be at the Marriott Hotel at ten the next night, Wednesday, February 18.

Kirby went to the Casa Commisso to pick up his expense money. But things had been delayed and Romeo was not yet ready to leave Toronto. The next evening, at the Casa Commisso, Kirby met with Remo, Michele, and Cosimo Commisso, who gave him $300 in cash. Kirby was told to meet with Romeo the next day at the Marriott Hotel in Stamford.

On Friday morning, February 20, Kirby met Corporal Murphy at Toronto International Airport. They took the noon American Airlines flight to LaGuardia Airport in New York. On arrival, Kirby and Murphy went to the Holiday Inn near the airport and checked into a room. Murphy later introduced Kirby to two FBI agents, who then accompanied them to nearby Darien, Conn., an affluent town about five miles northeast of Stamford, where they again took a room at a Holiday Inn. Here they met FBI agent John Schiman, who knew Kirby as "Jack Ryan". (Kirby went under many names; Cosimo Commisso had introduced him to Romeo as "George".) RCMP officer Murphy and FBI agent Schiman then drove Kirby to the Marriott Hotel in Stamford.

The next day at the bar of the hotel, Kirby had his meeting with Romeo and Vince. Melia was reluctant about meeting at the bar, and seemed concerned about police surveillance. He thought he spotted some policemen at the bar. Ironically, he ignored the real police officers, whom Kirby knew were there observing the meeting. Kirby later recalled that he had to stop himself from saying, "No, you dummy, those aren't the cops; the real cops are sitting opposite us on the other side of the bar!" But Kirby resisted this temptation and merely reassured Vince Melia that they were not being watched. When Vince offered to get Kirby a car and a gun as well as a room, Kirby replied that he didn't need wheels and didn't want anyone to know where he was staying. However, he did ask Melia to get him a .38 with a silencer as well as some money and a picture of Helen, the girl to be killed. Melia seemed to know all about the girl's movements on the next day. He gave Kirby her telephone number and two keys, one for her car and one for her house. He wanted her killed the following evening. Melia told Kirby to meet him at two the next afternoon at the hotel to get the money and the gun, and then the three left the hotel and went to the parking lot.

In the parking lot they approached a waiting Cadillac, where Vince introduced Kirby to an associate, Jerry Russo. After receiving $300 in cash, Kirby took off with Russo in the Cadillac to be briefed on the girl and be shown her house. Then, when Russo took him back to the Marriott, Kirby immediately called a taxi and went to the Holiday Inn in Darien, which was the headquarters for this joint FBI/RCMP sting operation. There he filled Schiman and Murphy in on what had happened. Kirby was of course body-packed, and the FBI had been discreetly taking surveillance photographs of the parking-lot meeting. Still, Murphy and Schiman needed Kirby's first-hand description of events.

And so it went. Meetings with Melia and his boys in Stamford, debriefing sessions with Schiman and Murphy in Darien. For two days Kirby shuttled back and forth as the plot unfolded. All this was secretly taped by Kirby and photographed by the FBI.

In his next meeting with Melia, Kirby was told that his fee had been reduced to $10,000, American (probably to allow for the exchange rate), but that if he could make it look like she was just a "missing person" he would get an extra thousand. In other words, the Melias wanted him to dump the corpse so it would never be found. Kirby agreed. Kirby was told not to kill Nafpliotis until after her "room-mate" left, because he was "family" and not to be harmed or involved in the murder. The room-mate, of course, was Nick Melia. Vince Melia told Kirby the time the room-mate was leaving and gave him a picture of the target.

In the Marriott parking lot, Vince Melia told Kirby that if he did a good job on the hit, the family might use him on a few other operations, including "burning places down" and other criminal enterprises. Kirby was handed $5,000 and a brown bag containing a fully loaded .22-calibre automatic with the serial numbers conveniently drilled out and equipped with a silencer. Annoyed that he wasn't given a .38, Kirby complained to Melia, who said that he was sorry, "but that's all we've got." Some mob!

Kirby shuttled up to Darien in a taxi with the photograph,

the gun, and the money. Meanwhile the FBI moved into high gear and arranged the final stages of this sting operation. On Monday, February 23, 1981, the FBI drove Kirby to the scene of the crime, 98 McMullen Street in Stamford, the home of Helen Nafpliotis. Kirby watched as the beautiful Greek hairdresser got into her white Datsun and drove off. The car was stopped on the highway by the FBI, and agent Schiman told Helen about the murder contract. She agreed to co-operate with the bureau by going into protective custody. In the meantime, Kirby drove back to Darien with the other FBI officers. He flew back to Toronto at ten that evening from LaGuardia with Corporal Murphy. Helen Nafpliotis and her car were safely in FBI hands.

About a week after the "hit" in Connecticut, Kirby met with Cosimo Commisso at the airport Howard Johnson's and told him that the girl was dead. Another meeting was set up for March 10 for further payment. On March 10, Cosimo Commisso paid Kirby $5,000 for the supposed murder. Later Commisso paid more – a bonus for disposing of the body – unaware that his conversations with Kirby were secretly being taped.

Not everything ran smoothly. Kirby recalls one occasion not long after this, when he thought the whole operation had been blown. Commisso said someone had reported to him that the girl was seen alive in Greece (this may, in fact, have been where the FBI put her). Melia family members were concerned that they had been ripped off. Without batting an eyelash, Kirby swore to Commisso that he had killed the girl and dumped her and her car in a pond. Kirby even called Commisso's bluff by offering to take him to the spot where he had ditched the car with the body in it. Commisso demurred, stating that he believed Kirby, and said the Melias had probably made up this story to avoid paying the rest of the money. This was a close call for Kirby, just as his most important police operation was to start. The Connecticut work with the FBI and RCMP was to be invaluable training for both the police and Kirby as they approached their next task.

The drama of the fake hit in Connecticut was merely to set the stage for Kirby's next murder contracts for the Commissos. This time there were to be two hits in Toronto. And the first target was to be an underling of one of the major organized-crime leaders in Ontario. The object of the RCMP sting on these operations would be to bring down the entire Commisso family with the co-operation of one of their hit men, Cecil Kirby, and of one of their targets, who was also one of the leading members of the Mafia in Canada, Paul Volpe.

CHAPTER FIFTEEN

Cecil Kirby, the Commissos, and the Police Go on the Great Fox Hunt

WHEN CECIL KIRBY, fully body-packed by the police, went to see Cosimo Commisso on March 10, 1981, to get the rest of the money for the Connecticut hit, he was surprised to hear that Commisso already had another victim for him to murder. He was just checking on the man's address so Kirby could kill him. Meanwhile, as we have seen, Kirby collected $5,000 for the previous hit, the balance (the bonus for disposing of the body) to be due on April 1 (appropriately enough, on April Fool's Day). A meeting was arranged for Kirby and Commisso at Cosimo Commisso's home on Tuesday, March 17, 1981. Because the police hoped the Commissos would really destroy themselves on this operation, they decided to let it continue and did not move to arrest anyone on the Connecticut hit.

On St. Patrick's Day, 1981, Kirby went to Commisso's home and picked him up. Speaking right into Kirby's hidden tape recorder, Cosimo Commisso told him that he wanted to have Peter Scarcella, a close friend of Paul Volpe's, murdered. No reason was given. They then drove to Scarcella's apartment in Mississauga. Commisso pointed out the building and gave Kirby a description of Scarcella's car and the last three digits of his licence plate. He also took Kirby to various locations around Toronto where, according to Commisso, Scarcella could regularly be found. The police followed the pair everywhere, wondering what on earth was going on.

On March 27, Commisso told Kirby to wait a week before killing Scarcella, whom he again emphasized was close to Paul Volpe. They wanted to be especially careful on this one. They discussed various ways of doing the job efficiently. In the meantime, Commisso asked Kirby to undertake a routine enforcement assignment, and beat up a man called Lillo. Finally, however, Cosimo Commisso made a far-from-routine suggestion. To the shock of Cecil Kirby, Commisso mentioned that in addition to Scarcella, they might want to have Paul Volpe killed. But this was to be discussed in a later meeting. The police were, to put it mildly, surprised and elated by the turn of events.

The next meeting of Kirby and Commisso was on Tuesday, March 31, at the Casa Commisso Banquet Hall. First Kirby was assured by Cosimo that he and Remo would have the rest of the money for the killing in Connecticut on April 1, as planned. Commisso instructed Kirby to keep watching Scarcella's movements so that he might be killed more easily when the time came. Then, again, Cosimo Commisso brought up the possibility of Kirby killing Paul Volpe at some future date.

On April Fool's Day, 1981, Kirby called Cosimo Commisso, but the money was not ready. A meeting was set up for Thursday, April 2, at the Howard Johnson's near the airport. This time, however, Commisso didn't show, perhaps because he spotted a police surveillance tail on him, and another meeting was arranged for Friday, April 3. When they met on the third, Commisso put Kirby off again, saying that Vince Melia was coming up from the States with the money on the following day. Clearly the Commissos were not planning to pay Kirby his complete hit fee too quickly.

On April 8, Cosimo Commisso and Antonio Romeo of Connecticut drove to a meeting with Kirby at the airport Howard Johnson's. Romeo stayed in the car, while Commisso met with Kirby inside. Cosimo still didn't have the money, and since he was off to Vancouver on mob business, he suggested Kirby contact his younger brother Michele to get the payment when it finally arrived from Vince Melia. Commisso told Kirby to keep "checking" on Scarcella, and said that Michele would tell him within the week whether or not the killing should take place. Cosimo said that Remo Commisso wanted yet another man killed, but that Remo Commisso probably would "look after it himself." This may have been the Paul Volpe hit. Remo Commisso has killed people many times on his own, but in more recent years has depended on hit men in order to insulate himself. So the hit referred to here must have been of unusual significance, possibly that of Paul Volpe, for him to consider undertaking it himself.

Cosimo Commisso then stated dramatically that there was soon to be "a war in Toronto", and he wanted to be sure that Kirby was on his side. He must have been afraid that the Volpes or their allies the Luppinos would try to buy Kirby off. The "war" could only refer to the consequences of the murder of Paul Volpe in Toronto. In fact, the proposed killing of Paul Volpe by the Commissos would have been the opening round of such a war.

Nothing more happened until April 14, when Kirby and Cosimo met once again at the airport Howard Johnson's. The money was still not forthcoming. Furthermore, Cosimo told Kirby to "hold off" on the Scarcella matter for the time being. Kirby and Cosimo then drove to a location near the Casa Commisso where Enzio Fimognai, an associate of the Commissos, gave Kirby $100, far short of the $2,000 still due for the Connecticut hit.

On Tuesday, April 21, Kirby met with Michele Commisso, since Remo had told him that Cosimo was "tied up". Michele still had no money for Kirby, but told him that it would be ready on Thursday of that week. Michele also said that he had been talking with Vince Melia in the United States, and that Melia was giving them the run-around on the money because some valuable jewellery was missing from Helen Napfliotis's apartment. (She had taken the jewellery before she went into FBI protective custody.) Michele Commisso then questioned Kirby to make sure that Napfliotis was really dead. Kirby reassured him, and was then told that Vince Melia was due up on Saturday, April 25, to attend the wedding of his cousin. He would be at the Casa Commisso for the reception and would bring the money with him at that time. Michele said that no final decision had yet been made regarding the Scarcella killing.

On Thursday, April 23, Cosimo Commisso met Kirby once again at the airport Howard Johnson's and gave him $1,000, promising the rest after Vince Melia came up to Toronto on Saturday. Cosimo told Kirby to "pass on the Scarcella deal for a month or two," but that there was someone else he wanted killed. He would give Kirby the new name on the following Wednesday. Commisso then offered to put Kirby on the Commisso family payroll at the rate of $500 per week, with bonuses for certain major crimes committed for them. Not a bad deal, considering that this was to be tax-free income.

Vince Melia did arrive in Toronto for the weekend wedding, and on Wednesday, April 29, Cosimo Commisso met with Kirby at their usual spot, the Howard Johnson's. Melia had told Commisso that they thought the woman was not dead, and therefore he would not pay any more. He also referred to the missing money and jewellery. Kirby allayed Commisso's fears by claiming that he had taken the money and jewellery in order to make it appear that she was just a missing person. Kirby was convincing.

Commisso then paid Kirby an additional $1,000 out of his own pocket, but told Kirby to "pass" on Scarcella for the time being. When Kirby asked the identity of the other man that the Commissos wanted killed, Cosimo Commisso whispered in his ear that they wanted him to kill Paul Volpe. The Commissos had made the fateful decision to move against one of the most powerful crime bosses in Toronto. Earlier that year, according to a rounder who was present, Paul Volpe had told a Commisso soldier that he was "tired of these fucking Calabrese." Apparently, the Calabrese were tired of Volpe, too.

The rest of the April 29 meeting – and all of the subsequent meeting between Kirby and Cosimo on May 15 – was taken up with supplying Kirby with the information he would need to kill Volpe, and with discussions of how the killing was to be accomplished. Commisso promised to pay $20,000 for the murder, and told Kirby that if Paul Volpe's wife, Lisa Dalholt, happened to be present at the time, then it was up to him whether he killed her as well.

The Special Enforcement Unit detachment working with Kirby was divided on how to proceed. A meeting with Howard Morton, the Crown attorney assigned to work with SEU, was hurriedly arranged on May 15. Some of the SEU members suggested that the police simply kidnap Paul Volpe for the day, and then have Kirby pretend he had carried out the murder. They also thought it would be useful to have Remo, as well as Cosimo Commisso, admitting to the plot on tape. An incredulous Morton said there was no legal way to detain Volpe, but suggested that they simply go to him and ask him to co-operate. Paul Volpe knew and liked one SEU officer, Sergeant Al Cooke, of Metro Toronto police, and it was suggested that he be one of the officers to approach Volpe.

During the early-morning hours of the next day, May 16, 1981, Sergeant Al Cooke and Corporal Mark Murphy of the RCMP arrived at Paul Volpe's mansion in Schomberg, Ontario, to warn him of the plot against his life and to ask his co-operation in ensnaring the would-be killers.

Volpe had purchased the handsome brown-and-gold Tudor mansion, complete with a turret, from a county court judge in 1980. It was set back quite a distance from the road, with a well-paved and well-lit entrance drive. On the front lawn, which was always immaculately landscaped with many evergreens, there was a huge flag-pole, reflecting Volpe's patriotism. Volpe called his humble abode "Fox Hill" – Volpe is Italian for "fox" – and he had set up an office in the basement, equipped with sofas, chairs, espresso-maker, and slot machine. Here, too, Volpe kept his "gun collection", as he had called it before the Waisberg inquiry. Sliding glass doors looked out onto a tennis court and a large private pond, stocked with over three hundred ducks. The property was floodlit. There were elaborate security devices, fences, guard dogs, and listening devices. The estate was like a castle under siege. But here Volpe felt more secure from media and police attention than he had in his more modest home in Toronto's fashionable Bayview area, where he and his wife had lived for several years before.

As the plot on his life revealed, all the security was justified, and the police were now on hand to provide even more. When Sergeant Cooke and Corporal Murphy told him hit man Cecil Kirby had been contracted by the Commissos to kill him as soon as possible, Volpe was at first both sceptical and surprised. "Why would anyone want to kill me?" he asked incredulously. The police officers patiently explained that time was of the essence, and explained that they needed his wallet so that Kirby would be able to prove he had killed him. According to Al Cooke, Volpe handed over his wallet without even looking at its contents. He had really been taken off guard. Cooke and Murphy then asked him to accompany them to RCMP headquarters on Jarvis Street, where they wanted Volpe and his wife to spend the day in hiding while the operation against the Commissos proceeded.

The trio which produced the award-winning CBC-TV *Connections* series on organized crime: (from left to right) the author, James Dubro, research director and associate producer; co-producer Martyn Burke; and co-producer William Macadam.
(Toronto Sun)

A 1970s police surveillance photograph showing Paul Volpe and Nathan Klegerman leaving the Colosseum Restaurant at Yonge and Walton streets in downtown Toronto.

A police surveillance picture of Paul Volpe on the streets of Toronto in the mid seventies. The streets, restaurants, and malls of downtown Toronto were where he did business.

(Arrows) Charles Yanover (left) and Murray Feldberg (right) waiting in line to pay their respects at the funeral for Paul Volpe's brother Eugene in the mid seventies.

Paul Volpe checking to see who is watching him at the funeral of his brother Eugene. Volpe was always on the lookout whenever he was in public.

Cosimo Commisso, the eldest of the Commisso brothers and one of the leaders of the Siderno Mafia in Ontario, gave Cecil Kirby many of his instructions.

Rocco "Remo" Commisso caught by a *Connections* surveillance camera coming out of his headquarters at the Casa Commisso Banquet Hall in Toronto.
(CBC-TV / Norfolk Productions)

Domenic Racco after he emerged from prison in 1978. He became one of the leaders of the Siderno group in Toronto and was active in the cocaine trade.
(Norfolk Productions)

Commisso hit man and enforcer Cecil Kirby, being filmed for *the fifth estate* in 1984.
His face is hidden to protect his identity, as there is a contract out on his life.
(Gordon Stewart)

Stamford, Conn., hairdresser Helen
Nafpliotis, the proposed victim of
one of many Commisso murder
plots. She escaped death because of a
joint F.B.I./R.C.M.P. sting operation
against the Commissos and one of
their Connecticut associates, Vince
Melia.
(*Hartford Courant*)

This photo from the front page of the *Globe and Mail* on Tuesday, November 15, 1983, shows police examining the body of Paul Volpe in the trunk of his car at Toronto International Airport.
(*Globe and Mail*, Toronto)

Pietro Scarcella, longtime Volpe associate, was the last known person to have seen Paul Volpe alive. He lunched with Volpe at an Italian restaurant in the Woodbridge Mall on the day of his murder.

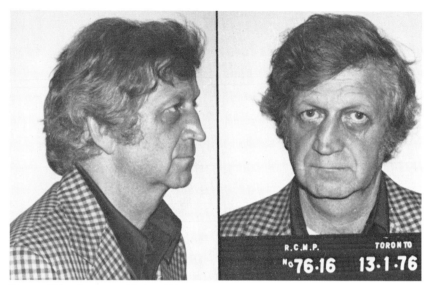

Former Volpe lieutenant Nathan Klegerman is now in hiding.

Former Volpe associate Angelo Pucci, photographed by *Connections* surveillance cameras, is selling real estate in New Jersey after pleading guilty in New Jersey in early 1985 to a charge of operating under a void corporate charter.
(CBC-TV / Norfolk Productions)

To the surprise of both the police officers present, Volpe agreed to spending the day incommunicado at RCMP headquarters with his wife, Lisa – with one condition. This was that his wife not be told about the hit contract and that a cover story be invented to explain to her why the day was to be spent with the RCMP. The officers agreed, leaving Volpe to tell his wife whatever he pleased. So Paul Volpe, one of the most powerful mob leaders in Canada, and his wife spent the day in the second-floor mess at RCMP headquarters in Toronto, chatting with the officers.

This ready co-operation with the police, as well as his willingness to strike back through official channels instead of using his own muscle and power to retaliate against the Commissos for their lack of respect, was a major breach of mob etiquette, and it was to cost Volpe dearly when the extent of his co-operation became generally known on the street. Volpe lost a lot of face over this with his underworld colleagues, even with such old friends and underlings as Chuck Yanover, who said "it was a breach of the mob code of ethics," and Natie Klegerman, his old and trusted lieutenant. However, Paul Volpe's assistance was crucial to the operation's success.

Later in the morning, while Paul Volpe was socializing with the Mounties, Cecil Kirby, body-packed and armed with Volpe's wallet, made his way to Remo Commisso's home to ensnare him in the sting. At this point the police had more than enough evidence against Cosimo Commisso, but lacked hard evidence against Remo Commisso, for whom his older brother was acting as a kind of insulation. It was decided that Kirby's final sting would be to obtain admissible evidence on the murder contracts against Remo Commisso, who, as we have seen, was considered to be the real leader of the Commisso family. Kirby and Remo went down to the basement washroom to chat, and Remo put on the water tap to counter any possible bugs. (Luckily, this didn't seriously affect what was recorded on Kirby's body-pack.) Kirby told Remo Commisso that he had just killed Paul Volpe and his wife; that they were lying dead behind their home. As proof, he showed Remo Volpe's wallet. At first Remo Commisso was very annoyed, asking why Kirby had come to his house, especially with such incriminating evidence as the wallet. He ordered Kirby to get rid of it – to throw it down a sewer or something. Kirby replied that he needed money to get out of town quickly. Remo Commisso made several exculpatory statements (as they were called in the eventual court proceedings) and told Kirby that his brother Michele Commisso would meet him at five and give him $1,000 so he could fly to Florida until the heat died down in Ontario. Remo ended the meeting by saying, "Don't worry, we will take care of you. You know we respect you like a brother. Don't worry." Remo then went on to acknowledge, for the first time on tape, his involvement in the original plan to kill Pietro Scarcella, who, he now acknowledged to Kirby, was no longer to be hit because "he is with us now."

At 5:05 P.M., Michele Commisso met with Kirby at the airport Howard Johnson's and gave him $1,100 for his escape. Immediately after this meeting, police in Toronto arrested Cosimo, Remo, and Michele Commisso. Meanwhile, in Connecticut, Vince Melia and one of his associates were arrested by the FBI. The complicated continental sting had been successfully completed. The police were elated; Kirby was greatly relieved; the Commissos were furious; Paul Volpe was stunned.

Faced with such documented, first-hand evidence of their guilt – all on tape – and hoping to have the charges reduced against their younger brother Michele (who after all had played only a minor supporting role), Remo and Cosimo Commisso manfully decided to admit their guilt. They were, after all, realists. They pleaded guilty to all of the plots: the plot against Helen Nafpliotis, the one against Pietro Scarcella, and the one to assassinate Paul Volpe. They were also later tried and convicted for the sixteen offences mentioned earlier, on information provided by Kirby. Michele Commisso was given a reduced sentence and is now back out on the streets after serving over a year of his time. Remo and Cosimo Commisso got long prison terms. When combined with their sentences on the many other bombings, extortions, and murder contracts they organized with Cecil Kirby and with other hit men and enforcers, their sentences added up to over fifteen years. They tried to get these sentences reduced by promising to give up their Canadian citizenships, but negotiations on this terminated after the Italian government made it plain that it would not accept them back in Italy. Vince Melia was finally extradited to Canada and convicted for his part in the Connecticut hit operation.

Not long after the Commissos were convicted for trying to kill him, Paul Volpe phoned the RCMP to say that it had come to his attention that certain bikers from Kirby's old gang, Satan's Choice, who had a contract out on Cecil Kirby's life, knew where the RCMP was hiding him. They strongly felt that Kirby should be exterminated for having worked as an informer against them and other organized criminals. Volpe politely suggested that the RCMP change Kirby's hotel before the hit men got to him. The police moved Kirby and thanked Paul Volpe for this additional assistance (above and beyond the call of duty, some would claim). It was Paul Volpe's way of saying thanks to the police and to Kirby. It was also an act of graciousness not very common in the criminal underworld, where co-operation with the police under any circumstances is considered a forbidden option. Volpe, who distrusted the police at the best of times, and who particularly hated informers, or "stool pigeons" as he had called them in his first *Connections* interview, must have had to do a double swallow before he made this particular call to the RCMP. But his life had been spared, and he was grateful.

Not long after Paul Volpe's tip-off to the police, Cecil Kirby, who was now living in hiding, decided it was time he paid a visit to Paul Volpe to thank him personally for his assistance. After all, he had, in a way, saved Volpe's life, and he felt it was time that the two of them got to know each other. Volpe might also be useful in other ways. And so Cecil Kirby, shaking off his police protection, drove up to Fox Hill for a meeting with his one-time hit target.

The meeting between Cecil Kirby, the youthful hit man, enforcer, and ex-biker from a lower-middle-class northern Ontario family of English heritage, and Paul Volpe, the wealthy, middle-aged, Toronto-born-and-bred, Italian crime boss, must have made an interesting study in contrasts. Kirby was shorter (five-foot-eight at best) and muscular, with a youthful dress and manner. He was more comfortable in an Adidas suit or T-shirt, while Paul Volpe always wore the latest in gentlemen's fashions. Paul Volpe had an earthy, natural charm and a confidence that came partly from being over six feet tall and well built; he was a physical presence. Kirby worked out in a gym and jogged daily. His charm comes from an affected gentleness, which masks a chilling lack of emotion. Kirby never shows great anger or great happiness. Beating someone with a blackjack, putting a bomb in someone's car, breaking legs, all were done with the same cool efficiency and lack of feelings. While under police protective custody in a hotel in 1982, Kirby did get publicly angry. He attacked his girl-friend of the time, Linda Caldwell, and beat her almost senseless. But this was a typical, non-verbal expression of hostility. Instead of letting anger out verbally, as it comes up every day, as most people do, he lets it build and burst out all at once. He had no conscience about his enforcement work; it was just a job. It would have been difficult to put together two less similar underworld personalities, though they were both native-born Canadians from Ontario who had spent their entire adult lives in criminal endeavours.

After initial pleasantries were exchanged, Volpe led Kirby to his hide-away study in the basement, which looked out onto the pond and tennis courts. Volpe told Kirby he was grateful for what he had done, and added that if there was anything else he could do for him, Kirby just had to phone and he would help in any way he could. Kirby then thanked Paul for helping him by alerting police that the bikers had discovered his hide-out. It was a cosy scene, proving to some extent that there is, indeed, honour among thieves.

Kirby was to visit with Volpe several times at Fox Hill. During one of his visits, Paul's hot-tempered German shepherd, Caesar, bit Kirby on the leg. "Caesar is a serious dog," Volpe was fond of warning visitors to his premises, including *Connections* co-producer Bill Macadam and his cameraman.

As a result of Kirby's co-operation and work with the police, the Office of the Attorney General of Ontario offered him round-the-clock police protection, a modest stipend of $23,500 per year with the suggestion of a rather large lump-sum payment when he finished testifying for the Crown, and, most importantly, immunity for past crimes he committed in Ontario. (Kirby himself admits to committing over a hundred serious indictable offences, but these were crimes for which the police had no independent evidence against him other than his own confessions.) The latter provision, immunity from prosecution, became quite controversial in Canada after veteran *Globe and Mail* crime reporter Peter Moon revealed in a front-page story that this also protected Kirby from being charged for the 1977 bombing of the Wah Kew Chop Suey House, which resulted in the death of Chong Yin Quan, the cook, and the injury of Sunny Lem, the owner. The controversy was further fuelled by press reports about Cecil Kirby beating his girl-friend while under police protection. It was reported that Kirby's police escorts did nothing to stop the savage beating and, according to one account, may have prevented the hotel manager doing so. Kirby was not charged with assault, and the inference was that he was being protected by the police against prosecution for ongoing criminal offences, not just past ones.

This investigative reportage on Kirby, mostly by Peter Moon in the *Globe and Mail*, combined with the furore at the time over the RCMP deal that gave $100,000 to mass-murderer Clifford Olson in exchange for his help in locating the bodies of some of his victims, led to a public outcry against the police in Canada for supporting and even rewarding murderers for their assistance or co-operation. *Maclean's* magazine devoted a cover story to the alleged national scandal on February 1, 1982, headlined "Why Police Pay Criminals", and devoted considerable space to both the Olson and Kirby cases. Famed criminal lawyers Edward Greenspan and Clayton Ruby, both of Toronto, came down particularly hard on the Kirby immunity deal. Said an outraged Ruby in a *Globe and Mail* interview:

Kirby is the most outrageous abuse of prosecutorial authority that ever existed, far more so than Olson. I think McMurtry has done the worst thing ever done in the administration of justice in the history of Ontario. Olson, at least, has been put in jail, so the public is protected against a dangerous man.... But in Kirby's case he is free to walk the streets with the blessing of the Attorney-General of Ontario and at public expense.

Eddie Greenspan, who is editor of *Martin's Annual Criminal Code*, in his interview with the *Globe and Mail* published January 20, 1982, echoed Ruby's comments:

The bottom line with Olson is that he is serving life in jail and will never, never get out.... But Kirby shocked me, because his case is the one that should be getting all the attention Olson is getting.... In Kirby we have an out-and-out criminal who never does a day in jail and gets blanket immunity. He confesses to crimes, one of which I understand is murder ... so that he can put away people who may be similar to him. What is society's gain to deal with a man like him? ... We give him, an evil man, total immunity from murder prosecution, pay him $200,000,

give him a car, holiday, the right to beat his common law wife
whenever he sees fit in the presence of law enforcement officers.
We have disgraced ourselves. I think all of society has suffered
by the Kirby deal.

Greenspan's facts are less than accurate. Kirby didn't confess to "murder" but to an "unintentional killing", no lump-sum payment has been given to him, and he does not have "blanket immunity", as he can still be prosecuted for any criminal activities he did not disclose, crimes committed after his agreement with the Crown, and crimes committed outside of Ontario. Greenspan also neglects to say in his condemnation of the Kirby deal that he is the lawyer for the very people Kirby's evidence put in jail. In fact, Edward Greenspan had been the lawyer for Cosimo and Remo Commisso for close to ten years. In a recent interview, Peter Moon said that this omission in the reported interview was "my fault.... I left it out because of space problems. I guess I did Greenspan a disservice." In his own defence, Greenspan says that "everyone knows I represented the Commissos." In a salvo aimed at the former attorney general, Greenspan adds: "I found it interesting that Roy McMurtry never revealed that he himself has acted for the Raccos and the Commissos." What he means is that Roy McMurtry, when he was in private practice as a criminal lawyer, defended some members of the Siderno group, including Mike Racco's brother (and Domenic's uncle), Joe Racco, and Domenic Racco's two colleagues present at the Newtonbrook Plaza shootings. But this was for a brief period back in 1972. Still, Eddie Greenspan is not in the best position to objectively judge the Kirby immunity deal, especially considering the number of years he has served as the lawyer to the Commissos, Kirby's one-time employers and victims of his testimony.

On Friday, January 29, 1982, in response to the clamour created by the *Globe and Mail* stories, Attorney General Roy McMurtry (now the Canadian high commissioner to the United Kingdom) called an unprecedented briefing meeting in his office for selected reporters. Peter Moon was not invited, though he found out about it and went anyway. In this extraordinary meeting with the press, McMurtry attacked "Canada's national newspaper" in the harshest terms, stating that its stories on Kirby "have done a disservice to the administration of justice and created difficulties for the police in their investigation of organized crime." With the Attorney General at the press conference were top officers from the three police forces in Toronto and senior Crown attorneys. They explained that ongoing operations were being severely compromised by the publicity, and that Kirby's life was now in even more danger.

The Attorney General followed up this meeting with the press with an extraordinary series of letters, stating all the facts as he knew them and directly attacking a *Globe and Mail* editorial ("What's the Charge? Exorbitant!" January 21, 1982) that criticized the immunity deal with Kirby. In his four-column response, published in the "Letters to the Editor" section of the *Globe and Mail* on Thursday, January 28, 1982, Attorney General McMurtry answered many of the charges that had been raised by the *Globe and Mail*, as well as by Eddie Greenspan, Clayton Ruby, and others. This is part of his official response to criticism of the Kirby deal:

Your editorial "What's the Charge? Exorbitant" (Jan. 21) is an unfortunate distortion of the facts surrounding the undertaking by senior Crown officials not to prosecute Cecil Kirby for offences which he had previously committed and which he fully and truthfully disclosed to the police but in respect of which there was no admissible evidence against him.

Cecil Kirby is a man with a criminal background and was a former enforcer for organized crime in Ontario. In late 1980, Mr. Kirby approached a member of the RCMP and offered to provide information concerning organized crime in Ontario as well as information with respect to several unsolved crimes.

As a result, senior officers of the Metropolitan Toronto Police, the Ontario Provincial Police and the RCMP met senior Crown law officers from the Ministry of the Attorney-General.

During this period, Mr. Kirby was approached by an organized crime family to murder an American woman. Mr. Kirby was willing to act as a police operative to gather evidence of this contract killing conspiracy. My Crown law officers, after discussing the matter with me, decided with my full concurrence that an undertaking not to prosecute was in the best interests of the administration of justice for the following reasons:

1) Apart from evidence supplied by Mr. Kirby himself, which is not admissible against him, there was absolutely no other evidence whatsoever to connect him to crimes he committed. In fact, there was no evidence whatsoever leading to any suspect for these offences. They had been fully investigated at the time they were committed and put on hold because there was no evidence against anyone. The fatal explosion case referred to in The Globe and Mail took place four years ago, and there not only was no independent evidence connecting Mr. Kirby to the crime, but no likelihood at all that any would be forthcoming.

2) With respect to all of the offences, Mr. Kirby was acting as an enforcer for organized crime. Mr. Kirby was prepared to disclose fully everything he knew about who hired him and why, and to testify in any criminal proceedings arising out of his disclosures. All of Mr. Kirby's revelations either have been investigated or are being thoroughly investigated at this moment. Accordingly, it would be inappropriate for me to comment on this aspect any further.

3) Organized crime presents a most serious challenge to law enforcement agencies. Until the revelations of Mr. Kirby, we had been frustrated to a large extent in obtaining evidence to prosecute its leaders for a large number of serious offences covering a broad range of criminal activities. Mr.Kirby presented the first real break-through in penetrating the conspiracy of silence that shrouds organized crime activities.

Having been given this undertaking, Mr. Kirby, at great risk to himself, continued to meet the heads of Toronto and New England organized crime families....

Mr. Kirby has not been given immunity in the sense that he is free to commit offences without fear of prosecution. The undertaking not to prosecute was limited to past crimes with respect to which there was no evidence against Mr. Kirby save that which he himself provided in a manner which made that evidence inadmissible against him. That is not immunity in the sense that your editorial would have us believe....

It is true that Mr. Kirby and his family are being protected at public expense. This is necessary by virtue of the fact that I am advised that there is currently a contract out on Mr. Kirby's life because of the assistance he gave police in gathering evidence against organized crime in Ontario.

Insofar as your reference to Mr. Kirby's having assaulted his girl friend, I wish to advise you that your allegation that two of the officers prevented the hotel manager from entering the room is not true. Your allegation, that he beat his girl friend while his "police body-guards" apparently took no action, is similarly untrue.

You quoted Mr. Greenspan as stating, "In Kirby, we have an out-and-out criminal who never does a day in jail, gets blanket immunity." I am sure that a defence counsel with Mr. Greenspan's experience is not suggesting that simply because Mr. Kirby has committed offences he should be put in jail irrespective of whether there is any admissible evidence which could be used in a prosecution against him. As I have indicated there was no admissible evidence which could have been used in a prosecution against Mr. Kirby. If either Mr. Greenspan, criminal lawyer Clayton Ruby or your editorial are suggesting that Mr. Kirby should simply be locked up without trial, then I can only say that I find your position rather astonishing, to say the least.

The giving of an undertaking not to prosecute is an extremely rarely exercised discretion and one that must be used with great caution only after a careful review of the circumstances. In this case, I am satisfied that the undertaking would not have been given if it had not been clearly in the public interest.

In a more succinct assessment of the facts, McMurtry in a letter to *Maclean's* magazine, published February 21, 1982, said: "The fact is Mr. Kirby was a vicious tool used by organized crime in Canada to enforce its criminal conspiracies. . . . He was turned into a police operative," continued McMurtry, "and, as the police have said, this represented the biggest break in the fight against organized crime in Ontario's history." In a further attack on media reporting of the case, McMurtry slammed the press: "The only thing that the considerable press attention at this time accomplished was to bring an untimely halt to a crucially important probe into the vicious conspiracies of organized crime. That investigation, and not the largely inaccurate publicity, is what was in the public interest." That ended the debate on the Kirby affair for some time.

Two years later, the CBC-TV program *the fifth estate* did the exclusive television interview with Kirby for which the Attorney General was also interviewed. During the interview he forcefully restated the case for giving Kirby immunity ("He literally sent terror ... throughout the ranks of organized crime, and immobilized a lot of the activity that was going on") and revealed for the first time that the immunity agreement for past crimes covered only crimes committed in Ontario (Kirby had also bombed in Montreal and operated in Vancouver) and that giving Kirby a "substantial amount" (hundreds of thousands of dollars) to help him to resettle and relocate had been considered, but this had not been finalized. The program, as mentioned earlier, was shown nationally on the CBC on March 6, 1984, but was blacked out in the Toronto area so as not to affect the continuing proceedings against the Commissos. It was after the airing of this program on Kirby that the Commissos decided to plead guilty to all the charges outstanding against them, based on Kirby's information, in exchange for a reduced sentence and the reduction of charges against their younger brother Michele. The *fifth estate* program on Kirby was then updated and broadcast in the Toronto area on April 25, 1984.

Here is what Cecil Kirby said about the immunity deal on that program when he was questioned by co-host Bob McKeown:

McKEOWN: But you got a pretty good deal, immunity from what you say are a hundred offences, expense money, protection. You've got the promise of a lump sum, and a new identity afterwards.

KIRBY: Yes, but I might die for all of this.

McKEOWN: You wouldn't talk to us unless we paid you. That's not a bad deal, is it?

KIRBY: Well, we all have got to live somehow. I'm not living the life of crime now. I can't. I'm working as a police informant for the RCMP, you know. If they don't want to support me when I'm going to court, what else do I do? Do I go back to a life of crime right now? I can go back out on the street and be a criminal again. I don't know for how long, but I can.

McKEOWN: There are some who would say that the only difference between your life of crime and the life you're now leading as a police informer is that you've got a better deal now. That this is a more lucrative arrangement for you.

KIRBY: No, it's not as lucrative ... because I could be making still more money if I was a criminal on the street. I was making an average of $50,000, $75,000 a year tax-free through criminal activities with these people. I've hurt a lot of people, injured some people.

McKEOWN: Killed people?

KIRBY: Not intentionally.

McKEOWN: Killed people, nonetheless.

KIRBY: Yes, but not intentionally. And now I believe I have done some good. I've saved the lives of three to five people, and possibly more, in the future, that could have been killed by these people.

McKEOWN: This deal whereby you've got immunity for a hundred – by your own admission – a hundred indictable crimes including extortion, arson, assault, killing – whether intentional or not – somebody else, that deal has been called a disgrace. Can you understand how people think that?

KIRBY: Sure I can. They believe I should be hung.

McKEOWN: Should you not be in jail for a very long time?

KIRBY: Well, putting me in jail would be just like hanging me. It would be killing me.... I wouldn't live very long in jail, so they might as well just take me out and get the satisfaction themselves of hanging me, if that's what they want. But then ... by killing me does that stop these people? For punishing me for my crimes, does that stop them? It doesn't. They continue on ...

McKEOWN: In return for all that – the expense money, the protection – what have you given them?

KIRBY: What have I given them? I have succeeded in helping them put fourteen people in jail for over seventy-five years.

McKEOWN: Is it good enough, that because a man like Cecil Kirby is willing to be a stool pigeon, a "rat" in your own phrase ... to turn in his former friends, colleagues, associates, because he sees it as being a better deal than a life of crime, is that enough to get you off the hook? Should immunity be based on something like that? Your whim?

KIRBY: It's immunity. It's ... a time between then, and maybe when I am going to be killed. It's just more time. I've just given myself more time before I'm going to be killed. That's all it is.

McKEOWN: Over what period of time will they be looking for you? When will they forget about Cecil Kirby?

KIRBY: When I'm dead. After I'm dead. A short while after

I'm dead. Contracts don't expire. They are always enforced.

When Kirby was asked what his former mob and biker colleagues would say about him, he replied in typical fatalistic, and probably realistic, fashion: "They would say he's a rat. He deserves to die. That's what they'd tell you. I'll bump into the wrong person one day when he's got a gun on him, and I'll probably be shot. It's a small world sometimes. You can't hide out in a cabin out in the bush all your life."

Kirby has made a very impressive witness in the cases where he has testified. Lawyer Edward Greenspan, who has cross-examined Kirby in several cases, said that Kirby "enjoys the game" of cross-examination and "enjoys being up against the best.... In a funny way, perhaps in another life, Kirby would have made an excellent lawyer," concludes an admiring Greenspan. When Greenspan told Kirby this after one of their sessions in court, Kirby was very pleased by the compliment from his adversary.

But Kirby has some legal problems of his own. The widow of the Chinese cook he inadvertently killed has been thinking of suing him for compensation through the Ontario Criminal Injuries Compensation Board for the death of her husband, and the insurance company for the Chinese restaurant destroyed by Kirby's blast is attempting to retrieve its damages from Kirby through the courts. Kirby responded, in this action, by naming Cosimo and Remo Commisso as "third parties". In a rather amusing statement of claim against the third parties, which he filed in the Supreme Court of Ontario in January 1983, Kirby took the position that, while he may have been the one that blew up the Wah Kew restaurant, he was merely doing so "at the request of and while in the course of his employment" with the Commissos, or the "third parties". In other words, by blowing up places and people for the Commisso crime family, Kirby was simply a conscientious worker doing his job. If anyone is liable for the damages to the building, the Kirby statement of claim goes on to say, then it would be these "third parties", the Commissos, and not a humble employee, Cecil Kirby. The case continues in the courts, though neither the insurance company for Wah Kew nor their lawyers seem particularly anxious to vigorously pursue the matter.

The issues surrounding the Kirby immunity deal and the tactics used by the police in their fight against organized crime remain unresolved. But the real focus of the debate should be not on Kirby or on the granting of immunity, but on the existence, guidelines, and operations of the élite Special Enforcement Unit, for the SEU is now the main police weapon against organized crime in Ontario.

CHAPTER SIXTEEN

Death on a Sunday Afternoon

S UNDAY, NOVEMBER 13, 1983, was a normal working day for Paul Volpe. One of his bodyguards and friends, Tony Iatti, was away on holidays, but he intended to do his rounds anyway. He left his home in the morning, dressed casually in a white T-shirt, corduroy pants, and a light brown jacket. He wasn't wearing a hat as he usually did. He told his wife, Lisa, that he would be home about one that afternoon. As usual, he would take the car, a BMW sedan leased in Lisa's name. His first meeting was with his trusted associate and sometime driver, Mississauga gambler and occasional union organizer Pietro Scarcella. They met at their usual spot, La Sem Patisserie and Pizzeria, in the Woodbridge Mall on Highway 7, at eleven, to discuss an ongoing operation. Then Volpe headed for the airport area to meet some unknown business associates. He was never heard from again.

Cecil Kirby was on a plane on Sunday, November 13, coming in from his hide-away to Toronto to meet with his lawyer and prepare for some testimony. He came through Toronto International Airport (now called Lester Pearson International) and walked right by Paul Volpe's car.

Natie Klegerman was on the lam in Los Angeles, keeping away from Toronto because of outstanding warrants for his arrest for his involvement in a diamond deal and a scam of Chuck

Yanover's against the North Koreans (see Addendum, Part II).

Chuck Yanover himself was a guest of Her Majesty at Kingston Penitentiary for his part in several plots against foreign governments and a bombing in Toronto.

Remo and Cosimo Commisso were also in jail in Kingston, for the aborted Connecticut hit and the first contract on Volpe. They were just about to face a preliminary hearing for the long list of hit and enforcement contracts for which they were charged as a result of Cecil Kirby's confessions to the police. Their lawyer, Eddie Greenspan, had been arguing in court that very week, as part of a "breach of undertaking" suit, that the Crown had reneged on a deal not to charge them again on Kirby's testimony alone. Their younger brother, Michele Commisso, was back on the streets in Toronto, having been released in the spring of 1983.

When Volpe didn't return home at one as he had promised, Lisa Dalholt began to fret. By nightfall he still had not returned, and she had a sleepless night. By seven the next morning, Monday, November 14, she was beside herself. Paul had never stayed out all night without telling her. Not knowing what to do, she called Volpe's lawyer, David Humphrey, and sought his advice. She instructed Humphrey to do what he thought best under the circumstances. So Humphrey did what he considered was the only thing he could do – he immediately called the police. With Paul Volpe's brother Albert in attendance, he met with two Toronto intelligence officers in his office within the hour. Mention was made of the airport rendezvous Paul Volpe was supposed to have had on Sunday. The next thing Humphrey heard from the police was that they had located Volpe's car at the airport parking lot at Terminal 2. The police needed permission to check the trunk. Could he get such permission from Mrs. Volpe? Humphrey phoned Lisa Dalholt and said that the police needed to check the trunk of the car. A routine matter. She agreed. It was early afternoon, November 14.

Barry King deplaned from his Ottawa flight at about four in the afternoon on November 14 and walked towards the car he had left on the second level of Terminal 2's interminable parking garage. Before he could reach the parking bay he was stopped by a Mountie. "I'm sorry, sir, you can't come in here. There's been a murder."

"Well," said King drily, looking at the swarms of police

surrounding the area, "if there's been a murder, you'd better let me in. I'll probably be in charge of the investigation." He pulled out a card that identified him as a police superintendent, head of the homicide department of the Peel Regional Police. His own car, he discovered, was parked opposite the $40,000 1982 grey BMW sedan, licence plate SHK 869, that was now the focus of all the police attention.

Only about an hour earlier, Peel Deputy Chief William Teggart, who in the early 1970s was the first senior Ontario police officer to make public the massive extent of mob activities in Ontario, had shown up at the parking spot, summoned by one of his constables. As Teggart approached the car, the light on the phone in the sedan flashed. The call was for Paul Volpe, but Volpe wasn't about to answer. He was lying in the trunk with at least two small-calibre bullet holes in the back of his head. His white T-shirt was soaked in blood, and there was so much blood caked on his neck that one police observer thought at first that he had been garrotted. He had a serene look on his face. There was no sign of a struggle. He had been dead for some hours.

The killing had been professionally done, though the body appeared to have been moved several times at considerable risk of detection to the killers. Chemical analysis of hair and a piece of fibre found on Volpe's blood-soaked body suggested that there were at least two hit men and possibly a hit woman involved, but this evidence could have been in the car long before the murder, since police forensic people also found traces of animal hairs on Volpe's clothes, probably from his own dogs. It appeared that Volpe was taken by people he trusted in an unguarded moment. There is no doubt that he was murdered early Sunday afternoon, within hours of his Woodbridge luncheon meeting with Scarcella, at some spot away from the airport. The car (most likely with his body already in the trunk) was deposited at the Terminal 2 parking lot before the nightly security check by the RCMP, which keeps computer tabs on all vehicles parked overnight. Since Volpe frequently met people near the airport, usually in a room at a nearby hotel, it was not unusual for his car to be parked there. The car had been discovered Monday at 2:40 P.M., not many hours after Volpe was reported missing, by Peel Regional Constable Linda Herder and OPP Constable Jim McKenzie. At 2:55 P.M., Sergeant Fernandes of the Iden-tification Unit of the Peel Regional Police spotted blood stains on the back fender, opened the trunk with the key provided by Metro police, and discovered the body of Paul Volpe.

The funeral of Paul Volpe, which took place on Thursday, November 17, was intended to be a modest affair by Mafia standards. Only personal friends of Lisa Dalholt, family, and a few mob associates and rounders were invited. It was to be a private event. No major mob figure showed up at the funeral itself, although several mobsters from Hamilton had earlier come to the funeral home. The procession was to start from the Trull Funeral Home at 2701 Yonge Street.

As it happened, Paul Volpe's funeral was to make almost as much news as his murder. The only people who showed up in vast numbers were the media. Since Volpe was a major crime leader, his funeral was to be a media event, and television reporters and cameramen jostled with each other for the best place to shoot videotape and to interview the mourners. Suddenly, as the funeral party was getting into the limousines, a man lunged at one of the cameramen, Dan McIvor of the CBC National news, punching him and kicking him in the crotch. McIvor fell to the ground in great pain. His expensive camera, broken, lay beside him. Sheila MacVicar, the National News reporter, ran to his assistance as other reporters and cameramen screamed for police assistance and videotaped the events. The police, on the scene to escort the funeral procession, were a few minutes in coming, while someone from the media stood in front of the limousine carrying the assailant so that he could not get away. When the police finally arrived on the scene, they ordered an ambulance for McIvor and took the attacker into custody. It was Paul Volpe's sixty-year-old brother, Joseph Anthony Volpe.

It was a very emotionally charged situation. As the police took Joe Volpe in for questioning, he shouted to reporters and cameramen present, "If you put a camera in my face, then I'll put mine [sticking up his fists for the remaining cameras] in yours." As a result of his attack on the CBC cameraman, Joe Volpe missed the funeral of his brother. He was busy being arraigned for assault, for which he was later convicted.

All this drama was prominently carried on the national television news that evening. The attack by Joe Volpe on McIvor made the otherwise quiet funeral a national event. The next day the *Globe and Mail* carried a dramatic picture of Sheila MacVicar hovering over the inert body of her cameraman. The

Volpe funeral was a front-page news story across the country.

By physically attacking the cameraman, Joe Volpe had broken a cardinal rule for conducting a mob funeral, especially one that was designed to be low-key. As a Mafia member was heard to say on a police wire-tap in discussing the incident, "He just drew attention to himself, that's all he did." The mobsters, like everyone else, watched the event on television, and compared the murder to *The Godfather* in their conversations. The funeral of Paul Volpe was a major topic of discussion while they planned the hit on young Domenic Racco, which was to occur just three weeks later. Paul Volpe, even in death, was causing controversy among other mafiosi.

There were other reactions to the murder from mobsters who knew Volpe well. Chuck Yanover, who had worked for Paul Volpe for over eight years, was not particularly grieved by the murder. He saw the events as a matter of setting things straight. "Paul got what he deserved, nice guy or not, since he did what he did when he broke the code of ethics," said Yanover in a letter from jail dated July 20, 1984. He meant that Volpe should not have helped the police in their sting of the Commissos by giving them his wallet and hiding at RCMP headquarters. "Paul was like a whore trying to quit the business. A trick always comes along; it's only a question of price.... It is in the rules and I would expect no different for myself, except I wouldn't be as easy a target." This is a hard line coming from an old Volpe friend and long-time associate.

Ironically enough, hit man Cecil Kirby was more sympathetic to Volpe. Kirby had saved Paul Volpe's life once, and Volpe had saved his life. Reflecting on Volpe's murder, Kirby was gracious: "Yes, I liked Paul Volpe. He never did me any harm. I did him a favour, and he'd do me a favour. I guess we are even now. It's too bad I couldn't save his life again.... I liked the man, even though he was a gangster.... He had a tough image and his own code of ethics, which he broke to help me.... He valued human life, in his way." Later, meditating on why Volpe was killed, Kirby speculated that it had to do with greed and envy, and that the earlier contract of the Commissos against Volpe was simply being fulfilled. "In the mob," Kirby reminded me, "contracts to kill do not expire until the person is dead." And Kirby ought to know. As for his being at the airport the day Volpe's body was deposited there, he said with a smile that it was "just a coincidence ... the world can be very small sometimes."

A veteran police intelligence officer, who had spent many hours following Volpe and listening to his phone calls, took a strangely sentimental view of Volpe's death. It was as if he had lost a personal friend. "Paul didn't deserve to die this way, even though he was a bandit," he solemnly told me. And then he added with a note of irony, "Half the intelligence officers in the city can be laid off now.... Paul engendered that much paperwork."

This is a line that Volpe's own lawyer, Dave Humphrey, took. "The police," he told me, "will miss all that overtime." In clear admiration of his former client, Humphrey added, "He was a very bright, intelligent, engaging person ... [who had] a great capacity for charm and a good sense of humour."

Deputy Chief Bill Teggart, of the Peel Regional Police, who was at the murder scene at the airport and has worked on organized-crime cases for several decades (he led the police investigation that nailed Peter Demeter for the contract murder of his wife), is less in awe of Paul Volpe. "Paul Volpe was an organized criminal; he lived in that jungle and died in it," he says, neatly summing up what to him is a very simple matter. He does not mourn for a "thug" like Paul Volpe.

The massive investigation undertaken by Teggart's homicide department has involved over twenty-five police officers from Peel Regional Police for almost two years under the able direction of Superintendent Desmond Rowland, Staff Inspector Jim Wingate (who worked on solving the Demeter case under Bill Teggart in the 1970s), and Detective-Sergeant Darcy Honer. They have travelled to a number of Canadian and American cities such as Montreal, Atlantic City (where Peel was joined by RCMP analysts), Trenton, N.J., and Philadelphia. The investigation has also involved extensive participation by a number of law-enforcement agencies, including the FBI, organized-crime strike forces in several major U.S. cities, the Montreal police, the New Jersey State Police, the Metropolitan Toronto police, and the RCMP.

It has been an all-out, thoroughly professional investigation that has left no stone unturned. Murder investigations are not new to Peel. As investigating officers have pointed out, there have been fifty-six homicides in the Peel region between 1974 and 1985, including the famous Demeter case, and only two remain unsolved in 1985. Curiously, the two unsolved murders both involve bullet-ridden bodies of people associated with the mob, who have been found in the trunks of their cars at the Toronto airport. The first unsolved mob murder was the 1979 slaying of mob rounder and well-known gambler Eddie Neuff, who was found in his car at the airport, his head riddled with many bullet holes, shortly after he had been heavily involved in some scams with known organized-crime figures in Toronto. Some police officials speculate that the same killers may have done both the Volpe and the Neuff jobs. The body with bullet holes in the head deposited in the trunk of a car at the airport appears to be a kind of executioner's signature.

As for the other unsolved murder, that of Paul Volpe, police have interviewed Volpe's friends, relatives, and associates, and others around the world. While they have interrogated Volpe intimate Angelo Pucci, they have not yet found Nate Klegerman, who is now hiding somewhere in Europe. Lawyer Earl Levy, the president of the Criminal Lawyers' Association, who had lunch with Volpe several days before his death, was interviewed, as were Volpe's widow, Lisa Dalholt, long-time Volpe enforcer Tony Iatti, and many other Volpe acquaintances and intimates. Needless to say, Pietro Scarcella, the one-time Volpe chauffeur and general aide, who was the last person known to see Volpe alive, has been interrogated more than once and watched very closely by police. Others who have been involved with Paul Volpe as both victims and collaborators, in land deals in Toronto and New Jersey, and those involved with Volpe and Klegerman in diamond deals throughout the 1970s and '80s, have also been interviewed and are under constant police scrutiny. Many more remain to be interviewed, such as Harold Bordonaro, a long-time friend of Volpe's, who himself was convicted of a major fraud a month before the Volpe murder, and Chuck Yanover, still in jail for fraud and a bombing. The police have yet to seriously interrogate Remo and Cosimo Commisso on the Volpe murder. They should certainly talk to Michele Commisso, now out on the streets, as well. Very few remain above suspicion in this massive, world-wide police investigation.

In February 1985, an RCMP intelligence analyst completed a top-secret, in-depth report on the murder for the Peel Regional Police. In this lengthy and thorough analysis, the RCMP set out the three most likely theories as to why, how, and by whom Paul Volpe was killed. The Peel police have been seriously following up the leads here as the major focus of their continuing investigation. These scenarios cannot now be revealed without seriously jeopardizing ongoing police operations.

Why was the man of respect killed? In criminal terms, Volpe's weaknesses were showing. The fact that Remo and Cosimo Commisso had ordered Volpe's death in 1981 became public knowledge, and Volpe apparently didn't have the muscle to discipline this breach of respect – or perhaps the will to use it. Many of Volpe's key people were either in jail or on the lam, and in any case he chose to do nothing. Volpe had also lost a good deal of ground through his co-operation with the Mounties over the Kirby contract; in the underworld the feeling was that Volpe was altogether too cosy with the law enforcers. To use his own word, Volpe was in the process of becoming a "stoolie". A week before he was killed, Volpe had a meeting with RCMP intelligence officer Corporal Mark Murphy in his basement office. They had wine and discussed the state of the mob. The encounter was part of a new RCMP intelligence program of talking to gangsters in their homes, and it was not Volpe's first such meeting with Murphy since the aborted hit. Finally, it looked as though Paul Volpe was beginning to inform on some of his criminal colleagues. He was using his new informer role to give the RCMP enough documents and information on one particular associate with whom he was feuding so that this former associate would be charged with a serious crime. The street does not like informers.

In addition to his other problems, Volpe was facing a challenge in Toronto from the Montreal Mafia. Montreal mobsters such as Frank Cotroni were beginning to move into Toronto's boxing, exotic-dance, and union rackets, to Volpe's chagrin but apparent helplessness. Some Montreal mobsters were meeting with certain people at the airport in Toronto, a day before Volpe was killed, to try to pressure them (by brute force, in one case) into allowing Montreal operators into the body-rub parlours near the airport and in Windsor, Ont. They had killed people who had gotten in their way in Toronto before. One Cotroni hit man, Réal Simard, was arrested and convicted of the murder of a wayward mobster at the Seaway Inn in Toronto in November 1983, shortly before the Volpe murder.

This killing had to do with a gangland battle over nude-dancing booking agencies. As well as being a Cotroni killer, Simard was a co-owner of the Prestige Agency, which brought girls into Ontario from Quebec for strip shows, and his victim, Joseph Heroux of Longueuil, Que., was with a rival booking agency. In addition, Simard shot Heroux's associate in the topless-dance business, Robert Hetu, three times, but Hetu survived to testify as the chief witness against Simard at his trial. Some suggest that Simard, who was still on the street in Toronto at the time of the Volpe murder, might have done one last job for the Cotronis before going to jail. It is also known that four men, one with close ties to Frank Cotroni, roughed up and extorted a Windsor-area tavern-and-motel owner named Peter Barth (also known as Peter Belmont) in Brampton on November 12, 1983, just twenty hours before Volpe was killed. The SEU and the Peel Regional Police are looking into a connection here between Montreal activity in Ontario, the Barth beating, and Volpe's death.

Frank Cotroni has been closely allied with Johnny Papalia of Hamilton. Cotroni had been observed by police intelligence meeting with Johnny "Pops", who, though a suspect, is far from the prime suspect. "Papalia is suspect number eleven on a list of the ten most likely suspects," one investigating officer has said. Pops is closely allied with some of Paul Volpe's rivals, including Remo Commisso and other Sidernese leaders.

The Peel investigators are talking frequently to Montreal police to follow up on the Montreal angle to the Volpe murder. Staff Inspector Jim Wingate and his colleague Inspector Noel Catney, the head of Peel Regional Police intelligence, recently spent four days in Montreal discussing facts and scenarios with Montreal police intelligence and homicide units.

There are other credible theories about the killing. For example, New Jersey figures prominently in the top-secret RCMP analysis of the murder. Some say that the Volpe execution had something to do with a falling-out between Volpe and the Bruno Mafia family of New Jersey, over Atlantic City land deals. As we have seen, the old don, Angelo Bruno, and several of his lieutenants had themselves been brutally murdered in the preceding months. Someone in business with Volpe in land deals in Atlantic City could have been trying to get his money back, and killed Volpe in desperation, or someone who had a lot to lose in any ongoing investigation into Volpe's operation in Atlantic City might have wanted him out of the way in case he talked or brought added heat on those deals. The police are certainly taking the New Jersey angles seriously, and are working closely with the FBI and the New Jersey State Police on some very interesting New Jersey leads.

The most obvious explanation for the murder, of course, is Cecil Kirby's theory that the Commissos simply carried through their first contract. This is the scenario that has the most credibility with the police. Remo and Cosimo Commisso cannot be counted out just because they are incarcerated. Organizing murders from jail is certainly not an uncommon occurrence these days. And the Commissos have the kind of reach and muscle in the criminal world of North America that would have made this all too possible. They could have tapped into their hit-man exchange program with U.S. affiliates, just as Domenic Racco did in 1976. Jailed for the attempted murder of Paul Volpe, they certainly had both the motive and the means to carry on with their plan.

There is new, hard wire-tap evidence to support this Commisso involvement in the murder of Volpe, uncovered in the Halton-Hamilton joint-forces operation on the Domenic Racco murder that followed Volpe's murder by three weeks. A close look at the wire-taps of the principals indicate that the hit man hired by Racco's rivals, the Musitanos, was in Collins Bay Penitentiary with Michele Commisso for two years. Domenic Musitano, in discussing the background of the Racco murder with his criminal colleagues, implicates the Commissos in both the Racco and the Volpe murders. Domenic Musitano, in a conversation in jail with his brother Antonio on February 5, 1984, makes this revealing comment: "They [the police] might connect us with each of these.... Yeah, not on that one [the Racco murder] but on the first one too [the Volpe murder?], because they [the Commissos] were supposed to be paying for it, now they won't.... I gotta tell Mike [Michele Commisso, who got out of jail for his part in various Commisso murder conspiracies just before Paul Volpe was murdered]."

It is quite possible that Domenic Musitano is linking the two murders here. Detective-Sergeant Darcy Honer, the head of the Peel homicide department, has said that this section of the tape was "certainly very, very interesting.... Clearly Musitano is carrying on something for the Commissos with respect to Racco's murder.... There seems to be some inference about the Volpe murder, too." Another police source states flatly: "Cleary the Commissos were involved.... They [the Musitanos] certainly seem to be talking about the Volpe killing in relation to their work with the Commissos." This is a lead that Peel is now following as the investigation continues. The Commissos and their Siderno allies are certainly prime suspects in the Volpe investigation.

One of the problems with the theory that the Commissos were behind the Volpe hit is that Remo and Cosimo were facing a preliminary hearing for the series of hit contracts and enforcement activities, brought down on them as a result of Cecil Kirby's evidence. The Commissos' lawyer, Edward Greenspan, was in the process of trying to have the charges dropped against his clients on the basis of an alleged earlier deal with the Crown on the first cases; the deal was that Kirby wouldn't be used as the sole source by the Crown for laying future charges. Greenspan was charging in this "breach of undertaking" suit that the Crown had reneged on this deal, and that therefore his clients could not be charged for these crimes. As a result the Commissos were naturally trying to keep out of trouble at the time: they were trying to present as clean an image as possible. When they were brought to a preliminary hearing session on Tuesday, November 15, 1983, just a day after Paul Volpe's body was discovered, they seemed genuinely disconcerted by the timing of Volpe's murder. It could be that an old hit contract had been executed when they didn't expect it, or their surprise was just an act designed to fool the police who were accompanying them to the hearing. In any case, they certainly realized that it made their current case look hopeless. Also, on January 11, 1984, Judge Arthur Meen found that Edward Greenspan's allegation that there was an undertaking with the Crown was incorrect, a ruling that was later upheld by the Ontario Court of Appeal. As a result the Commissos gave up any real defence against Kirby's new charges.

However, when one lives as Paul Volpe did, there is no end to the possible suspects. For example, Volpe most likely had Ian Rosenberg and Joan Lipson killed in 1977. Revenge for something like this would be a powerful motive for someone close to Ian Rosenberg. Other Volpe victims, as well as relatives of victims, may also have been moved to this ultimate act of revenge.

Still, the three motives under most active police scrutiny are rivalry from the Sidernese factions in Toronto, primarily the Commissos; a falling-out with other organized-crime associates or rivals over some New Jersey land deals; and a conflict or rivalry with the Montreal mob over certain areas of Toronto. A combination of two of these motives is also very possible, for example a Commisso alliance with a Volpe land-deal associate to get rid of Paul Volpe, by this time a police informer against them.

Whatever the actual motives for the Volpe killing, clearly the killers had carefully thought out how to execute the murder and make a swift getaway. One of the killers seems to have been someone Volpe knew well, because he was so clearly taken off guard. It was no accident that the car was found at the airport, as the killers probably made their way back to the States or to Montreal on the first plane out after they deposited the body in the airport parking lot. The execution was well thought out by professional hit men working for criminals who had allowed no margin for error in the murder of such an important organized-crime figure.

In many respects Volpe's killing had become inevitable. Volpe's power, which rested on respect for his connections and for their ability to create mayhem, was eroding. As he climbed the ladder towards respectability, Volpe started to believe his own PR about being a "businessman", and he let his enforcement arm lapse. He undertook a life of crime to achieve acceptance and respectability, and that very desire probably did him in. The lessons of Volpe's death are that retribution is never far away and cannot be evaded, and that brute power is vulnerable to power that is even more determined. Volpe's death closed a certain era in Toronto's underworld; it's difficult to say whether the tougher, harder men who succeeded Volpe will learn or can learn the lessons of his death.

For the police, the files are still very much open. They are hoping against hope that some mob informer or participant will talk. A break could occur at any time, for any number of reasons. Police intelligence units in Canada are keeping a very watchful eye (and ear, as police are currently wire-tapping some of the suspects). As one of the chiefs of the investigation, Staff Inspector Jim Wingate, recently put it, "The majority of this type of murder is solved by someone eventually rolling over [that is, finding an inside source, an informer, who turns on his former criminal colleagues for personal monetary gain or some other advantage such as having charges dropped against himself] at some stage of the game.... It will probably be very costly, too," Wingate added with a touch of resignation, "but we just have to keep plugging away, that's all."

CHAPTER SEVENTEEN

The Fall-out: Life in New Jersey and Death on the Railway Tracks

S HORTLY AFTER Paul Volpe's death, things began to dete-
riorate for some of his associates and rivals. For example,
one Volpe business associate, Angelo Pucci, had to undergo two
major trials based on earlier transactions with Paul Volpe. On
the other side of the coin, one of the mob leaders who put
up money for the 1981 contract on Volpe's life, Domenic Racco,
was taken for the proverbial ride himself, not long after Paul
Volpe's execution.

I) Life in New Jersey
One of Paul Volpe's last land deals, a case that was still pending
at the time of his death, involved the old CITY-TV building
on Queen Street East, owned by one of Pucci's companies. It
was a classic Volpe-Pucci real-estate transaction, involving a cast
of exotic characters and a complex series of deals. It had all
started when Angelo Pucci and Paul Volpe decided to sell some
of their considerable Toronto land and building holdings in order
to put more money into Atlantic City. Paul Volpe approached
a real-estate wheeler-dealer associate by the name of Vince
Salvatore to find a buyer for the CITY-TV building, one of their
more lucrative properties. Salvatore, who lives, according to his
lawyer Earl Levy, "like a king, in a huge property that requires
nine furnaces," came up with buyers from Indonesia, who were

represented by Mississauga lawyer Sam Wetston. From this point on things got rather complicated.

Wetston signed the offer for $4.5 million. Then he forged another offer to show his clients, stating the price at $5.9 million, hoping thus to pocket a neat $1.4 million for himself. (Wetston, needless to say, was disbarred and sentenced to a jail term of two years after this affair became public.) So the Indonesian money intended for Paul Volpe and his associate Angelo Pucci went through a crooked lawyer, through the arrangements of a flamboyant Italian intermediary, who got a hefty commission for the deal. To guarantee his commission, Salvatore registered the mortgage, which was assigned to Durham Realty, Volpe's company. One police investigator says of Salvatore's business style, "The guy can't even purchase a cup of coffee without putting at least five mortgages on it." The Indonesian buyers put a $200,000 deposit on the deal, which went to Salvatore and then to Pucci as a mortgage advance. All the papers for this series of transactions were left in the custody of the one party that all sides trusted: Paul Volpe. This deal was agreed upon in January 1981.

The plot thickened when Angelo Pucci requested a delay in the execution of the deal for tax reasons, and later accused Wetston of not living up to the agreement. Pucci then made another deal to sell the property to the Sunshine Group and then to Dylex and others. Salvatore found out about this second sale of the same property and obtained a Certificate of Lis Pendens, which he registered against the title to the property to hold up the second sale. There was then a meeting between Pucci and Salvatore, during which Pucci offered Salvatore $200,000 and another piece of property in Midland. Meanwhile the original papers stayed with Paul Volpe, who was now unavailable, since he was by this point in jail for ninety days for illegal possession of wire-tap equipment. Volpe, of course, had an interest in the original deal closing, as he was to get part of Salvatore's sizeable commission.

So Salvatore, Wetston, and Volpe wanted the original deal to go through, but Pucci wanted the second deal to go through. Pucci's lawyers sent Volpe a letter requesting the original papers back in a sealed envelope. Volpe, in turn, took the papers to his own lawyer, John Rosen. Meanwhile, the people behind the Indonesian money found out about the second sale of the property and went to the Peel Regional Police (several of the principals were resident in Peel). As a result of the mess, Vince Salvatore, Paul Volpe, and Angelo Pucci were charged with conspiracy to commit fraud and theft (of the $200,000 mortgage advance money).

When the whole complex matter finally came to trial in the spring of 1984, Paul Volpe was already dead. Salvatore and Pucci were acquitted of the charges. The second sale of the CITY-TV building went through.

Meanwhile, Operation Condor, the New Jersey State Police effort to keep the Volpe group out of Atlantic City, had continued. On January 4, 1984, after many years of investigating the transactions surrounding many of the land transfers made by Paul Volpe and his associates in New Jersey, and acting under the specific orders of the governor and the superintendent of the state police, New Jersey authorities were finally able to get a grand jury to return an eleven-count indictment against Angelo Pucci. Since Paul Volpe had been murdered six weeks earlier, his name was dropped from the indictment.

What happened next is a perfect example of how the American criminal justice system ends up in conflict with itself, and operates to frustrate the objectives of the laws it is supposed to administer. The sequence of events went unnoticed by the media and by certain high-level police officials.

When the indictment came down, the New Jersey Attorney General's office was very proud and issued a press release about the catch:

Attorney General Irwin I. Kimmelman announced today the indictment of an Atlantic City real estate investor who is a Canadian citizen on charges of evading personal and corporate income taxes by filing false corporate returns and by failing to file personal tax returns.

Donald R. Belsole, Director of the State Division of Criminal Justice, identified the defendant as Angelo Pucci, 614 Delavan Avenue, Margate, New Jersey. Also indicted was Pucci's corporation, Topland Holdings, Ltd., 440 Guarantee Trust Building, Atlantic City.

Colonel Clinton L. Pagano, Superintendent of State Police, said Topland Holdings was a partner in a real estate venture with a corporation owned by the late Paul Volpe, another

Canadian citizen, who was found murdered on November 14, 1983, in Toronto.

Both Belsole and Pagano said the investigation is continuing into real estate transactions in Atlantic City and into potential tax violations.

Belsole said the 11-count State Grand Jury indictment, which was handed up today, charged Pucci with six counts of evading personal income taxes; Pucci and his corporation with two counts of filing false and fraudulent corporate returns; Pucci with two counts of false swearing by virtue of signing false corporate tax returns; and Pucci with one count of acting under a void corporate charter....

The matter was investigated by the Intelligence Unit of the State Division of Taxation, by the Casino Intelligence Unit of the State Police and by the Casino Prosecutions Section of the Division of Criminal Justice. The evidence in the case was presented to the State Grand Jury by Deputy Attorney General Helen E. Szabo.

Pucci and his lawyer rushed into action. They plea-bargained with the Attorney General's office and managed to have the eleven-count indictment reduced to one count – namely of acting under a void corporate charter – to which he pleaded guilty. This "crime" was of a highly technical nature; basically, Pucci or his accountant forgot to update the paperwork on the company with a state office. It was just the kind of small thing that the state police were counting on in Operation Condor to get at some organized-crime associates. But this guilty plea was dismissed after six months when Pucci's attorneys applied for implementation of New Jersey's Pre-Trial Intervention Program (PTI) for first offenders. PTI results in the technical exoneration of the accused and wipes away any record of the conviction after six months. Thus Pucci successfully avoided actually having a conviction on the books, and any record of operating under a void corporate charter was crossed off the books in July 1985. Pucci then successfully applied for "L-1" status, which means that he is an investor representing a Canadian business in the United States. The L-1 status allows Pucci to go back and forth and live anywhere in the United States until December 1986, when the status comes up for another three-year renewal.

Now Angelo Pucci is happily living and working on real-estate deals right in Atlantic City with the apparent blessing of the office of the Attorney General, who admitted that "we didn't get him on much." It is very difficult for the average, honest, law-abiding, unconnected Canadian who wants to work in the United States to get a visa or a green card. However, Pucci managed to get his L-1, even though he was technically guilty of operating under a void corporate charter and was a known associate of a major Canadian mafioso – and even though he was considered an undesirable by the state. Colonel Pagano, who was unaware of the sequence of events surrounding Pucci's plea-bargaining until he was interviewed in his office in Trenton, N.J., on February 4, 1985, was shocked to find out the disposition of the case. He stated that the PTI system was "for first offenders, to reduce the calendar of the court and not for this type of situation." Pagano went on to say that the Volpe-Pucci incursion into Atlantic City-area real estate was "not a Mom and Pop squabble on Saturday night" – which is what PTI is meant for – but a very expensive investigation into organized crime." Clearly outraged, Pagano continued: "PTI was not meant for people like Angelo Pucci, and I am not happy about it." Still, he doesn't think that all the police operations were in vain. "We interrupted a lot of this activity [the buying and selling of land in and around Atlantic City] by organized crime, including the Volpe activity, because a number of investors backed away after the media exposure."

The U.S. Department of Immigration and the federal organized-crime strike force in New Jersey are currently investigating Angelo Pucci's immigration status with a view to finding a way to get him out of the country and back to Canada before the PTI is in full effect. According to Immigration special agent John Drastal of the Newark strike force, the American immigration authorities are deferring to the request of the Internal Revenue Service that they be allowed to proceed with an investigation of Pucci before steps are taken to seek Pucci's deportation from the United States. An IRS special agent, also on the special federal organized-crime task force operating out of Newark, is currently reviewing the Pucci file. If the IRS doesn't charge Pucci, then Immigration will move to challenge his L-1 visa status on the basis of Pucci's close association with Paul Volpe. There is even some talk in New Jersey of trying to turn Pucci into an informer, or "turning him around", to work for the task force, but this appears a long shot. Pucci does not have a green card, which allows a Canadian permanent residence in the United States, and he is unlikely to be offered one under the circumstances, according to Immigration and police sources in New Jersey.

So much for Operation Condor. The whole Volpe-Pucci matter is currently under study by the federal organized-crime strike force. Whether the Internal Revenue Service or the U.S. Department of Immigration will be any more successful than the State of New Jersey has been is anyone's guess. With some difficulty, it might be possible for the U.S. government to overturn the decision of the New Jersey Attorney General's office to allow Pucci to live and work in Atlantic City.

II) Death on the Railway Tracks

Meanwhile, Paul Volpe's execution had other consequences as things started to fall apart for some of Volpe's rivals. Within three weeks of the murder of Volpe, a Hamilton mob faction run by Hamilton bakery store owner Domenic Musitano, who is allied to Volpe's old friends the Luppinos, decided to take out Domenic Racco, who was moving in on their drug trade.

Domenic Musitano, with the assistance of his nephew Giuseppe Avignone, owned and operated D&M Scrapyard on Beach Road at Woodward in Hamilton. Anthony Musitano, Domenic Musitano's brother, who was serving a life term in the Millhaven maximum-security prison for conspiracy to possess explosive substances, continued to offer advice and counsel to the group on mob business. In fact, it was on the premises of the Millhaven Penitentiary in Bath, Ont., that the conspiracy to murder Domenic Racco began to unfold.

The conspiracy and the events that followed can be clearly reported since wire-tap authorizations – obtained for a completely separate investigation into the Musitanos' drug activities by the Hamilton-Wentworth Regional Police, the Halton Regional Police, the Ontario Provincial Police, and the RCMP – intercepted and recorded many conversations that took place at Domenic Musitano's residence at 48 Colborne Street in Hamilton, at D&M Scrapyard, and at Anthony Musitano's cell and the visiting area at Millhaven Penitentiary. In all, sixty-one conversations were recorded, and these formed the basis of the Crown's successful case against the Musitanos for Domenic Racco's murder. The conspiracy to murder Racco was allowed to proceed, as the police were unclear about the meaning of the evidence they had gathered, and prior to Domenic Racco's death they had no suspicion that he was about to be murdered.

However, the police did know something was up. Paul Volpe's murder and funeral is discussed by Racco's killers as they plan the hit – as a kind of positive reinforcement. While Racco's murder is probably unrelated (though the Commissos' name comes up in the planning of the murder and there are references to the Volpe murder by the conspirators), having to do with a squabble over Hamilton drug territory and money, the general climate in Toronto and southern Ontario set by Paul Volpe's murder certainly made it a lot easier to go ahead with the killing of this son of one of the most respected Mafia leaders in Canada, the late Mike Racco. Of course, the very fact of Mike Racco's death in 1980, of cancer, also made it easier, and young Domenic, with his drug-taking and his bad temper, was becoming a bit of a wild card in organized crime in southern Ontario.

The nature of mob relations in southern Ontario follows a clearly defined hierarchy. The Musitanos would never have moved against Mike Racco's son without first having sought the counsel and permission of a higher authority, most likely the Commisso family of Toronto and other senior Sidernese Mafia leaders.

Conversations initially recorded between Domenic Racco and Domenic Musitano were clearly discussions about some illegal transaction, and they also made clear that Domenic Racco owed the Musitanos a large sum of money, which the Musitanos were having a difficult time collecting. On November 21, 1983, Giuseppe Avignone visited his uncle, Tony Musitano, in Millhaven, accompanied by Musitano associate Giuseppe Chiarelli. Their concern about Domenic Racco, "the one from Toronto", had reached a boiling point. Avignone's suggestion that "we'll take him for a ride" met with general acceptance. The recent murder and funeral of Toronto mobster Paul Volpe had set a precedent for them to follow. The discussion then turned to who would do the job.

CHIARELLI: ... Who's gonna do it?
AVIGNONE: ... It's up to you.
MUSITANO: What's the name ... Mike?
CHIARELLI: He can't do it no more, Tony.

MUSITANO: His brother?

AVIGNONE: No – Rosario is too scared ...

Tony Musitano then suggests an acquaintance from Millhaven who knows Michele Commisso, who was due out on December 7 and who might be interested in the job.

AVIGNONE: Um, tell this guy when he comes down to kill him he owes me nothing.

MUSITANO: He can look after that when he comes out, that's no problem. ...

AVIGNONE: Tell him ... [inaudible] tell him we gotta that [pause; inaudible] you guys want December 7th?

MUSITANO: Uh ...

AVIGNONE: For December the 7th?

MUSITANO: Yeah.

AVIGNONE: Tell him to get a hold of me as soon as he comes out – the next night after that he's happy.

MUSITANO: I guess Hanrahan's is busy, eh [pause]. I'll give him the number of the yard?

AVIGNONE: Yeah the number of the yard, tell him to call me.

MUSITANO: You gonna be at the yard?

AVIGNONE: I'll be at the yard the next day. I'll be at the yard when he calls if anything goes. ...

Between November 21 and December 7, a flurry of conversations between Racco and Musitano indicated that the problems between them needed to be dealt with. A meeting was arranged for December 7 at the Holiday Inn on Trafalgar Road in Oakville, midway between Toronto and Hamilton. Earlier that afternoon, William Rankin, who was to play a major role in the killing of Racco, was released from Millhaven Penitentiary on parole under mandatory supervision. He was the only prisoner released that day. Two women and a man met Rankin and took him to Hamilton in a rented brown Pontiac station wagon.

Meanwhile, the December 7 meeting between Racco and Domenic Musitano, monitored by the police, took place. They did not resolve their differences, and they agreed to meet again the following evening.

On the afternoon of December 8, Rankin and a companion, Peter Majeste, left their women friends in a motel in Hamilton and drove to the Holiday Inn in Oakville to meet a drug connection of Rankin's. Unable to find the connection, Majeste and Rankin returned to Hamilton.

At about the same time, in Millhaven, Tony Musitano received visitors, Giuseppe Avignone, Joe Spanno, Vince Nicoletti, and Joe Chiarelli. The upcoming hit was discussed in further detail.

AVIGNONE: Tonight we are busy eh? Don't you two disappear.

MUSITANO: What's on tonight?

AVIGNONE: Going for a ride. Just in case, you know just in case we forget to [inaudible]. . . . So you are sure this guy knows what he has gotta do? That bastard's not going to get it all cash after he does it.

MUSITANO: Yeah, well I hope so you know.

AVIGNONE: Well, when you told him half up front.

MUSITANO: Well you can work that out with him Thursday?

AVIGNONE: He's gonna come around and . . .

MUSITANO: I know. He knows that. He knows nothin's for free. . . .

That evening William Rankin and Peter Majeste returned to the Holiday Inn in Oakville, where Domenic Racco was meeting with Domenic Musitano. Majeste stayed in the car while Rankin went in to make positive identification of Racco. The pair then staked out Domenic Racco's apartment at 1333 Bloor Street West in Mississauga, obviously intending to kill him when he returned home. Giuseppe Avignone and some other Musitano associates waited nearby in another car. But Domenic Racco escaped his fate that night, for instead of going home, he spent the night at his sister's.

On the morning of Friday, December 9, Racco visited his lawyer, Meyer Feldman, and received a cheque for $21,506.83, the proceeds from a mortgage on some property owned by Racco that used to house the family bakery business on St. Clair Avenue West in Toronto. He deposited $1,000 in his account and took the rest in cash and an $8,000 certified cheque. Just prior to his meeting with Musitano, scheduled for nine that evening, Racco checked in with his parole officer at RCMP headquarters in Toronto, and then he headed to Oakville. The meeting with Musitano was short, and Musitano left Racco sitting in the bar of the hotel.

Witnesses later placed Rankin's brown station wagon in front of Racco's apartment late at night on December 9 and in the early-morning hours of Saturday, December 10. At half past midnight, Racco phoned his girl-friend, but her mother told him she was not in. From evidence presented by the Crown "it can be ascertained that sometime subsequent to 12:30 A.M., Domenic Racco returned to 1333 Bloor St. West. He parked his car in the front parking lot at this apartment and, as he exited his car, Racco was forcibly abducted and taken to an area north of Derry Road in the Town of Milton by William Rankin and at least one other person." Three sets of footprints were found leading to Racco's body, which was discovered at 10:30 A.M. on Saturday, December 10, 1983, lying across an abandoned railway spur. Only two sets of footprints led away from the scene. Domenic Racco had been shot five times at close range in the head and chest with a .38-calibre hand-gun. The body was supposed to have been hidden in an abandoned shed about half a mile up from the place where it was actually found, and where the Musitanos figured it would not be discovered until the spring at the earliest. However, Rankin and his associate had botched this part of the job. The awkward placing of the body in plain view was to cause problems, and eventually helped lead the police to the killers.

At 9:22 A.M. Saturday, after the murder but before Racco's body had been found, Rankin reached Avignone, his contact with the Musitano group, at the D&M Scrapyard, and said, "I've got to talk to you." A meeting was set up at the Tim Horton doughnut shop on King at Caroline Street in Hamilton. Rankin demanded his payment of $20,000. As the Musitanos had discussed in Millhaven, not all of it was going to be in cash and not all of it was to be delivered at once.

By Monday, December 12, the news of Domenic Racco's murder was in the headlines. In spite of this, Domenic Musitano tried to pass Racco's certified cheque for $8,000 to Edward Greenspan, the Toronto lawyer. Musitano had counted on the body not being discovered for some time, but of course this was not the case, and he still needed the money to pay Greenspan, who was acting for Tony Musitano in his appeal from a conviction for a nasty series of bakery bombings in the Hamilton area from 1976 to 1980. They were part of a protection-extortion racket for which Tony Musitano was eventually sentenced to life. Domenic Musitano sent his nephew Giuseppe Avignone to Greenspan's office with the cheque, after phoning the office to say that Avignone was coming. The police, of course, had Avignone under surveillance and followed him to Greenspan's office. Greenspan was not in, so Avignone presented Francesca Briggs, Greenspan's secretary and assistant, with the cheque, made out to D. Racco. However, the signatures endorsing the cheque on the front and back were different, showing that Musitano had not received it from Racco himself. Rankin had taken the cheque from Racco's body after he killed him. After consulting with Greenspan by phone, Francesca Briggs explained to Avignone that Racco, a former client of Greenspan's, had been murdered over the weekend, and they could not accept the cheque. Avignone became excited and nervous and said, "I don't know anybody by that name. I don't know anyone that was murdered. I know nothing about any murder. I don't know anything about it, I am just a messenger." Avignone became so distraught he had to be shown out of the office, as he almost went in the wrong direction.

However, despite this bungling, the police were still not certain of the Musitanos' conspiracy against Racco. Edward Greenspan could not co-operate with the police in the course of their investigation, as he was prohibited from disclosing information required by the police by virtue of solicitor-client privilege. Greenspan takes a strict, legalistic view of dealings with the police when it concerns clients. "Any transaction between a lawyer and his client is privileged, until a court determines otherwise," says Greenspan, and he adds, "We [lawyers] are duty bound not to run off to the police.... You must presume it is privileged." Greenspan also says that he "wouldn't give them [the police] an interview" unless he were subpoenaed and ordered to do so by the courts. Francesca Briggs left Greenspan's employment within three days of these events. She had been specifically cautioned by Greenspan on the importance of lawyer-client privilege, but she nevertheless allowed herself to be interviewed by the police about the cheque. This was against the express orders of her former boss, who now says flatly: "Francesca Briggs had no business talking to the police." Until they interviewed

Briggs, the police did not know about the cheque, which to this day has never surfaced. Greenspan now maintains that he would never accept a cheque signed by a client who had since died, "whether from natural causes or as a result of murder." (Edward Greenspan himself adheres rigorously to tradition and to strict guidelines for running his criminal law practice. He follows the English legal tradition and will not, for instance – unlike many other criminal lawyers in Canada – socialize with a client, if he can reasonably avoid it.)

The involvement of the Musitanos in Racco's death slowly became more evident to police over the next two months (though they did follow other avenues of investigation as well), as hit man Rankin's erratic behaviour became more and more of a problem for the Musitanos. He hung around Hanrahan's Tavern in Hamilton, drinking and bragging about his "connections". Rankin even told his parole officer he was working for D&M Scrapyard. Given a brown Dodge by Avignone as partial payment for his assignment, Rankin had a serious accident in Hamilton on December 22. The vehicle, travelling in the south curb lane, suddenly swerved into the centre lane, then crossed back to the curb lane, striking a telephone pole. Rankin and two of the occupants fled the scene, but a fourth person, James Dixon, was left trapped in the vehicle. The plates on the car were stolen, but the car ownership was still traced back to D&M Scrapyard. The Musitanos did not need this kind of attention.

Meanwhile, Rankin's friend Peter Majeste was arrested for driving without a licence in the brown Pontiac station wagon that was seen in front of Racco's apartment on the evenings of December 8 and 9, 1983. The car was seized because of the overdue rental on it, and this gave police and the Centre of Forensic Sciences a chance to examine fibre samples that were taken from the seats. After a comparison with clothing worn by Domenic Racco at the time of his death, it was found that there were wool and animal fibres from Racco's clothes on the seat of the car, and polyester fibres from the upholstery of the car seat on the jacket worn by Domenic Racco.

It was Rankin's increasingly persistent demands for money that led to the following conversation between Domenic Musitano and Giuseppe Avignone:

MUSITANO: What's he say? What's up?

AVIGNONE: He said he'll be there at eleven o'clock tonight.

MUSITANO: Alright, as long as it's done right. I told him that.

AVIGNONE: I told him, if the fucking thing is on, the money you're going to get paid [inaudible]. What the fuck, he lost the muffler already.

MUSITANO: [inaudible]

AVIGNONE: [whispers] We kill him. Well if he does, that's that. If he does that, you know, once we know he does [whispers] we gotta kill him. . . .

The surveillance by the police was becoming increasingly obvious to the Musitanos and they were becoming nervous. A family conference was held at Millhaven Penitentiary on February 5, 1984, with Domenic Musitano in attendance:

TONY MUSITANO: Yeah, been busy.

DOMENIC MUSITANO: Ah everything's quiet. A lot of heat.

TONY: Yeah I've been reading the paper with that guy there.

DOMENIC: Ah fuck, he's crazy.

TONY: Huh?

DOMENIC: Listen, why'd these guys ever send that fuckin' guy to do it, to work for them?

TONY: Who?

DOMENIC: That guy you sent down, that fuckin' apple – what's his name?

TONY: I dunno.

DOMENIC: Billy-y-y.

TONY: Yeah, yeah yeah.

DOMENIC: He's going around Hamilton braggin' that he worked for them [the Commissos].

TONY: Oh yeah!

DOMENIC: I ain't, if they connect him with me, it will come down on your fucking head. . . . I'm tired of giving him the money.

TONY: Twenty thou . . .

DOMENIC: Ah – and now – they worked back his name.

TONY: Screws [street slang for the police]?

DOMENIC: Screws. . . . But I heard this before that he [Rankin] goes out in Hamilton braggin' in the fuckin' joints, you know, bars, that he is working for the Commissos so ah . . .

TONY: Cuz he was in with Michael [Michele Commisso].

DOMENIC: I don't know who he was in with, I'm just telling

you, tell those guys [the Commissos], if the guy goes near them, he's no fuckin' good. He's N.G. – period.... Drunk. Drunk every day – smashed my car – everything else.

Despite Domenic Musitano's threats to take care of Rankin, and his efforts (monitored by the police) to find out where Rankin was staying in Hamilton, events dragged on unresolved for another month until the unlucky Rankin had another entanglement with a telephone pole while driving a car. In the back seat police found a photograph of Rankin with Tony Musitano that had been taken in Millhaven Penitentiary, with a significant message on the back: "Domenic: As you can see your brother sends his *respect* with me to you. Yes, he's the person I listen to and respect. His words and mine concur. No other person, family or otherwise. You were told to help me so please do not ever attempt to project the illusion that I am responsible to you. Talk to Tony. Capice! Bill."

This handwritten note proved to the police that Rankin was working under the direct orders of the Musitanos. Also, because it was signed by Rankin himself, the photograph and message on the back became valuable potential evidence against Rankin and both of the Musitanos. Up to this point, the police evidence had been based on wire-taps and mere circumstantial evidence.

The evidence had finally accumulated to the point where the police and the Crown were ready to move. On March 20, 1984, warrants were issued for the arrest of Giuseppe Avignone, Tony Musitano, Domenic Musitano, and William Rankin for murder and conspiracy to commit murder. A search conducted at 48 Colborne Street located two loaded hand-guns under the basement staircase. Both were .38-calibre; one was a Smith & Wesson, later determined to have been the weapon that fired the bullets that killed Domenic Racco.

All of those arrested pleaded guilty to charges of conspiracy to commit murder in a Milton courtroom on February 18, 1985, and were sentenced to prison terms of five to twelve years. In the sentencing, Mr. Justice Coulter Osborne stated: "It was apparent that other persons than the accused decided that Domenic Racco must be killed." Judge Osborne was, of course, referring to the senior Hamilton and Toronto Mafia men who, according to the etiquette of the Mafia, must have sanctioned the hit of the son of one of the most respected dons of southern

Ontario. Significantly, Judge Osborne did not name these co-conspirators, even though the police wire-taps and bugs do suggest that the Commisso crime family of Toronto had some involvement in the planning of the killing. Other dons in southern Ontario, especially in Hamilton, were also consulted. There is no doubt that the earlier murder of Paul Volpe made the taking out of Domenic Racco much easier. The climate in Toronto was becoming one of violent, final solutions to various mob rivalries.

CHAPTER EIGHTEEN

The Mob
in Transition

T HE PAUL VOLPE organization is now totally shattered.
Nathan Klegerman is on the lam, hiding in Israel or
in Antwerp, according to the latest intelligence (though he spent
some time in Los Angeles before he went overseas), avoiding
the charges awaiting him in Toronto on a caper with Yanover
and yet another diamond fraud. He's sure to be out of town
for a long while. Yanover is in jail and awaiting a new trial
for his alleged role in the bombing of a Toronto disco.* Angelo
Pucci, having avoided a record through the graciousness of the
New Jersey justice system, is safely ensconced in Atlantic City,
buying and selling real estate while supervising his Toronto real-
estate empire from afar. Ian Rosenberg is dead, brutally murdered
along with his girl-friend Joan Lipson.

Murray Feldberg, a Volpe loan shark, and Ron Mooney, a
Volpe card man and professional thief, have both died recently,
of natural causes. According to the latest word on the street,
Raymond "Squeaker" Greco, a long-time Volpe enforcer, Toronto
drug dealer, and all-round thug, is now living and operating
(mostly on stock frauds and drugs) out of Amsterdam. Other
Volpe stalwarts still live in Toronto, such as Sam Shirose, the

---

*In the late seventies Yanover struck out on his own. For a look at the adventures of this
engaging rogue, see Addendum, Part II.

card man, Tony Iatti, Volpe's long-time bodyguard and enforcer, Pietro Scarcella, the associate who remains the last person known to have seen Volpe alive, and the three Volpe brothers who remain in Canada, including Albert Volpe (who lately has been trying to get his Yugoslavian casino going again). But with Paul Volpe gone, the heart and brains of the Volpe group are gone as well, and the group is in total disarray.

Within weeks of Volpe's murder, as we have seen, Domenic Racco was himself brutally murdered. But there are other mob groups to look at in Ontario and Canada.

The senility of old man Giacomo Luppino, the elder don of southern Ontario, was confirmed in the fall of 1984 by the annual report of the Criminal Intelligence Service of Canada to the police chiefs' annual meeting in Niagara Falls, Ont.: "The senility of another leader [Don Giacomo Luppino] has contributed to important organized crime contacts being disrupted between Hamilton, Ontario, and Buffalo, New York."

But Giacomo's sons, Paul Volpe's old friends Jimmy, Antonio, and Natale Luppino and their brothers, Rocco and John Luppino, are still very much on the scene, able and willing to play a role in the criminal life of southern Ontario. They also have excellent connections in the old country. Significantly, their brother-in-law, Domenic Rugolo, is currently active in the Mafia in Calabria.

Another of Paul Volpe's old friends, and his one-time sponsor in the Mafia, Hamilton lawyer Harold Bordonaro (born Ignazio Bordonaro, the son of old Mafia don Calogero "Charlie" Bordonaro, who was arrested in Hamilton in 1922 for his participation in Black Hand bombings), who has been living in Toronto since 1979, has fallen on hard times as well. In October 1983, shortly before Paul Volpe's murder, he was busted, with two other lawyers and a land developer from Hamilton named Frank Silvestri, for a sophisticated land development fraud in Welland, Ont., involving close to a million dollars in mortgage funds. He is now serving a 3½-year sentence in jail. But Bordonaro is far from finished. His father was an important old don, he is closely associated with all the mob powers in the Toronto-Hamilton area, including Johnny "Pops" and the Luppinos, and his emergence from jail will be closely watched by both police intelligence and his colleagues in the Mafia. Bordonaro may yet emerge as one of the key players in organized crime in southern

Ontario, now that he doesn't have to play at being straight.

Bordonaro may well have more finesse and strength than Johnny "Pops" Papalia, who carries on in Hamilton and Toronto after yet another lengthy prison term. Coincidentally, shortly after Pops got out of prison in 1982 for an extortion conducted with Vic Cotroni and Paolo Violi, the victim in the case, Stanley Bader, who had testified against these mob bosses in 1976, was shot to death in his Florida retreat after receiving a phone call that warned him: "Look over your shoulder – you won't live out the week.... This is revenge for five years ago." Pops is no angel, and it is rumoured that the Bader murder may have been his calling card. Pops has a long memory and a long reach. Yet muscle alone is not enough, and he lacks the tact of some other mob bosses in Canada. He is also getting on in years, after close to five decades in organized crime.

Harry Bordonaro also has a real chance to emerge as a major force because of the recent incarceration of Frank Cotroni of Montreal, who had long been planning a big move into Toronto and Ontario. Frank Cotroni's power is further eroded by the fact that his older brother, Vic Cotroni, who had been the Godfather of Montreal since the 1940s, died of cancer in September 1984, at seventy-four. Frank Cotroni is now behind bars awaiting a trial for drug importation in Connecticut, which will probably put him away for another ten years, considering he already has a long record for drug trafficking.

Sicilian mafioso Nick Rizzuto, who had Paolo Violi killed in 1978, has now displaced Cotroni as the Godfather of the Montreal Mafia and as the "man of respect" in a city with a long history of mob activity. But at this moment, Rizzuto has his hands full, consolidating his position and respect in Montreal, where he spends three months a year, and in Venezuela, where he lives and runs a business during the rest of the year. He is too busy to concern himself with an Ontario take-over.

However, there is still the powerful Siderno group in Toronto, some of whom are closely allied to Nick Rizzuto and others in the Montreal Mafia. Killers Remo and Cosimo Commisso are safely in jail for at least the rest of the 1980s for their numerous conspiracies to murder. Remo Commisso was recently moved from Kingston Penitentiary in Ontario to a Quebec prison, Archambault Penitentiary, after a drug incident in jail involving his brother. This move is making it a bit more difficult for

Commisso to run things back home; however, it is now a lot easier for him to liaise and plan ongoing and future operations with his connections in the Montreal Mafia. The younger Commisso brother, Michele, now in his late thirties, is already out on the street in Toronto.

There are also a number of other serious men in the Siderno group willing to take power since the deaths of Mike and Domenic Racco and the imprisonment of the Commissos. There is Rocco Zito, an old associate of both Nick Rizzuto of Montreal and Tomasso Buscetta of Italy (the Sicilian Mafia boss who is spilling the beans in Palermo, causing so many problems for the Mafia in Italy and the United States), who in 1969 worked with Zito on drug importation in Toronto. And there is Giuseppe Indelicato, who, though Sicilian, is in the Siderno group and is a friend of Zito's. He is also a well-established crime figure in Toronto, having served time in the 1960s with Johnny "Pops" for heroin importation. There is also Eugenio Rocco Scopelliti, a fifty-year-old convicted drug-trafficker with some clout in the Sidernese Mafia. And long-time Sidernese boss Cosimo Stalteri is waiting in the wings in Toronto, though he is still wanted in Italy on a manslaughter charge. There are many, many more, too numerous to mention here, in the Calabrian and Sicilian crime groups in the Toronto area, who may yet emerge as major figures.

It may also be interesting to watch the fall-out from the recent death, in May 1985, of seventy-five-year-old don Santo Scibetta, scion of the old southern Ontario Mafia family (his brother Joseph Scibetta was involved in extortion activities in Hamilton and Buffalo in the 1920s), a major don in his own right, and an old friend and supporter of Harold Bordonaro and the Luppinos. He had been observed many times meeting with Giacomo Luppino and Charlie Bordonaro, two of the oldest dons of southern Ontario, and he once even accompanied these senior mafiosi on a visit to Buffalo to see don Stefano Magaddino, the Godfather of Buffalo and northern New York State and the long-time head of the Mafia's ruling commission in the United States. In the 1970s, as a "businessman", Scibetta accompanied Premier William Davis on his trade trip to Italy. Whoever inherits his mantle of "respect" in Hamilton and southern Ontario will be worth watching closely. It could be Harold Bordonaro when he emerges from jail in 1986.

And then there are the many Sicilian drug importers who

connect directly to Palermo and live very unobtrusively in Toronto and other centres in southern Ontario, quietly importing and distributing heroin and other narcotics. Some of these even live in such small cities as St. Catharines and Welland. Any one of them could emerge from the shadows as a major figure on the Mafia scene in the Toronto-Hamilton area.

There is obviously lots of Mafia leadership material left in Ontario and Quebec for the tradition to continue.

However, the murder of Paul Volpe does mark the end of an era in organized crime in Toronto and southern Ontario. This is not to say that things would not have changed anyway, but only that the death of Paul Volpe and the events that followed accelerated a turning point in criminal life. The days of the ascendancy of the "respected" Mafia leader in Canada, whether Italian-born or Italian-Canadian, are really numbered. In fact the prominence of the Mafia in organized crime in Toronto and southern Ontario is itself seriously under the gun, both figuratively and literally. This is not only a Toronto and southern Ontario phenomenon; it is a North American phenomenon as well. This does not mean that the Mafia is close to death, for the Mafia is alive and well in most major cities across the continent, in spite of the world-wide offensive against it by the FBI and the U.S. government; by the Italian government and the Pope; by the Crime Probe in Quebec (where the death of Vic Cotroni has left a major void in national and international connections, though smaller men are vying for his power and respect); and by the SEU in Ontario. However, other forces are taking a bigger piece of the organized-crime action in Toronto and in large American cities. These include the Chinese and Asian gangs and the criminal biker gangs, to name but two who are challenging the old concepts upon which "respect" and criminal ascendancy have hitherto been based.

The criminal biker gangs in Canada – specifically the Outlaw Motorcycle Club and the Hell's Angels (both international in membership and activities, having chapters throughout the United States and Canada as well as overseas), and their allies such as Satan's Choice in Ontario – have been on the rise in the organized-crime world for the past fifteen years. With people like Cecil Kirby moving directly from the biker gangs to the mob as enforcers and hit men, it is easy to show a direct link with the traditional Mafia. But these gangs are also becoming powers unto themselves. They are heavily involved in the drug trade, prostitution, and theft, as well as in traditional enforcement activities, and in recent years they have tried to clean up their act and operate in the world of three-piece suits and respectability. Certain bike-gang leaders have been accorded the same respect hitherto granted by the criminal underworld only to Mafia dons.

The FBI recently announced at a Police Biker Intelligence function in Toronto that the biker gangs are now its second priority after the mob in the United States and are considered an "organized-crime family". The FBI has said that in this area it is following the lead of the joint-forces biker squad in Ontario, in which over ten members of the RCMP, the OPP, and the Toronto police (and the Hamilton police at times) co-operate in a unit run by an OPP sergeant. This élite unit works on the biker gangs full-time, keeping close tabs on the gang leaders and members through surveillance, infiltration, and the use of paid informers. There are now over two hundred criminal bikers in Ontario alone. In the 1984 report of the Criminal Intelligence Service of Canada, the police project that bikers "are one of the major organized crime threats in Canada today" and that these gangs, which are described as "becoming increasingly sophisticated and wealthy," are involved in "all major criminal activity from murder to white-collar crime and in turn are investing profits into legitimate business."

In January 1985, the police in Ontario and Quebec moved simultaneously to arrest over a hundred members of the Outlaw Club and their affiliates in thirteen cities across the two provinces, including Hamilton, Montreal, and Toronto, on five hundred charges, ranging from conspiracy to traffic in drugs to illegal possession of firearms. To be even-handed, on April 11, 1985, police raided Hell's Angels clubhouses throughout Quebec and in Halifax, in an operation code-named "Arrow", arresting over eighty club members on narcotics and illegal-arms charges (though only seven were actually charged), while looking for the corpses of six Hell's Angels believed to be buried near one of the clubhouses. Five of the six bodies found two months later over a ten-day period in June 1985 had chains around them and concrete blocks attached to their feet; they were stuffed into sleeping bags. They had all been shot several times. The bodies, including all six of the missing Hell's Angels and, in addition, the corpse of the former wife of a biker, were dragged from the St. Lawrence River in Quebec. One stretch of the river has now been dubbed "the Hell's Angels cemetery" by the locals.

The Hell's Angels have since taken their own legal action against the Quebec Provincial Police for alleged damages to their Lennoxville, Que., clubhouse as a result of the raid and the ensuing bad publicity. Said Hell's Angels lawyer Michel Dussault, "This was nothing but a big police fishing expedition to arrest and question people.... They had nothing on anybody." The police insisted that their information was correct, and for the first time in the force's 178-year history, they released names and photographs of the alleged victims before all of the bodies were discovered.

On May 2, 1985, a massive, three-year FBI investigation of the Hell's Angels, code-named "Operation Rough Rider", which involved FBI infiltration of the gang, climaxed with the arrests of over one hundred Hell's Angels in sixteen cities from California to New York on drug and arms charges. This kind of massive police move against biker gangs in the United States and Canada should limit their growth and power temporarily, but no one is sure of the long-term effect. There are serious rivalries between the two main clubs, the Hell's Angels and the Outlaws, which have resulted in major bloodshed (over the past decade alone more than fifty bikers have been savagely killed), and this, too, inhibits their growth potential and power. But they are clearly an organized-crime force to be reckoned with right across North America.

Another rising force in organized crime in Toronto and Vancouver, as well as in many U.S. cities, is the Oriental gangs and secret criminal societies (or triads, as they are known in the Oriental community). In southern Ontario the main group is the Kung Lok gang, which has about one hundred hard-core members, many no longer youngsters but well into their thirties and forties. Originally a youth gang, it is now heavily involved in extortion in the Chinese community, in drug importation and distribution, in Chinese theatrical and movie distribution, and in providing "protection" services (usually from themselves). Gangs like the Kung Lok of Toronto, which is currently run by Danny Mo, are also part of an international criminal movement. When Mo was sentenced in June 1985 for armed robbery, the Crown attorney called him "a dangerous individual with many gangland connections." He was sentenced to four and a half years for organizing a robbery. Judge Sydney Harris said, "He used his position as one of the leaders of the Kung Lok gang to prey on the Chinese community for personal gain." Kung Lok has allies and affiliates in Boston, New York City, San Francisco, and Hong Kong. The United States Presidential Commission on Organized Crime has recently held hearings on the Chinese and other Oriental gangs in the United States, some with Canadian ties, and will be making recommendations to President Reagan about the problem in the near future.

There are serious rivalries amongst the Oriental gangs, such as the one between the Vietnamese gangs and certain Chinese gangs in southern Ontario, which have led to more violence and gang warfare in the past few years. Recently there have been extortions in Vancouver and Toronto involving the murder of the victims (a husband and wife, who owned a restaurant in Vancouver, and a young student in Toronto). One Toronto gang leader was recently shot and seriously wounded by Vietnamese gang members. This has curtailed some of the strength of the Oriental gangs. Also, the police have moved to pool their efforts against Oriental gangs across North America, and in the Toronto area there is an Oriental Gang Squad led by Sergeant Barry Hill, which closely monitors the activities of the gangs through informers and surveillance of the leaders and members. But the Oriental gangs are beginning to break out of their own ethnic community and become a more general threat to the public.

In recent years there have been joint Mafia–Chinese gang operations in Toronto involving gambling, drugs, and extortion. However, tensions between the Oriental groups and the Italian Mafia exist as well. The Kirby bombing of the Chinese restaurant in 1976, which resulted in the death of the cook, was part of a Commisso family extortion attempt against a Chinese gambling ring. This shows that competing organized-crime groups in the same city can often prey on each other, with innocent bystanders such as the Chinese cook, who was not involved in the gambling ring, suffering as a result.

However, notwithstanding the emergence and growth of other organized-crime groups, the Mafia, as we have seen, is still very much alive and thriving in Toronto and southern Ontario, and is still a major threat.

The question facing Canadians now is how best to keep the

Mafia and other organized-crime groups from operating efficiently. Italy and the United States have recently launched all-out offensives on a national and even international scale to fight the power of the Mafia. Canada should be a part of this drive. The legal-assistance treaty signed by President Reagan and Prime Minister Mulroney at the so-called Shamrock Summit in Quebec on March 18, 1985, is a step in the right direction, allowing Canadian and American authorities working in the area of organized crime to co-operate more closely. But Italy and the United States have strong anti-Mafia and anti-racketeering laws that give the police something to work with. In Italy, any person who is shown to be a member of the Mafia can be arrested and jailed for a long prison sentence. Italian law allows even associates of known Mafia members to be arrested and jailed. Also – and this is most important – the assets of the criminal in Italy are seized by the state, whether or not it can be proved that the assets come from the proceeds of organized crime. In the United States, the 1970 Racketeer-Influenced and Corrupt-Organization Act (the so-called R.I.C.O. statute) allows similar confiscation of the proceeds of organized-crime activity, thus cutting off revenue for future criminal operations. Canadian Solicitor General Elmer MacKay suggested in an interview with the *Globe and Mail* in May 1985 that something similar is needed in Canada. "What may be needed to get at the gigantic profits [of organized crime] is a general power in Canadian law that provides for identification, tracing and freezing and forfeiture of assets." R.I.C.O. has also allowed U.S. Attorneys in a number of jurisdictions to charge a whole Mafia family (as they did with the Colombo family in New York City in 1984), as well as any member or leader of an ongoing criminal conspiracy (as they did when they arrested the leaders of the five Mafia families in New York City in March 1985).

These are all things for Canada to look at. Canada is hopelessly behind the United States and Italy in enacting serious legislation to control organized crime. The way to get significant legislation passed as a major priority by the government in Canada is to appoint a top-level commission to thoroughly examine the problem across the nation. There has never been a national commission on organized crime in Canadian history. And the mob doesn't pay too much attention to provincial borders in its operations. In the United States the Presidential Commission on Organized Crime is currently taking evidence across the country. Also, the Americans have had other presidential committees and Senate committees seriously investigate the mob on a national scale over the years. Much important legislation, such as the R.I.C.O. statute, has come out of these public investigations into organized crime.

Canada has never done anything close to this. Quebec's Crime Probe, which has run for many years since its heyday in the middle to late 1970s, did an excellent job in identifying the problem and in disrupting the activities of the Cotroni-Violi family. In Ontario, the Roach commission of 1963 and the Waisberg commission of 1974 focussed public attention for a week or two on specific organized-crime activities (gambling and construction-industry violence, respectively), but they were ineffective in the long term. In Ontario the establishment of the Special Enforcement Unit by the police and the Attorney General's Office in 1977 has done a lot to focus police attention on certain organized-crime leaders. But they do not really have any great public support or the back-up legislation with which to fight organized crime effectively.

A federal royal commission into organized crime would provide such legislative assistance. Former prime minister and current external affairs minister Joe Clark proposed such a national crime probe when he was in opposition in 1977, as did former prime minister John Diefenbaker. They argued that only a national crime probe could effectively deal with what is clearly a national problem of gigantic proportions. "A royal commission could subpoena witnesses; names and places could be brought out, but instead," Joe Clark went on, "the government is refusing action, pretending that the responsibility for inquiries is in the hands of the provinces.... What we are dealing with here is problems relating to violations of immigration laws, we're dealing with narcotics matters, we're dealing with questions that are clearly in the federal domain, and the federal government can't leave the Mafia to Prince Edward Island. It's going to have to take its responsibilities itself and act itself." Joe Clark should advise his prime minister to follow this advice soon, now that the Conservatives are in power.

Canada needs a R.I.C.O. statute and anti-Mafia laws very badly. Canadian police are divided in their opinions on the effectiveness of a national crime probe. Many think it would impair ongoing police investigations by showing the police hand ("displaying all our trumps," as one police source put it) and by taking up the time of key personnel. Yet without public support and public pressure these police are not going to get the necessary funds or strong anti-Mafia laws to fight organized crime. Ontario attorney general Roy McMurtry was very much on the defensive throughout the public debate in 1982–83 about his department's decision to give Cecil Kirby immunity because the public was generally poorly informed on the danger and scope of organized crime in Ontario.

One of the areas a national royal commission could look at is the feasibility of a national program to deal with witnesses against organized crime. This does not exist at present in Canada, and all such activities are the result of ad hoc agreements, which vary greatly from case to case. In the United States there is the Witness Protection Program, which, with all its flaws, does provide a national structure for those who would risk their lives to inform on mobsters. On the other hand, criminal lawyer Eddie Greenspan, who has defended his fair share of organized-crime leaders over the years, including Remo and Cosimo Commisso, Tony Musitano, John and Antonio Luppino, and Domenic Racco, feels very strongly that the government should "never make deals with murderers." Greenspan adds that he does not think that any special measures need to be taken against organized crime, and that the normal police investigative techniques are sufficient; he cites the American example as proof of the potential for abuse in the system of using mobsters (and sometimes murderers) to get at other mobsters. A national royal commission could examine this whole area to avoid the abuses that have been observed in the American system.

Such a commission could also look at the effectiveness of capital punishment in murder conspiracies involving mob bosses. The mob uses capital punishment regularly, as a weapon against informers and to eliminate problem people. Perhaps it would be appropriate for the state to use capital punishment in certain cases where it can be proved that the Mafia boss or organized-crime leader, such as a biker-gang leader, has deliberately ordered the execution of another human being. Putting Mafia leaders and other organized-crime leaders in jail for conspiracy to commit murder is not an effective deterrent, as they continue to run their operations and even order hits from jail. Former attorney general McMurtry of Ontario has admitted this, and it has been shown that Domenic Racco and Tony Musitano ordered hits while they were incarcerated.

As an alternative to such a drastic step as capital punishment, a commission could look at the possibility of making "life" in prison mean just that for organized-crime bosses who have been convicted of conspiracies to kill; it could find a legal way to keep these killers off the streets and out of power in the underworld by keeping them in prison *literally* for the rest of their lives.

The antiquated extradition treaty between Canada and Italy, negotiated in the nineteenth century, is another area that should be seriously examined by a commission. Any extradition treaty that allows a Mafia leader to live happily in Canada even though he is wanted for manslaughter in Italy cannot be quite right.

But perhaps most importantly, a federal royal commission into organized crime would be one of the best ways to expose and effectively get at the business, the official and the political connections of organized crime across the country, for all the nation to see and evaluate. Corruption of public officials and businessmen is one of the most pernicious areas of organized-crime activity, and the most difficult to uncover. Without corruption, organized crime could not thrive, and the efforts of the mob to corrupt police, judges, politicians, lawyers, and government officials are probably more deleterious to society than any other activity in which it engages. For the moment, the level of corruption in Canada lags some years behind that in the United States (and Italy), but this gap is closing. A commission could focus on this crucial area.

If our society is to effectively fight organized crime, the public must be fully informed, and the government and the police must have laws that give them the proper tools for the battle – without taking away the civil liberties of law-abiding Canadians. This can only be accomplished through a federal royal commission, which is the one thing that all major mobsters fear because of the inevitable public exposure and the concerted effort against them that would result. The time has come to put the Mafia and organized crime in Canada on notice that their criminal activities are no longer to be tolerated and that they face very serious consequences if they continue, as they have for all of the twentieth century in Canada, with murder, extortion, drug trafficking, assaults, and other major organized-crime activities.

The time has come to take a strong stand against the ongoing menace of organized crime. Mob rule should not be allowed to continue in Canada without a major counter-offensive.

A Profile of Two Canadian Mob Originals

THERE ARE TWO unique Canadian mob characters – one of the past and one of the present – whose careers deserve closer scrutiny. While both Rocco Perri and Charles Yanover have worked with other mob groups, both are also highly charismatic, enterprising independents as well. Their stories, presented below as an Addendum, provide a rare glimpse of two Canadian criminal originals.

PART I

Rocco Perri, Canada's "King of the Bootleggers"

ROCCO PERRI, the self-styled "King of the Bootleggers" of southern Ontario in the Roaring Twenties, was born of a humble family in Reggio, Calabria, in 1890. He emigrated to Canada at the age of thirteen in 1903, and he soon became just one of thousands of young Italian immigrants holding down the poorest-paid and most laborious of jobs – that is, when he could find one. First, he slugged it out on the Dundas stone quarry, and later he worked as a construction worker on the Welland Canal. In 1912 he came to Toronto, where he fell in love with the wife of his landlord, the witty and vivacious Bessie

Starkman. By 1913, although he could barely afford a pair of shoes, Perri managed to steal Bessie from her husband. She was a thirty-year-old Jewish immigrant from Poland and the mother of two daughters. She must have seen some potential that was not readily apparent to others in the penniless and transient twenty-three-year old. Certainly they both had dreams.

In 1915 Rocco and Bessie moved to Hamilton after a short stint in St. Catharines, where Perri worked in a macaroni factory. The Hamilton location was no accident. The combination of agricultural and industrial activity in Steel City and the surrounding fruit belt attracted a large number of Italians. Like Rocco Perri they were initially attracted by the construction work available on the nearby Welland Canal, and many stayed on.

By 1916 Perri was a small-time operator. With Bessie helping out, Perri ran a small grocery store on Hess Street in Hamilton, where they sold olive oil and Italian specialties to neighbourhood Italian immigrants. This was at the time of a temporary Prohibition act in the province of Ontario. The sale of alcoholic beverages was banned as part of the war effort, and Rocco and Bessie turned the back of their store into a bootleg joint, selling whisky at fifty cents a shot. Getting access to liquor was simple enough.

Prohibition was not some collective madness that seized all of North America overnight. For fifty years the temperance movement had been growing in popularity in rural areas, urged on by the axe-wielding, saloon-busting tactics of Carry Nation and the fire-and-brimstone preachings of former-baseball-star-turned-evangelist Billy Sunday. But temperance efforts had been hampered by the multitude of jurisdictions – provincial, state, and federal – that blanketed the continent. After the First World War, the surprising political victories of populist movements like the United Farmers' Party of Ontario assured the temporary success of the temperance movement, but the almost total rejection of Prohibition by the growing urban populations should have been cause for alarm. As it was, Prohibition in Canada passed unevenly from province to province. The Ontario Temperance Act was passed by the provincial legislature in 1919.

Until limits were placed on the prescription privileges of family doctors, pharmacies were the only legitimate outlets for liquor. The humorist Stephen Leacock, an outspoken critic of Prohibition, acidly remarked that if you wanted a drink in Ontario, "it is necessary to go to the drugstore, lean up against the counter and make a gurgling sigh like apoplexy.... One often sees these apoplexy cases lined up four deep!"

The U.S. Congress passed the country-wide Volstead Act on October 28, 1919, over President Woodrow Wilson's veto. But while the United States went completely dry, Ontario supporters of Prohibition had little to celebrate. The British North America Act of 1867 may have made the sale of intoxicating spirits a provincial concern, but it left the distillation of alcohol for export and the excise revenue that accrued a federal responsibility. The feds were not about to give up such a lucrative source of tax dollars. So while most of the American distillers and breweries were broken up and driven out of business, the production of Canadian alcohol barely sagged. In fact it soared. Most of Al Capone's whisky came from Canada – from the Windsor area across the river from Detroit. In this area alone, per capita consumption of liquor increased from a pre-1914 level of nine gallons to a staggering 102 gallons by 1924. And technically it was illegal to drink!

Obviously most of the liquor being produced was finding its way into the United States and to mobsters like Al Capone – although he never admitted it. Once pressed about his Canadian suppliers, Capone replied, "Do I do business with Canadian racketeers? Why, I don't even know what street Canada's on."

The Canadian government allowed any exporter with the flimsiest of credentials to purchase from a Canadian distillery, as long as the shipment was destined for an offshore location that did not have Prohibition legislation in place. Cuba and the West Indies were the preferred locations. The situation was so clearly ludicrous that one boat was advertised as leaving for Cuba four times daily. Canadian excise was paid and the Customs officials who oversaw the loading of the shipment and the departure of the boat were satisfied. In the middle of Lake Erie the cargo might be intercepted by a fast trawler, or more usually the boat would put in at one of the numerous ports and unload its cargo, never having left Canadian waters.

By the time Prohibition came into effect in late 1920 in the U.S. (nearly a year after formal ratification by Congress and three-quarters of the states of the Eighteenth Amendment to the U.S. Constitution), Rocco Perri had learned the rudiments of the bootlegging business and was tussling over the marginal profits in the Hamilton area. When the potential profits of the American market made the bootlegging business worth killing for, Perri's organization was already in place. The competition was being either absorbed or eliminated. Perri was ready for big-time racketeering, and when the big American mobsters sought a source of Canadian whisky, it was Rocco Perri they had to deal with.

During the early days of 1919, Perri's name first received public attention. During a New Year's Eve party at his apartment above his store on Hess Street North, a guest, Tony Martino, was killed outside. (The other guests were uncooperative, and the assailant was arrested four years later in Pennsylvania only because of a stroke of luck.) Less than one week after the killing, on January 6, 1919, Perri was fined $1,000 or six months in jail by magistrate George Frederick Jelfs, who was an authority on the illicit sale of alcohol, a noted social reformer, and the author of *Commentary on Sin* as well as *Offences Under the Liquor Control Act*. It was a relatively inexpensive conviction, but an invaluable lesson. Thereafter, Perri let his men handle the dirty work and take the risks.

Charles Wood, a retired staff superintendent of the OPP, served as an Ontario Temperance Act special officer during the 1920s, raiding stills and bootleggers throughout Wentworth County (later on, as chief of detectives with the OPP, he solved the famous Evelyn Dick case). He personally stopped Rocco Perri many times but could never actually catch him with the goods. Perri was too smart to get personally involved. "He may have been the King of the Bootleggers but he never drove a car full of booze in his life," said Wood. It became part of Perri's legend that he was never actually present when shipments changed hands, but was always lurking nearby in the shadows, ready to offer a bribe or throw bail for his boys.

One evening in 1926, Wood and some fellow OTA officers received a tip-off that a shipment was being unloaded in Hamilton harbour. Scouting around, they stumbled on the *Atum*, the largest and most recognizable of several boats owned by Perri, being unloaded at the docks near the foot of Wellington Street. The launch, the whisky, and a high-powered truck were seized, and two men, Patsy Lasconi and John Sullivan, were arrested. Just as the officers were leading Lasconi and Sullivan away, Perri, who had been watching events unfold from the sidelines, approached. Taking aside Bob Bryant, the officer in charge, so their conversation could not be overheard, Perri offered a bribe. Wood cannot report what the bribe was, only that it was refused, and since there were no other witnesses, a charge could not be laid.

The papers are full of accounts of Rocco or even Bessie Perri arriving at court to put up bail for some vague acquaintance they had happened to loan a car to – unaware, of course, that the individual was going to use it to transport alcohol. For instance in September 1924, when John Rosse and Andrea Catanzaret of Wood Street in Hamilton were arrested with five one-gallon tins of whisky in the back of their touring car at Bay and York streets, it was Bessie Perri who signed the bail bond for their release. The Perris' actions not only ensured loyalty but demonstrated their unerring sense of promotion. Rocco Perri once bragged that he had lost over $80,000 the previous year in shipments and vehicles seized by the authorities. Perri discovered you could be the King of the Bootleggers if you simply called yourself that.

The purchase of a nineteen-room Hamilton mansion at 166 Bay Street South proclaimed the Perris' new wealth from bootlegging. Stocked with Oriental carpets, a $2,000 piano, and a billiard room, it was the envy of the neighbourhood and visible proof of Perri's upward mobility. And it was no wonder that he was gaining wealth. Perri was buying cases of bonded 60-proof whisky at distilleries like Gooderham and Worts in Toronto for as little as $18 a case and reselling them, landed in the United States, for $120 a case. He shipped up to 1,000 cases a day.

It was hard to miss the Perris' presence in town. Rocco was described as a Canadian "Little Caesar", renowned for his exclamatory ties, fat cigars, and sporty race-track outfits, and according to the papers of the time, for "grinning an Italian grin." Superintendent V. A. M. Kemp, the commander of the RCMP's "O" Division in western Ontario, described Perri more clinically in a letter to an inquiring U.S. Attorney: "Italian; height 5'3", weight 165 lbs; stocky build; clean shaven; straight black hair; receding off forehead; bald spot on top of head; small boil scar on left cheek; very swarthy complexion." In a perplexing footnote, the Mounties added, "It has not been definitely ascertained as to whether or not this man has suffered the loss of any toes, but it is believed this is not the case." He was usually accompanied by his petite and spirited wife, Bessie, draped in Tiffany jewellery.

The legend grew, but sometimes even legends make mistakes. In Toronto, September 29, 1923, police surprised a crew unloading sacks of whisky bottles from a boat near the foot of Leslie Street. Several shots were fired in the dark, all by the police, it was later proven. One of the boat's crew, John Gogo of Hamilton, was killed. As usual Rocco Perri was close by, but this time his alibi did not prevent his arrest. The trial caused a sensation, and Perri was discovered by the media. His relaxed and witty responses under examination made excellent copy. Pressed to name his occupation, Perri replied, "Macaroni salesman."

"Do you ever take anything in your truck besides a little macaroni – a little whisky?" suggested the Crown attorney.

"Prove it!" smiled Perri amid the courtroom's laughter. The incident ended with Perri's acquittal, but may have helped convince him that guns and police shoot-outs only brought bad publicity.

In February 1924, OTA officials were the first to try out Perri's new notoriety with a raid on his house in Hamilton. However, Perri had taken the precaution of installing a secret room under the cellar. Unaware of the subterranean room, the OTA officials came up empty-handed.

Jack Larenchuk and two members of a rival Ukrainian bootlegging operation, perhaps believing the news reports that Perri was unarmed, also embarked on a futile attempt to raid Perri's home. The ensuing shoot-out marked the first time that Hamilton city police had fired their guns in over twenty years. It began late one night in May 1924 when a suspicious-looking car was spotted by police cruising in the southwest section of the city. Following at a distance, police watched the car turn into an alley at the rear of 166 Bay Street South. The officers split up to cover the alley and watched three armed men emerge. Seeing the police, the men took flight up Bold Street. The police started in pursuit and some shots were exchanged, one of which wounded one of the fugitives. Under cover of darkness the rest of the men made good their escape. A squad of police was called to comb the area, but no traces were found. Then an intruder was reported in the backyard of a house on Robinson Street. Surrounding the house, the police swept the backyard with the beam of several flashlights. A figure was located lurking under the back porch, and the call to surrender was answered by a hail of bullets. From all sides the police returned the fire. There was no further reply. Waiting until the first light of dawn to move in, the police found the corpse of Jack Larenchuk, still clutching a partially loaded .38 hand-gun.

The police were hardly surprised to have a dead body on their hands. After all, Larenchuk had been caught trying to break and enter at the residence of one of Hamilton's most notorious citizens – 166 Bay Street South, the home of Rocco Perri. This was not the first corpse connected to Perri. His climb to the top had been strewn with the bodies of rival bootleggers and enemies.

Complaints about the city's open secret – Perri's bootlegging activities – were few, however; perhaps too many benefited from Perri's presence to initiate any action at that point. The warning to Perri, however, was clear enough and he soon beefed up his personal protection with a pair of bodyguards, William "Bill the Butcher" Leuchter and John "the Mad Gunman" Brown.

The murders of bootleg runners Joe Boitovich and Fred Genesee in November 1924 refocussed public attention on the violence taking place between the Italian and Ukrainian rivals for the Hamilton liquor trade. The murders occasioned a sensational interview with Perri that was printed in the *Toronto Star*, headlined "'King of Bootleggers' Won't Stand for Guns" (November 19, 1924). Perri was described as "suave, immaculate and unperturbed":

His eyes shone with amusement when asked "Who killed the two men?" His carefully groomed shoulders rose slowly in the gesture of perfect Italian indifference and then he spoke. "Who knows? Rocco Perri did it I suppose? Everything that happens, they blame on Rocco Perri. Why is it? Maybe because my name is so easy to say. From what I heard Joe Boitovich was put out of the way because he was a squealer. He was a Polack. He said too much and he has paid the price. Genesee, I do not know, I think there was a woman in the case. I think it was spite."

"There is a report that Boitovich and Genesee were killed in connection with a bootleg war?" suggested The Star. "Bootleg war, that is funny," replied Bessie Perri [incorrectly identified

as his Italian wife]. *She reached toward her silent husband and patted him easily on the back. "You tell them Rocco that there is no war. You are the King of the Bootleggers. That is what they say. You should know."*

Mr. Perri was quick to respond. "There is no bootleg war!" he declared with abrupt emphasis. "Next they will be saying it is the Blackhand or the vendetta."

He was asked to differentiate between the two latter terms. "The Blackhand – that is to put away a man if demands for money are not met. The vendetta – that is to kill a man for revenge."...

Mr. Perri began to tell something of his own business. "My men," he said, "do not carry guns. If I find that they do I get rid of them. It is not necessary. I provide them with high powered cars. That is enough. If they cannot run away from the police, it is their own fault. My men do not use them.... The man who does not play the game as it should be played will not get far. Pure liquor, fair prices and square dealing. Those are the requisites of the trade. I have played the game and ..."

He did not end the sentence verbally but the indulgent survey which his eyes made of all the attributes and rewards of wealth which surrounded him in the form of fine furnishings and costly clothes spoke volumes....

He went on to say that if a man squealed on him he would find a way to punish him. "That is the law of the Italians. We do not go to the police and complain. That is useless. We take the law into our own hands. I would kill a man on a question of honor, but not if he merely informed on me. We believe that we have a right to inflict our penalties. Sometimes it is necessary to kill a man. But I have never done it and I don't want to."...

"You have heard that there is honor among thieves," she [Bessie Perri] *said soberly, "but maybe you do not know that there is such a thing as principle among bootleggers. Yes, we admit we are bootleggers but we do our business on the level."*

The disclosures hit like a bombshell. Newsboys were mobbed, and newsdealers were sold out in fifteen minutes. A curb market sprang up with papers selling for as much as $2 apiece. Latecomers or those unable to afford the price of a copy gathered around demanding to be read titbits of the interview.

At Queen's Park, Attorney General W. F. Nickle held a hurried news conference with General Williams of the provincial police and the law department. The law library was ransacked for volumes that might contain some basis for a warrant on a charge of conspiracy to break the law, in the absence of any proof of breaking the law. In the end they were defeated and forced to declare: "It is not a breach of the OTA for a person to say he is a bootlegger. A boast is not proof of guilt."

Temperance workers and Hamilton's clergy urged Perri's deportation for his shameful confession and the brazen effrontery with which he publicly defied the law. One wag, however, suggested that Perri's success be rewarded by placing him in charge of the enforcement of the Ontario Temperance Act.

Rival bootleggers were less sanguine about Perri's newest publicity and the heat it drew for all of them. "Rocco Perri, he talk too much, he busta da biz," complained one competitor. Certainly it lit a fire under the police for a while as they tried to redeem their reputations. Asked if they could ever stop the bootlegging, one officer replied sarcastically, "Sure, if we can stop and search every car, wagon, and truck entering the city."

Despite Perri's disclaimer about moonshine in his newspaper interview ("Many hundreds of cheap bootleggers selling poison liquor. That is bad. It drives men crazy. They commit crimes."), his next run-in with the law was over a batch of poison brew. At least thirty-five people died in one night throughout the Niagara Peninsula. A warrant for Rocco Perri was issued for the unlawful slaying and death of John Lyons of Oakville on July 31, 1926. Perri obligingly turned himself in shortly thereafter. The Crown's case against Perri was based on a Jamestown, N.Y., grand jury indictment that connected Perri to a massive liquor-smuggling syndicate. Links between the two cases were difficult to prove, so despite the manslaughter conviction of four of Perri's men, the poison moonshine case against Rocco was thrown out of court by magistrate Jelfs for insufficient evidence. This was the same judge who had presided at Perri's only previous conviction.

But the authorities found other ways at getting at Perri. Quite by accident they managed to get him on his bookkeeping. This came out of the federal Royal Commission on Customs Violations, set up in 1927 after the province of Ontario replaced Prohibition with restricted government distribution of booze. The commission had the power to subpoena witnesses.

Testimony given at the royal commission identified a "J. Penna" as a frequent purchaser of Seagram's and Gooderham and Worts products for export. Further evidence by OTA officials ascertained that Frank De Pietro (also known as Di Pietro), a Perri driver who had recently been arrested by the OTA officers, had been delivering a load of Seagram's whisky assigned to J. Penna. Moreover, De Pietro's car was registered to Mrs. Bessie Perri. Penna's name came up again in connection with a load of Gooderham and Worts whisky that was seized from Perri's boat, the *Atum*.

Charlie Wood, who was part of the team making the bust, remembered the night well, even after sixty years. Wood and his colleagues Everett Smith and Bob Bryant were tipped off through an informer that a shipment would be arriving in Hamilton harbour that evening. Scouting about, the OTA officers found the *Atum* in the process of transferring eighty-one cases from the ship. They were then being delivered to the shore by one of Perri's fleet of swift launches and loaded onto one of Perri's fifteen high-powered trucks. The *Atum* was nearly sixty feet long and was the largest and most recognizable of Perri's boats. OTA officers moved quickly and seized the launch, the cases of whisky, one of the trucks, and two of Perri's men, Patsy Lasconi and John Sullivan. Perri himself, as usual, was lurking nearby as all this was happening.

Perri and his wife were subpoenaed to testify before the royal commission on April 1, 1927. Bessie appeared first. Asked if she operated a liquor business in Toronto under the name of J. Penna, she replied with a curt "No." She also replied in the negative about a series of telephone calls made from her house on a daily basis to a number of distilleries and breweries. She had no knowledge of the calls, she lamely replied.

Rocco Perri was then called to the stand. This was the moment everyone had been waiting for. The Crown planned to use his King of the Bootleggers appellation against him, and the press was on the look-out for new sensational headlines. Both were satisfied by Perri's performance.

The interrogation started innocently enough: "Is Mrs. Bessie Perri your wife?" But Rocco's answer shocked the room: "I have lived with her for many years.... We are not married." This was 1927, after all, and pandemonium ensued.

When order was finally restored, Perri was asked more mundane yet more pertinent questions about various phone calls and house guests from New York City, Chicago, Buffalo, and elsewhere. Joe Penna of Buffalo, it turns out, was one of his guests who frequently used his phone. As Perri could not admit to making the calls to the breweries and the distilleries, it was of course the house guests, he explained, who had made the calls.

When asked about a club in Niagara Falls, a noted bootlegging joint that had his name on its books, Perri denied all knowledge of the place and suggested that perhaps someone was using his name. When asked about this interview in the *Toronto Star*, during which he admitted his involvement in the bootleg business, Rocco flabbergasted everybody by announcing that he had finally told reporters what they wanted to hear to keep them away from his door. Reminded that he had signed the interview, indicating it was a true representation of the discussion that had occurred, Perri claimed that his imperfect knowledge of English had prevented his proper understanding of the written interview. The *Star* testified that the interview had been read back to Mr. Perri before he signed it – several times, in fact. Oh yes, smiled Perri, but they had read it to him while his wife was playing the piano, thus preventing his understanding.

Exasperated, the commission tried another tactic: Perri's finances. "My wife keeps all my money!" he replied. "Except for the cash in my pocket, it all goes into her account." It seemed that the real power behind the throne was finally revealed, but later events were to prove this wrong.

Bessie Perri was recalled to the stand and asked to produce her account book. The only entry had been three weeks earlier and showed a balance of only $98.78. She assured the commission that she had no other accounts in her own or any other name.

Perri's tax records were subpoenaed. They revealed that in 1922 he had successfully appealed a small assessment, levied as income tax. In 1923 he paid no tax. He showed only a small income in 1924 and had not paid taxes in 1925 and 1926 because his wily solicitor, M. J. Riley, was fighting the assessment on the grounds that income tax could not be collected from bootleggers as they were engaged in an illegal business. But the real surprise came with the discovery that the Perris had close to $1 million on deposit in a local bank under the name of Bessie Starkman.

When the commission closed its investigation on May 13, 1927, it recommended that warrants be issued immediately for the arrest of Rocco and Bessie Perri on eight counts of perjury each for violating their oaths – oaths that carried the same force as in a court of law. Efforts to locate the Perris failed, however. It was rumoured that they were in the United States preparing to sail for Italy. Others said they were still in Hamilton. On June 4, 1927, four Italian men were arrested leaving the Thorncliffe race-track in Toronto in a car belonging to the Perris. Under interrogation they claimed that Bessie Perri had lent them the car the previous day in Hamilton to attend the races. The search began anew.

But once again it was Rocco Perri who turned himself in. Committed to trial on eight charges of perjury each, Perri and Bessie had no way out of this one. Both were convicted and served six-month sentences in 1928.

When the Perris returned to Hamilton, Prohibition and the world that went with it were winding down. The OTA was abolished while the Perris were in jail in 1927, partly as a result of the royal commission. The U.S. stayed dry until 1933, but the Depression took away a lot of the demand and most of the profit. The Perris started to think about diversification.

Returning home late at night from a party on August 11, 1930, the Perris parked their car in the garage behind 166 Bay Street South. Both of them got out and while Rocco was still on the driver's side of the car, Bessie was felled by two shotgun blasts at close range. Clues were scarce and the assailants were never found.

The funeral that followed remains unrivalled in Hamilton. Thousands of curious on-lookers crowded the lawns and ver- andahs of Perri's neighbours. Many more lined the route of the procession to the cemetery to catch a glimpse of the fifteen flower cars and the $3,000 silver casket. The blinds on the bereaved's car were drawn tight.

Various theories have been advanced to explain how Perri escaped that night in his garage. Charles Wood, the provincial police veteran of the period, believes that Bessie Perri was branching the Perri gang into narcotics to make up the shortfall in the liquor business. Rocco was known to have strong feelings against the dope business, and Wood believes that a rival gang in the narcotics game took out Bessie to forestall any competition. Others, who share the assumption that Bessie was really the brains behind the family business, believe that rival bootleggers were responsible and cite the apparent decline of the Perri empire as evidence.

For some inexplicable reason all these theories bury Rocco as a force to be reckoned with along with Bessie in 1930. Confidential RCMP documents reveal, however, that Rocco Perri and his bootlegging business continued to flourish in Ontario, albeit with less flamboyance and publicity, during the post-Prohibition Depression of the 1930s. Obviously another explanation can be found for Rocco's survival that night.

Since Rocco was the beneficiary of Bessie's estate, there was naturally suspicion at the time that he might even have had his wife murdered, just to loosen her grip on the purse-strings.

A letter buried in the RCMP files, obtained under the Access to Information Act, contains gossip from the widow of one of Rocco Perri's Toronto lieutenants [unnamed because she may still be alive] that the word on the street was that Rocco had his wife murdered.

Evidence at the 1927 Customs commission made it clear that the money was in Bessie's name. But it now appears that this was a convenient fiction used by Rocco all along to avoid income taxes and persistent interrogation about his occupation. Despite the transparent nature of the tale, to one and all he remained a "retired macaroni salesman", living off his wife's investments.

This convenient arrangement was to continue with Bessie's successor, Mrs. Anne Newman. The pretty and mysterious Mrs. Newman was also a Polish immigrant of Jewish descent, but this time several years younger than Rocco. First described in newspaper clippings in 1938 as Rocco Perri's housekeeper, Anne Newman, it can now be revealed, was more than just Rocco Perri's mistress. She served as his major link with the mobs in Chicago and Detroit and organized the delivery of bootleg liquor through Canadian Customs. A bomb attempt on Perri's life in March 1938 demolished the porch of the house on Bay Street, and investigation would reveal that the house was then owned by Mrs. A. Newman of Richmond Hill. RCMP documents reveal that other possessions, such as car registrations and telephones, were also in Mrs. Newman's name.

It is not known if Bessie Perri was as closely involved in the direct oversight of the business as was Anne Newman, but it is clear that Perri used both women as fronts to cover his involvement. So in the end whether Bessie was killed by Rocco to get at the money or mistakenly killed by rivals, the death of Bessie Perri neatly closes the first chapter in Rocco Perri's history as the kingpin of southern Ontario's underworld before the Second World War.

The boom years that coincided with Prohibition called forth a certain brashness and optimism. Business was good and the bootlegging business was even better. In the 1930s Prohibition petered out, but so did the economy. As a reflection of the grimmer and greyer times, the strutting braggadocio of Rocco Perri disappeared altogether. The business had changed and Perri changed with it. When the Ontario legislature abolished the OTA in 1927, it replaced it with closely controlled government distribution, the forerunner of the Liquor Control Board. Alcohol was available but on a very restricted basis. In 1930, the Canadian government had finally relented to pressure from the Americans and cracked down on the manufacture of alcohol for export. Rocco Perri and others had to turn to stills to supply their customers. The quality could never come close to that achieved by the professional distillers, whose product was so highly valued that a market for Canadian whisky exists to this day in the United States. Moreover, the manufacture and storage of home-made hooch in quantities sufficient to be profitable posed great risks of detection. Small stills had existed throughout Prohibition, serving the local neighbourhoods with the cheap rot-gut, or "white mule", that Rocco had been so contemptuous of. But business was business. The discovery of an illegal still on Concession Street in 1932, in a house that had once belonged to a local justice, and the arrest of three known associates of Perri proved that the King of the Bootleggers had gone into the moonshine business – but in a very large way. The still that was seized had the capacity to turn out 26,000 imperial gallons of "white mule" a month. This was more than many small legitimate distilleries. It was estimated that the weekly profit was $5,000.

As it transpired, Perri kept busy after 1933, when the United States abolished Prohibition. Overnight the flow of illicit whisky resumed but this time in reverse. Careering from one extreme to the other, the United States went from total Prohibition to total access. Suddenly it became a source of inexpensive quality liquor. The restricted nature of alcohol sales in Ontario created a thirsty market and a source of bountiful profit that Perri was once again well placed to serve.

The dash and élan of the heyday of Prohibition bootlegging had no place in the new arrangements of the 1930s. Smuggling a load across the Niagara River undercover at night had a certain romance, but too many risks to sustain a business.

Through his mob connections, Rocco Perri got his liquor from a source in Chicago. Specially constructed high-powered cars, which could carry up to 300 gallons of liquor at a time without showing the load – even to careful scrutiny – travelled the distance to Detroit. There they confronted the only possible obstacle to a dry market as far east as Montreal, Canadian Customs. Sometimes those paid to notice such things can conveniently look the other way.

RCMP documents obtained under the Access to Information Act dramatically reveal that Perri controlled not only the Ambassador Bridge that connected Detroit to Windsor but the tunnel that ran beneath it as well. Between 1933 and 1940, when the RCMP finally broke up the ring, Perri ran illegal distilling equipment and gaming tables, as well as liquor, across the river as though it was the Burlington Skyway.

A secret memo to the commissioner of the RCMP, dated August 26, 1939, and titled "Irregularities of Customs Officials", recommended the immediate arrest of the "principal co-conspirators Rocco Perri and Anne Newman before they go into hiding." On August 31, at 5:15 P.M., Perri and Newman, driving in Anne Newman's car, were stopped and arrested at the corner of Nina and Bathurst streets in Toronto (they had moved to Toronto after two bomb attempts on Perri's life in Hamilton in the previous year). In Windsor, five Customs officials were arrested and charged with bribery and corruption in the performance of their duties, along with two of Perri's associates, Sam Motruk and Sam Miller. The arrests climaxed a six-month investigation by the RCMP.

Ironically, the investigation began as a result of rumours that Perri had died in a fiery car crash in Ann Arbor, Mich., on December 4, 1938. Two men were burned beyond recognition, and the car was traced to Hamilton. Perri, however, was safe at home, having just miraculously survived, on November 23, the second bomb attempt on his life in one year. After the previous attempt, in March, during which the front of his house was dynamited while he was out, he had purchased a new house on Hughson Road. This time the bomb was in his car, which was parked in front of the new house, and it had exploded as soon as he started the ignition. The car was totally demolished and two bystanders were severely injured, but Perri, still leading a charmed life, was thrown clear with only minor scrapes.

Investigation of the crash in Ann Arbor revealed that the car was driven by Bill "the Butcher" Leuchter, Perri's long-time associate, and the passenger was a nephew of Anne Newman. The inquest determined that their deaths had been accidental, but that the car had contained an enormous amount of alcohol. Everyone knew that Perri was in the bootlegging business, and RCMP documents make clear that they suspected Perri's organization was the source of a large part of the illicit alcohol and other contraband in western Ontario. But how was he doing it?

It was not until three members of Perri's bootlegging ring agreed to become Crown witnesses that the RCMP learned of the huge scope of Perri's operation. The RCMP memo on the informers' statements indicates astonishment that the corruption of Canadian Customs officials in Windsor went as far back as 1933 and had possibly even prevailed for a considerable time prior to that date.

The three informers were David Michael Armaly, Victor Bernat, and Milton Goldhart. All had taken part in the Perri bootlegging business, Armaly as a Customs officer and driver and Bernat and Goldhart as drivers. Armaly was the key Crown witness. He had recruited his fellow officials to the conspiracy before he was dismissed from his post for incompetence. Later he took up driving for the ring. Bernat had always been a driver and though considered insignificant, he was able to offer some corroborating testimony for Armaly's story. Goldhart's testimony was considered to be the more damaging of the two because he dealt directly with Anne Newman. All three men were crucial to the successful prosecution of the Perri case. The federal deputy minister of justice admitted in a confidential letter to the attorney general of Ontario that "there is little or no direct Police evidence."

But the police were not the only ones aware of the slender nature of the Crown's case. RCMP informers in the underworld reported that Perri's arrest had caused "a violent furor amongst the underworld as far away as Chicago." In an urgent memo marked "Secret", Superintendent Kemp, the commanding officer of "O" Division, advised the commissioner that the witnesses might be tampered with or eliminated:

It has been strongly intimated from a source believed to be reliable that definite steps may now be expected by those whose interests have been affected, to make some attempt to ensure that certain of the Crown witnesses are not available for the forthcoming trial.... In view of what we know as to foreign elements here, and in the United States who are interested in this case, it is felt that the information received is not exaggerated, and should be acted upon.

The RCMP was under no illusions. The two most recent attempts on Perri's life were hardly needed as reminders that people in Perri's league played for keeps. Superintendent Kemp insisted that the chief witnesses and informers be placed in protective custody in secret locations, with the RCMP picking up the full tab. Armaly and his wife and four children were put in a summer cottage outside Ottawa. Bernat was put up by the RCMP detachment in Amherstburg, Ont.; Goldhart, who was from Toronto, was placed with the Lindsay, Ont., detachment. But in the case of Goldhart the worst fears of the RCMP were realized. He disappeared shortly before the trials began, never to be seen again.

The commissioner was even more worried, however, about keeping down the costs of lodging the informers. Superintendent Kemp assured him that since the case was to be heard in September, they would only be in hiding for a month at most. Concern that the case be tried as quickly as possible was the main reason for the deputy minister of justice's hurried letter to the Ontario attorney general. The $3-per-day costs for the witnesses seemed a heavy burden for the deputy minister, though the RCMP later paid Crown attorney Tom Phelan a daily rate of $300 for his attendance at departmental hearings on the trials. As it turned out, the trials did not actually begin until January 1940, thus costing the RCMP many $3 per diems. The controversy over these payments to informers raged in the press, and the public was up in arms at the generous treatment of the witnesses – which included immunity from prosecution. Cecil Kirby, the RCMP informer of the 1980s, was not the first bad guy to be supported by the force. Armaly and Bernat were hardly paragons of virtue. Before the end of the trials, Armaly confessed to forgery, illegal gambling, cheating on welfare, taking bribes, and fraud, among other illegal acts. Armaly had such a chequered career that Perri's counsel, Joe Bullen, KC, of Toronto, closed his cross-examination of Armaly with one short question: "Is there much short of everything in the Criminal Code of which you are not guilty?" Armaly replied with a lame "I don't know." Bernat had a long criminal record and was equally disreputable.

But the stories the three informers had to tell were certainly worth the price. For the first time in his long criminal career, Rocco Perri faced the real possibility of ending up behind bars for many years for some pretty serious crimes. Armaly, Bernat, and Goldhart represented a real chink in Perri's otherwise impenetrable armour.

Dave Armaly had become a Customs officer in 1930. In order to pay off a gambling debt of $35, he agreed to let a car belonging to Sam Miller, a Perri associate, through Customs. It was easy money and Armaly was soon letting cars through regularly for the Perri ring. Warned by a telephone call from Detroit which car to look for, Armaly would let the smuggler know which traffic lane he would be working. Between 1935 and 1936 Armaly claimed to have waved close to two hundred cars through Customs for Perri's associate Sam Miller. But Armaly was only observing part of the flow. Since he could not always be on duty at a traffic lane, Armaly claimed he recruited other officers, including the senior bridge officer, to the conspiracy. It was not until 1936 that Armaly was able to confirm that he was actually working for Rocco Perri of Hamilton.

In March 1936, Sam Miller introduced Armaly to Anne Newman. Armaly claimed that he initially refused to work for a woman, until she mentioned that she worked for Perri. Armaly immediately agreed to go on working. His meetings with Anne Newman continued even after he was dismissed from the Customs Service in May 1936, as he served as a liaison between her and the other Customs officers. Most of his meetings were with Newman in front of the Norton-Palmer Hotel in Detroit, but on several occasions, when Perri himself attended, they met at his house. Now unemployed, Armaly managed to keep his family fed by deducting a small fee from the money he delivered to the other Customs officials. Armaly soon started to drive for Sam Miller.

During the trial, Armaly testified that he had made over twenty trips to Chicago, occasionally with his wife, to haul liquor to Detroit. At this point the car was usually turned over to another driver to clear Customs, in case Armaly was recognized by one of his former colleagues not on the take.

In Chicago, Armaly loaded five gallon tins of booze into the specially constructed car at Joe Terrelli's garage at 121 East 123 Street. The telephone number at Terrelli's was entered as evidence as one of the numbers dialled frequently from Perri's Hamilton residence. Asked by the Crown where he stayed while in Chicago, Armaly responded, "The Westin and the Alcatraz." Blushing at the courtroom's laughter, he realized his mistake and mumbled, "The Alcazar."

Armaly continued to drive for Miller until early 1938. At that time he had a run-in with Miller over a car accident on the way to Montreal in which several gallons of alcohol had been lost. Miller refused to pay him his fee, and Armaly walked out. Armaly took up with Milton Goldhart, who was running a few cars now himself for Victor Sola, a nephew of Joe Terrelli's in Chicago, but Armaly continued to meet Anne Newman. Armaly claimed to have met Bill "the Butcher" Leuchter the morning of his fiery demise to arrange for clearance through Customs on his return from Chicago. The deaths of the two men, coming so close after the recent attempt on Perri's life, shook Armaly. When an RCMP officer approached him in 1939 about an entirely separate issue and asked about his connection to Sam Miller, the officer got a totally unexpected confession.

Victor Bernat's testimony identified several of the Customs officers named by Armaly. Most of them he had met with another Windsor associate of Perri's, Sam Motruk. Motruk had found Bernat driving a bread wagon. The offer of $75 a week and a fast car to smuggle liquor was too good to refuse, but Bernat was only a minor cog in the wheel. The most sensational of his recollections was his report that "one of the Customs men, Gough, had threatened to take care of anyone who squealed to the police."

During the eight-day trial, Perri remained unruffled and calm, as he had throughout his long career. As he mugged for photographers and traded quips with the newsmen, it was just like the old days. Perri had all the confidence of a man with a secret weapon. Asked by reporters about the war then raging in Europe, Perri replied: "Canada is my country. Canada is part of the British Empire. I would fight for it. I left Italy more than twenty-five years ago. I don't remember much about it."

"What about those bombs, Rocco?" asked another reporter, referring to the numerous bomb attacks on Perri's life. Perri confidently replied, "There aren't any left in Canada," and grinned an Italian grin. "They've taken them all to Europe. They need them over there."

Part of Perri's arsenal was his defensive team, consisting of Joseph Bullen, KC, of Toronto and a young Windsor MP, Paul Martin. Attacking Armaly's credibility from the start, Martin (who later served many years in Liberal cabinets in Ottawa) recalls that attacking Armaly's credibility seemed like the most obvious tack to take right from the start. Even today, Martin does not think Armaly was a very impressive witness on whom to build a case. Armaly was particularly open to attack as a paid informer, a mercenary who would fabricate and say anything to get continued support. Martin particularly zeroed in on the fact that Armaly was on the RCMP payroll as an informer while he was also collecting welfare from the city of Windsor. Martin seemed to know minute details about Armaly's interrogation by the Mounties.

A worried memo from the RCMP officer assigned to the trial expresses concern about the source of Mr. Martin's facts:

Cross examination by Mr. Martin M.P. disclosed the astonishing fact that Mr. Martin was familiar with a certain interview which took place in the office of the writer, many months ago between Armaly, the other witnesses and myself, which was actually for the purpose of clearing up some obvious errors in their statements, and this was what Mr. Martin charged. Mr. Martin failed to follow up his questioning along these lines, otherwise I would have been forced to testify accordingly. I cannot understand in what manner Mr. Martin became possessed of his facts.

Superintendent Kemp in a secret memo to the commissioner

attempts to provide the answer: "I am not aware of how the information referred to came into the possession of Mr. Martin. In as much as Goldhart is missing, I can only assume that he was responsible for this." Paul Martin cannot recall how the information on the meeting at the RCMP headquarters in Toronto came into his hands, nor does he remember Milton Goldhart.

Goldhart's presence might have provided the corroboration the Crown was now desperately seeking to rebuild Armaly's credibility. However, since he was not available, not even his damaging preliminary statement could be introduced as there was no witness for the defence to cross-examine. Some of the relevant parts, which the jury did not get to see, have been obtained from RCMP files.

In a signed statement to Customs, Goldhart stated that Anne Newman was involved in all aspects of the bootlegging: that she went down to Detroit with him, arranged for the pay-off of Customs officials, arranged contacts in the United States, arranged for the disposition of the bootleg liquor in Canada, and in all things connected with the bootleg trade acted to insulate her common-law husband, Rocco Perri. Anne Newman, according to Goldhart, was the principal organizer and front for Perri. But since Goldhart disappeared before the trial actually took place, this testimony, unfortunately, could not be introduced. Was this why Rocco Perri was so confident? Without Goldhart the Crown's case was seriously weakened.

Victor Bernat's character was quickly discredited by the introduction of evidence that he had been involved in smuggling Chinese people into the United States. Bootlegging had romance, but alien-smuggling was despised. Those involved usually looted their desperate cargo of any valuables, and there were rumours that before the voyage the aliens were hidden in weighted bags to keep them out of sight. If the smugglers were spotted by the border patrol, the bags were simply slid overboard.

The demolition of the Crown's case was complete and the verdict was almost anti-climactic. Rocco Perri, Anne Newman, and the five Customs officials were acquitted. Only Perri's unfortunate Windsor lieutenants, Miller and Motruk, were convicted.

As a footnote, Dave Armaly's name appears one last time as a dead-pan aside in a follow-up memo in the RCMP files, released to me under the Access to Information Act: "At the moment Armaly is facing charges for defrauding Windsor relief agencies and will probably be sent to jail for at least a month."

Rocco Perri's freedom was short-lived, however. Despite his constantly professed desire to fight for Canada, when Italy declared war on the Allies in June 1940, Perri, who had never become a naturalized Canadian citizen, was interned at Camp Petawawa. There he stayed for the duration of the conflict with Italy. With his internment at Petawawa, Anne Newman apparently faded out of Perri's life and into obscurity.

He was released on October 17, 1943, by a special order signed by the justice minister, Louis St. Laurent. Rocco Perri gave every indication of leaving the criminal life behind. He took up a bachelor's existence in Toronto, becoming the doorman and janitor at a Bloor Street theatre.

Then suddenly, on Sunday, April 23, 1944, while visiting his cousin Joseph Serge in Hamilton, Rocco Perri disappeared. Complaining of a headache, he went for a walk, leaving his car by the curbside. According to Serge, he thought a walk in the fresh air would do him a world of good. It didn't. He never returned.

Since the war still raged in Europe, Perri's disappearance did not get much notice at the time. But it was the opening shot in a war taking shape on the home front as Mafia rivals sought to position themselves in post-war Ontario. Old scores were being paid off.

Within months, other former Perri associates fell victim to a rising new force in Hamilton's underworld. Louis Wernick, identified as the former dope king of Buffalo (and the RCMP source for the information that Perri "had been taken for a ride and was encased in cement in Hamilton Bay"), was found in a snowbank near Long Branch Race Track with five bullet wounds in the back of his head. Other Perri associates, Paul Doneff and John Durso, also disappeared, although Durso's car was found in the Welland Canal near Thorold.

And what of Rocco Perri? As an RCMP officer succinctly put it: "His body will not turn up until the bay dries up."

PART II

Charles Yanover, Con Man Extraordinaire

ONE OF THE PRIZE PUPILS of Paul Volpe and Nate Kleger-man, and one of the most colourful of the mob characters still around, is Charles "Chuck" Yanover, who drew even more heat from the SEU after the death of Volpe and the imprisonment of the Commissos. Yanover had been in jail when Volpe was killed, and in fact between 1982 and 1984 Yanover had plenty of troubles of his own, undergoing three major trials for three independent criminal operations, including an arson job in downtown Toronto, a coup attempt in the Caribbean, and an assassination scam involving North Koreans. While a key middle-management figure in the Volpe-Klegerman group for eight years, Yanover, in addition, like any good mobster of the 1980s, took what he could, where he could, when it came to cons and scams. As we have seen in the stories of Paul Volpe, Nate Klegerman, Cecil Kirby, and even the Commissos, the mob in Canada is not as highly structured and organized as most of us think it is. Many different groups operate simultaneously in many different areas, and many individuals within crime groups operate simultaneously in other criminal enterprises. The bottom line for all criminal operations is taking advantage of an opportunity when it comes along, and using "connections" to further the scheme or bring it to fruition.

Chuck Yanover is a colourful and fascinating chameleon. While he was trained by Klegerman and worked for Volpe, he excelled, in his own right, in ripping people off. This is typical of the above-average mob personality of today. Mobsters in Canada today, outside of the old-styled Italian Mafia structures, are breaking away from too much organization. Chuck Yanover is the modern mobster incarnate. It would be interesting then to take a look at his "free-lance" operations over the years, those undertaken outside his work within the Volpe organization (though he did tap into the organ-ization, as we shall see, for laundering some of his illicit profits), to give us a glimpse into the possible shape of things to come.

Yanover's is a classic case of chutzpah gone to wild and dangerous extremes. What he is best at is bull-shitting and boasting for profit, and making an excellent living out of telling tall tales of assassinating foreign leaders and overturning governments through elaborately conceived coups d'état. His adventures in Togo with a former

Canadian lieutenant-colonel, in Dominica with the Ku Klux Klan, and in Europe and Asia with assassins from North Korean intelligence were all in this vein. Though he has done more mundane local enforcement work in Toronto and its environs, what Chuck Yanover really enjoys is jetting around the world – Paris, Bangkok, the Philippines – on missions of international intrigue.

The Togo adventure began like one of those Greek tragedies on the usurpation theme, in which the children of the rightful ruler set out to restore the natural order that has been overthrown by a dictator who has killed their father and taken over the government.

On January 13, 1967, Lieutenant-Colonel Etienne Eyadema toppled the elected government of Sylvanus Olympio and set himself up as the dictator of Togo, a small African agricultural country of 2.5 million people, famous for its beautiful postage stamps. Togo is in west Africa, surrounded by the Gulf of Guinea and Upper Volta and Ghana, and was a protectorate of Germany from 1884 until 1922 when the British and French took over as part of the League of Nations activities following the First World War.

In the 1950s, Togo was divided into two countries: British Togoland became part of what now is Ghana, and French Togoland became on April 27, 1960, the independent state of Togo. The first president and the father of the new country was Sylvanus Olympio, who was assassinated in 1963 by a faction led by Lieutenant-Colonel Eyadema. In 1967 Eyadema abolished all political parties and set himself up as the dictator.

Eyadema now admits he had Olympio killed in 1963, and he has himself been the target of numerous assassination and coup plots over the past eighteen years of his despotic rule. The children of Sylvanus Olympio, who live in exile in Paris, certainly have motive enough to depose Eyadema, but they lack the political support inside the country and a base to effect this.

Thus, in 1977, they went to international adventurer and arms dealer Colonel Thomas Finan and his company, Teshi-Team. There were plans to kill Eyadema in Paris, and to engineer a coup in Togo itself by having mercenaries in strategic positions in Lomé, the capital, begin a military action. The Togolese army consisted of several thousand soldiers, but it was thinly spread out along Togo's northern borders. Only four hundred troops guarded the presidential palace in Lomé.

For the operations, Finan assembled a crack team of mercenaries from two continents. The team included former members of Britain's parachute regiment and Charles Yanover as part of the North American contingent. For Yanover, who used to advertise for mercenaries in the outrageously militaristic and sensationalistic *Soldier of Fortune* magazine ("Write C.Y. Associates at 334 King Street East, Toronto"), it was a tailor-made situation. The Togolese expedition was to be his first taste of the forbidden and alluring fruit of international adventurism, and was to supply him with a model for future operations that would prove both exciting and dangerous.

Yanover was brought into the Togolese project through Ji Shik Moon, a South Korean living in Toronto. Moon had been a sergeant and had served in Vietnam with South Korean forces, where he became familiar with weapons and explosives. He was introduced to Yanover by Barry "Bunks" Collart, who asked Moon if he would be interested in training military personnel in Africa and South Amercia. Moon expressed interest, and in September 1977, he and Collart went to Paris, where they linked up with Yanover, then went on to Basel, Switzerland. There the pair met with Colonel Tom Finan, who supplied them with money and plane tickets to Accra, Ghana. Yanover and Moon flew to Ghana and travelled by land to Lomé, where they met up with Collart. They did a reconnaissance of the presidential palace and decided that the best place to kill the president would be in an ambush on the road from the airport to the palace. They set October 13, 1977, as the target date. Though weapons were supplied and the planning process went ahead, involving more than ten mercenaries, it is unclear whether the whole escapade was in earnest or just a fake. Whatever the case, the president of Togo was warned of the plot through CIA sources and British intelligence, and he remained in a hideaway in Paris; Yanover and his fellow conspirators remained in Togo for eighteen days before being asked to leave by the authorities. No assassination attempt or coup attempt involving these mercenaries ever took place.

In 1978, when Canadian police were investigating the Togolese adventure in an attempt to lay charges (some of the planning may have taken place in Canada, which is a crime under Canadian law), they had trouble even proving that Yanover and Collart had been to Togo. Mysteriously, both Yanover's passport and Collart's had been "burned" and partially destroyed and the pages with the African visa were unreadable. Yanover claimed that his mother, Eve Yanover, accidentally tossed his passport on the stove in her house, and

"Bunks" Collart claimed a similar "accident". In a bail hearing in Toronto on a gun charge on May 18, 1978, Yanover was questioned closely by Crown attorney Howard Morton on the passport and the aborted Togolese mission. Yanover admitted being in Togo between September 2 and September 20, 1977, but only as a "tourist consultant" for Teshi-Team International Ltd. Except for articles in the *Sunday Times* of London, the *Toronto Sun*, and some French journals, little note was taken of the Togolese project by the general public. (As an intriguing aside, it came out at the same bail hearing, in an interrogation conducted by Morton, that Yanover was the Ontario agent for a Belgian arms firm, Fabrique Nationale, which, according to Yanover, was arming the Ontario Provincial Police among others. This was a result of Yanover's legitimate position as vice-president of R. E. Ross Firearms, a company owned by an associate who was engaged to his sister at the time. It could have proved a slight embarrassment for the OPP to have an organized-crime figure as its arms agent, but nothing came of this in the media as no reporter covered the bail hearing.) Charges were never brought against anyone on the Togolese expedition, but the next international adventure for Yanover was to prove more costly.

The overall plan, though somewhat simplistic, did have real potential, and it was conceived to succeed: a B-26 airplane was used; an international group of mercenaries was mobilized; arms were put into place; and a plan was laid to actually overthrow a government and assassinate a president.

Chuck Yanover saw in all these elaborate preparations – for which money was no object – a marvellous scam potential. Why not concoct his own plans to overthrow governments and to assassinate leaders, rope in some well-financed special interest that would pay through the nose to finance the coup d'état or assassination, and make elaborate preparations for the killing or coup without actually doing anything? In other words, why not pretend to be arranging an overthrow of a government or a hit and take the plotters with the loot for a walk? Yanover would use these schemers for a good score and make a mint, while enjoying himself wining and dining and travelling internationally at the expense of his victims.

Morally, Yanover found the idea of such scams quite appealing, in that the victims were extremists of the right and the left who deserved to be ripped off. All he had to do was bring in one or two other people on the plots whom he could control and trust to make the scams work. He would travel to the location where the coup or assassination was to take place, take surveillance and reconnaissance photos, and work out a seemingly workable plan, without ever really intending to do anything except rip off the original plotters. Yanover saw this as more fun and more profitable even than the diamond frauds at which his friend and mentor, Nate Klegerman, was so proficient. It was also a lot less risky, in that the victims were spies or crazies who could hardly go to the police for protection. Spotting the right victim for Yanover, as for Klegerman, was as important as planning the scam, and such desperate characters were made to order.

When he emerged from jail from the Veronac extortion conviction in 1981, Yanover took a job as manager of Cooper's, a bar at Yonge and St. Clair in Toronto (not far from where Paul Volpe kept an apartment in the late 1950s), owned by a Korean friend of his. It was when he was working here that he got involved in two bizarre plots: one to overthrow the government of the tiny Caribbean island of Dominica with the Ku Klux Klan and the Western Guard, and the other to kill the president of South Korea for North Korean spies.

One day at Cooper's, Yanover was introduced to two Canadian Klansmen, Wolfgang Droege and Alexander McQuirter. They asked him if he could help provide arms and get surveillance photographs for an invasion of Dominica that they were sponsoring. Yanover was intrigued by the idea, so in 1981, with Alexander Michael Gerol, his partner and co-defendant in a bombing case, he flew to Dominica with his trusty camera and took photographs of all the sensitive installations he could find. He came back to Toronto and handed the pictures to the KKK, giving them a vivid description of the island's geography as well. (When Yanover was later arrested for his involvement in the Korean operation, police found many of the negatives from his Dominican trip, and the photos that were missing were those found in the possession of Droege and McQuirter.)

The KKK had been working on the Dominican plan for some time. They had originally intended to seize the then Marxist-run island of Grenada and set up a white supremacist regime. They planned to embark on this invasion from Dominica. But they soon found out that Grenada was armed to the teeth with Cuban and Soviet weapons and was fully prepared for an invasion (from the U.S., which eventually did take place in 1983). The plotters, who consisted of senior members of the Ku Klux Klan of the United States and Canada as well as members of the racist Western Guard of Canada, discovered in their early reconnaissance that Dominica was a much easier, more vulnerable target.

The ringleader of the plot was U.S. Ku Klux Klansman Michael Perdue of Houston, Texas. Also in the plot were Canadian KKK Grand Wizard James Alexander McQuirter; Canadian Donald Andrews, former head of the Nazi-like Western Guard; Canadian Klansman Wolfgang Droege; Larry Jacklin; Torontonian Klanswoman Marian McGuire; and several U.S.-based KKK members. Under false pretences, Don Andrews even managed to have meetings with Eugenia Charles, then leader of the Opposition and now prime minister, known affectionately by her people as "Momma". Joining in the plot for reasons of his own was Charles Yanover.

Yanover helped with the reconnaissance of the island with surveillance photos and with arms. If the KKK were successful, which he knew was very much a long shot, he fancied himself as defence minister for the KKK government; at the very least, he hoped to be able to set up a casino on the island, with Paul Volpe. Yanover even tried to recruit Cecil Kirby for the project when he ran into him one day at Cooper's. Kirby, however, was too busy with Commisso bombings and enforcement work to undertake such a long voyage. Since the invasion was a long shot at best, Yanover decided to take the KKK for a walk and rip them off for a few thousand dollars.

However, the adventure was to be more short-lived than even Yanover had imagined. On April 27, 1981, when the invasion party of ten set off from the New Orleans area in a heavily armed boat for its ten-day, 2,000-mile trip to Dominica, it was intercepted by the FBI, who had been tipped off to the plan most likely by Cecil Kirby, who was by this time secretly working for the Mounties. Two Canadians were arrested immediately, Droege and Jacklin. McGuire was later arrested in Dominica; much later Yanover was arrested in Toronto, after a lengthy police investigation (by the OPP, not the SEU this time). The news department of CFTR, a Toronto radio station, had been informed of the invasion as it was in the planning stages, and it taped interviews with the plotters without informing the police. The reporter at CFTR also spoke with Miss Charles and the Dominican prime minister on behalf of one of the plotters. Miss Charles says, "A Toronto radio reporter acted as McGuire's contact with the mercenaries." Reporter Gordon

Sivell of CFTR was not charged but resigned from the station shortly after the plotters were arrested in Louisiana. Sivell was to write a book about his involvement with the plotters with former *Globe and Mail* employee and Toronto teacher Stephen Overbury; the book has never been published.

Dominica was a perfect target for these half-brained right-wing terrorists operating with mob support. An island of 290 square miles, situated between Martinique to the south and Guadeloupe to the north, with a population of 75,000, Dominica had received its independence from Britain only in 1978. Its economy is based on agriculture (bananas and grapefruits, mostly), it has a very small militia (unlike heavily armed Grenada), and it is vulnerable on all sides.

In May of 1981, Attorney General Roy McMurtry of Ontario ordered a "top-priority investigation" into Yanover's links to the Klan and their plan to take over Dominica, after police were tipped off. This resulted in charges being laid in February 1982 by the OPP against Yanover for conspiracy in Canada to break the law of another country. Yanover had accepted money in Canada for his assistance in the coup plans. Oddly enough, it came out in the newspapers at the time of the invasion, including the *Globe and Mail*, that a mobster (Chuck Yanover) was giving money ($10,000) to help finance the operation, rather than being paid by the plotters for his services. It was yet another Yanover scam, continuing even as he planned the Korean score and pursued his usual criminal activities.

It is interesting to note that Yanover himself views his Dominica coup plot as a rip-off of the KKK and not as a real plot to take over the island. The police and the Crown took another view (as they did later on the Korean assassination plot), which led to Yanover's subsequent arrest and conviction for "conspiracy to commit an unlawful act." Yanover did not know that he would never have become defence minister in the new government in the unlikely event that the plan had been successful, as one of the main Klan conspirators told Cecil Kirby at the time that they were planning to kill Yanover on the island after they took it over. The Klan obviously did not want a Jewish defence minister for its utopian state. Yanover's scam of the Klan was more realistic than was the Klan's plan to take over Dominica.

Considering Yanover's love of the intrigue of international adventurism, it is probable that he never had any intention, whether in Togo, Dominica, or on the later Philippines "assassination" plot, of really carrying out the assassinations and coups. His motivation was always to make money in a fun way with lots of exciting travel thrown in as well. It is a testimony to Yanover's talent that he can make even paranoid people such as the Ku Klux Klan and North Korean intelligence officers believe that he is serious in his intention to carry out assassinations or aid in a coup – even though his prime goal is to catch these international intriguers in his own sting operation. In all these cases, Yanover succeeded both in making considerable sums of money and in having a great time at the expense of the original conspirators. Yanover is the classic and consummate con artist, possessing considerable knowledge of human behaviour and motivations and a substantial charm and cunning that sucks certain people in. Klegerman was his role model, and Natie Klegerman is the consummate rip-off artist, whose victims often still believe in him after they have been taken. What Klegerman does in his diamond rip-offs, Yanover has effectively done in the murky and equally mysterious netherworld of international mercenaries and adventures.

Even while the Dominican plot was proceeding, in May 1981, Yanover was approached by James Choi, a friend of Ji Shik Moon, with a feeler concerning a possible assassination of the president of South Korea, Chun Doo Hwan. Choi's father had been a major figure on the South Korean political scene, a general of the army with some hope of succeeding to the presidency after the death of President Park at the hands of the head of the South Korean intelligence agency in 1980. However, Chun Doo Hwan took over, and General Choi fled with his family. James, his son (Jung Hwa Choi is his real name), lived in Mississauga, with his father.

James Choi was the liaison with the North Koreans who wanted to have President Chun Doo Hwan assassinated. Yanover convinced first Choi and then the North Koreans that he could organize and effectively carry out a successful plot to kill Chun if he were given enough money for his considerable expenses and his time. As his lawyer later told a hushed courtroom in Toronto, Yanover promised to "muster the Sixth Fleet for a three-pronged amphibious landing in the Philippines with helicopters and armies" to kill Chun while he played golf with the president of the Philippines, Ferdinand Marcos, in what has been called the "annual dictators' golf tournament".

The whole world was Yanover's stage for the Korean operation.

The North Koreans went to Yanover because of Yanover's reputation as an organized-crime operator and arms dealer. Yanover, in his initial meeting with Choi, convinced him that he was the right man for the assassination, that he had the resources and· skills necessary to pull it off. In May 1981, Yanover followed Choi to Vienna to meet with key agents of North Korean intelligence. While there, Yanover signed a contract with the North Koreans and Choi to kill President Chun in exchange for a large sum of money (between $200,000 and $400,000 in U.S. funds). This was unusual in at least two ways: it is extremely rare for a hit contract to be put in writing – it's not as if anyone could bring the matter to court if the contract were not fulfilled; and it is most unusual for Communist intelligence services to give large sums of money to their agents. KGB officers are notorious for their miserliness and most known cases in which they have bought people involved considerably lower sums. Yanover then returned to Canada and developed a plan.

In June 1981, Yanover asked his girl-friend, Christine Barnes, if she would "like to get some Chinese food." He neglected to tell her that they would be going to Hong Kong for the Chinese dinner and conspiring with North Korean intelligence to kill the president of South Korea in their spare time. Michael Gerol also came along. Wearing bullet-proof vests, Gerol and Yanover went to the Portuguese colony of Macao for a strategy meeting with the North Koreans and Choi. They were given two briefcases full of American $100 bills as an advance for the assassination. Yanover told the North Koreans that he would assassinate the president at a resort in the Philippines called Puerto Azul, where he knew the "annual dictators' golf tournament" would take place between July 6 and July 8, 1981.

Travelling to Manila, Yanover then took up residence in the Hotel Oriental with Gerol and Christine Barnes. At Puerto Azul, Gerol and Yanover took surveillance photographs on Gerol's camera, photographing the lay-out of the resort from the exterior and photographing the golf course itself from a hotel room they rented within the complex. Gerol also took pictures of the coastline from a boat. They then went back to Manila; Gerol, with a briefcase full of money, returned to Toronto. Yanover and Barnes travelled on to Bangkok with the remaining briefcase of cash, then flew to Amsterdam and stayed at the Okura Hotel. Barnes flew back to Toronto, and Gerol joined Yanover in Amsterdam.

At this point there was a slight problem, since they had difficulty getting the money exchanged by Dutch banks. (Suspicious of the source of the money, Dutch police contacted Interpol. Interpol, in turn, telexed Metropolitan Toronto police intelligence, who confirmed that Yanover was a "bad guy" but didn't mount an operation at this point.) However, arrangements were made with Nate Klegerman to convert some of the money (about $100,000 U.S.) into diamonds through his Antwerp connections.

Yanover and Gerol then went on to Vienna for another meeting with the North Koreans and Choi. They brought the photographs of Puerto Azul, and Yanover wore a hidden tape recorder, while Gerol secretly taped the meeting and provided armed security. At this point Yanover decided to alert the South Koreans to the potential danger to President Chun's life in the Philippines, and the South Koreans then cancelled President Chun's trip, sparing Yanover the trouble of having to pretend to kill Chun (or trying to kill Chun, depending on whose point of view one takes). In July 1981, the North Koreans put pressure on Yanover to fulfil his contract. Yanover stalled, hoping to bilk the North Koreans for much more money. He felt he had a good thing going.

Having pocketed hundreds of thousands of dollars already, Yanover now decided on a bold strategy that involved a double scam. He decided to try to get money from the RCMP in exchange for his services as a double agent, acting for the Security Service on behalf of Canada and the free world. Yanover brought his mentor and criminal colleague, Nate Klegerman, into the picture for this phase of the operation, as well as criminal lawyer Earl Levy. Klegerman was awaiting trial for two elaborate diamond frauds he had engineered. In addition to Klegerman, the defendants included Paul Volpe, Frank Volpe, Murray Feldberg, Mo Cooper, and Joe Volpe.

Klegerman suggested that Yanover demand that the charges be dropped against Paul Volpe, Joe Volpe, Murray Feldberg, and Klegerman himself as part of any agreement to help the RCMP sting the North Koreans. In addition, Yanover told Levy, who was to act as their agent with the RCMP, to demand $1.5 million and immunity from prosecution for himself and Michael Gerol in exchange for their becoming police agents.

Levy approached the RCMP, saying that he was representing a client, whom he identified simply as a "Mr. X". Yanover had told Levy the full story in a series of ten meetings in mid-July: the assassination plot, the contract, the photographs, the film and tape recordings available to confirm the story, the travels around the world, and the money received from the North Koreans. Yanover also told Levy that he never intended to kill anyone and that the whole thing was an elaborate "sting" of the Communists. Before he went to the RCMP Security Service (now the Canadian Security Intelligence Service), Levy warned Yanover that it was a criminal offence to conspire in this country to commit an offence outside of the country. Yanover and Klegerman decided that it was worth the risk. In early August 1981, Levy had a meeting with the RCMP Security Service, told them his client's story of the assassination, and said that "Mr. X" would give the tapes, photos, and films of his meetings with the Korean spies to the RCMP in exchange for immunity, $1.5 million, and the dropping of charges against Paul Volpe, Nathan Klegerman, and their colleagues on the alleged diamond frauds.

Requesting that charges be dropped against such prominent organized criminals as Paul Volpe and Nathan Klegerman was like waving a red flag before the RCMP. It was a great tactical error to introduce this demand at such an early stage. The RCMP had no choice but to inform the SEU, for it was SEU cases that Levy was trying to have dropped. The SEU in turn, demanded that the whole matter be turned over to them, as Yanover, Volpe, Klegerman, and Company were all targets of ongoing SEU investigations. Once the SEU took over the matter, Yanover and Levy didn't have a chance. In fact they set themselves up for an SEU investigation, which led finally to charges being brought against Yanover and Gerol for defrauding the North Koreans.

Initially, however, the SEU, through Staff Sergeant Ron Sandelli and Sergeant Al Oake, did negotiate with Levy, though they balked at the request for $1.5 million. On September 8, 1981, six days before the Volpe-Klegerman trial was to begin, Levy requested another meeting with the Mounties. Levy told Sandelli that on the previous weekend he had seen photographs, tape recordings, and a film relative to the plot. Levy wanted an answer right away, as "Mr. X" faced deadlines and was being pressured by the North Koreans to complete the assignment for which he had been paid. On September 16, 1981, Levy talked with Inspector Jim McIlvenna, the officer in charge of the SEU. McIlvenna offered "Mr. X" immunity from self-incrimination but nothing else. Levy pushed for the dropping of charges against Volpe, Klegerman, and the others.

Throughout all these conversations, Levy referred to Yanover only as "Mr. X", but the RCMP knew from the beginning who he really was, and now mounted its own operation against him, including wire-tapping and surveillance. This led to charges being brought against Yanover. Of course, at the same time, the OPP was conducting its own investigation of Yanover for his involvement in the Dominica plot, and this led to charges just two weeks before the SEU charges were made on the Korean fraud. Levy suggested to the SEU that "Mr. X" be allowed to continue with his scam of the North Koreans while under RCMP auspices and make a score. The SEU was outraged at the suggestion of helping Yanover "lift" the North Koreans. Levy's problem was that he was now dealing with the unit that had targeted his clients, not the Security Service, which at the time was in charge of security and intelligence matters. Levy hadn't realized that the minute the SEU took over the case, all likelihood of a deal ended.

The SEU began a massive world-wide investigation of the Korean caper that involved government and police agencies in South Korea, the Philippines, Thailand, Holland, France, Belgium, Martinique, and, of course, Toronto – as well as Interpol. Sergeants Sandelli and Oake were assigned to pursue all leads, including electronic and physical surveillance of Yanover and Gerol. In one instance, Sandelli and Oake followed Yanover to the Club Med in Martinique, one of their more entertaining and relaxing assignments. Yanover was tipped off to undercover police presence, but he just used this to increase his own credibility: "I am so important a criminal that I am being followed by the police at this very moment," he said dramatically to someone in Martinique.

In early October 1981, Yanover and Gerol went to Vienna once again to meet with Choi and the North Koreans and to continue their scam – but this time they were under police surveillance themselves. Yanover and Gerol wore bullet-proof vests and purchased a shotgun and a gas pistol. It was classic spy stuff, with special codes and clandestine meetings. Yanover, amazingly, convinced the North Koreans that he still intended to complete the contract, and managed to get even more money from them. He then tried to launder this money in Geneva, Amsterdam, and New York, as well as through Klegerman in Antwerp. Police traced $300,000 directly to Yanover and $100,000 directly to Gerol, after gaining access to banking records and safe deposit boxes in Toronto, New York, Geneva, and Amsterdam. When police in Paris stopped Gerol for an aggressive interrogation (instead of keeping him under surveillance, as Toronto police had requested, they brought him in and roughed him up a bit), the whole police operation was almost blown. But Yanover and Gerol didn't seem to connect this with the possibility that the SEU had been tracking them across Europe. In any case, they just carried on until they were arrested on February 24, 1982, for defrauding the North Koreans (just two weeks earlier they had been arrested by the OPP for their role in the Dominica coup plot). Yanover was released on $400,000 bail.

While convicting Yanover of the charges of defrauding the North Koreans, the judge was not entirely convinced that the "crime" warranted a harsh sentence. "These two men were not terrorists," Judge Lesage stated in his sentencing statement on February 17, 1984; "in fact they apparently frustrated the terrorists in their first attempt to assassinate the President." Judge Lesage didn't go as far as Yanover's lawyer, Irwin Koziebrocki, who had said in court that "some would call him [Yanover] a hero. Some would say he deserves a medal instead of going to jail." Speaking of the meetings with the North Koreans in Vienna, Koziebrocki seemed amazed at the success of Yanover's scam: "I'd suggest this was the first time in Austrian history that anyone agreed to a legal contract for this kind of action.... It was incredible and almost comical in certain ways. Here are these unknown Communists, sitting around in cafés in Vienna sipping cognac and offering bags of money.... To everyone's surprise these people gave him money."

The Crown, Michael Bernstein, took a less comic view of Yanover's activities: "He is a gun-runner, an extortionist, a bomber, a man capable of conspiring to overthrow a government, and a man who would cheat other would-be terrorists.... Mr. Yanover is well known for keen interest in mercenary adventurism." But the defence countered with the argument that Yanover was a "hero" who double-crossed the real terrorists to save the life of President Chun, "albeit with a profit motive." "When was the last time Your Honour heard of someone being charged with fraud for selling baking soda as heroin?" defence attorney Allan Gold asked, adding: "Would Mr. Bernstein have them charged with fraud for not selling the heroin?" Judge Lesage, while marvelling that "it boggles the mind that he [Yanover] would be able to do anything honest," said that while "the whole bizarre scenario was hatched by the victims [the North Koreans], the law protects the innocent, but it also protects the guilty – that is why these two are here." In other words, the North Korean spies who were trying to arrange the assassination of the president of South Korea were nonetheless protected by Canadian law from con artists like Gerol and Yanover. Judge Lesage then gave Yanover and Gerol two years and one year respectively to be served concurrently with their long prison terms (now awaiting a new trial) for allegedly helping to arrange the bombing of Arviv's Disco in January of 1980. James Choi, who originally brought Yanover to the North Korean spies, is currently hiding in Europe and is on the Ten Most Wanted list of the Toronto police for his role in the Korean caper.

Earl Levy, who is a partner with Koziebrocki as well as a participant in some of the activities brought out in the case, thinks the police handled the whole case very badly. He feels strongly that the SEU officers' desire to make cases against Yanover and Gerol overwhelmed their better judgment. Levy claims that "Mr. X" was not Yanover but Klegerman, his client on the diamond fraud case, who arranged his approach to the police on a deal. Levy feels that had the Security Service worked with Yanover, they would have gotten significant intelligence on North Korean intelligence operations in Canada and around the world that would have been of great assistance to Canada, the United States, and South Korea. Levy feels the Rangoon bombing, which killed half of South Korea's cabinet in 1983 and was arranged and executed by the North Korean intelligence service, might have been averted. "It might have been possible to save those lives," Yanover and Levy now say.

The North Koreans are controlled by the Soviet KGB, so an intelligence breakthrough here could have been of enormous importance to the free world. It does seem that the RCMP missed an opportunity, and threw away access to a great deal of information, which included pictures and film of North Korean agents operating in Europe and Asia as well as tape recordings of the North Koreans plotting against the life of the South Korean president.

"The Korean case is significant and bizarre," says the former SEU head, Inspector James McIlvenna, "because on the bottom line is the fact that a real assassination plot was attempted. . . . There is no doubt that the assassination plot was real." For McIlvenna, then, Yanover's story is a good example of SEU effectiveness in fighting organized crime in Ontario. Earl Levy disagrees with this assessment and says that "the fact that the photographs and films were taken ... [shows that Yanover was] only pretending to take part in the plot." Levy says he could not imagine people seriously involved in a plot to kill the president of South Korea taking photographs, taping conversations, and signing a contract.

Today, in 1985, Yanover is reviewing his criminal career from jail. Looking back upon the many years of his close relationship with Paul Volpe, Chuck Yanover, as we have seen, is strangely unsentimental, stating that Volpe "got what he deserved, nice guy or not." In a letter dated July 20, 1984, from his prison cell in Joyceville Penitentiary, Yanover goes on with his hard, unsentimental view of Volpe's murder: "It is in the rules" – that is, not co-operating with the police, informing on other mobsters, and assisting in a police sting operation against the mob – "and I would expect no different for myself, except I wouldn't be as easy a target."

Yanover does not identify in any way with former hit man and informer Cecil Kirby, who helped save Paul Volpe's life in 1981. In his first letter from prison Yanover made it clear that he did not like the *fifth estate* television piece on Kirby, which I had helped to produce. "About your program on Cecil Kirby, I will give you a piece of advice, not to mention his name and mine in the same context or breath for that matter. I do not wish to be compared to Cecil at all. There is no difference to you, but a lot to me. I wasn't crazy about that show and I will tell you why when I see you if you care for constructive criticism." Yanover had known Kirby from the days when he worked with the biker gangs on fencing stolen bikes. He now feels that Kirby betrayed everything that he stood for as a biker and hit man, and that by working with the police to ensnare the Commissos and others, Kirby is beneath contempt, a traitor who sold out his former colleagues in the underworld for money and an immunity deal. To Charles Yanover this represents a major breach in the underworld code of ethics, which condemns to death all snitches and informers.

But then Yanover and Kirby are quite different in their criminal styles. Yanover has been a talker: a con man and a scam man extraordinaire. Kirby has been a doer: ruthless hit man and efficient enforcer. Yanover respects the underworld code of silence and hates "stoolies", while Kirby has turned his back on this tradition and co-operated extensively with the police as a means of survival after leaving the employ of the Commisso family. Both have survived for years working with the predominantly Italian underworld in Toronto by preying on the weaknesses of others to make a livelihood.

And both are now, for all practical purposes (though for very different reasons), out of action in the criminal world: Yanover in jail and Kirby in hiding.

After mercenary missions in three continents, an eight-year stint as a middle-management figure in the Volpe mob, a period of fencing stolen goods for biker gangs and arranging dynamiting for the mob and others, as well as a period of selling arms all over the world, Yanover has few challenges left when he gets out of jail. The underworld he will face when he emerges from jail will be radically different from that of the 1970s. There will be no Paul Volpe, no Nate Klegerman, and – until 1989, when they probably will get out of jail – no Remo and Cosimo Commisso.

And most significantly of all, Yanover's credibility with the street will have been severely damaged by the scams he did against the KKK and the North Koreans, for not only didn't he deliver, by his own testimony he never intended to deliver in the North Korean plot or the Dominica plot. You cannot go on indefinitely as a free-lance mercenary and never deliver the goods. Previously, he relied on his reputation, based on years of enforcement work for the Volpes and fencing for the biker gangs. But that activity was in the late 1960s and early and middle 1970s. Since then, he hasn't really done anything, except run scams against various groups. And the North Koreans, in particular, are not known to be forgiving. They eventually tried to kill the president of South Korea in Burma in 1983, killing half of his cabinet. And they are assumed to be rather annoyed with Yanover for not only taking them for well over $600,000 (and money does mean something to Communists), but also surreptitiously recording their plots and taking pictures of meetings with their agents all over the world. As far as the North Koreans are concerned, Yanover is a real menace, and as they say in espionage jargon, very "eliminatable" or subject to "termination with extreme prejudice".

Charles Yanover does indeed have lots of good reasons to consider going straight and maintaining a low profile when he gets out of jail. Perhaps he will work in his father's clothing store or bankruptcy business. He could also become an informer for the police, though it is doubtful that he would betray his own code of ethics and become a stoolie. Charles Yanover maintains that he is not a Cecil Kirby and would not turn in or inform on his former colleagues or work with the police. This remains to be seen. On the other hand, Yanover could forget about going straight, join his old friend and criminal mentor Nate Klegerman (in Antwerp or in Israel, according to the latest intelligence, working in the diamond trade), and get back some of the money laundered in diamonds through Klegerman during the Korean scam. Yanover does enjoy the good life in Europe. When in Paris during the Korean caper, Yanover and Ji Shik Moon stayed at the most exclusive hotel in Paris, the George V (everyone else in this $1,000-a-night hotel wears formal clothes, but Moon and Yanover arrived in American jeans instead of the traditional tuxedos). Yanover loves to spend money wildly on champagne and beautiful women, and if he can hitch up with Klegerman in Europe, he might just be able to live the fantasy again for a little while – that is, if Klegerman has kept any money for his former "student" and colleague. After all, supreme con man that he is, it is very doubtful that Nate Klegerman ever intended to give Yanover back any of the money he laundered for him. Some say there is honour among thieves, but in the world of the confidence men, of "walking" as many people as you can as smoothly as you can, honour is not a top priority. In this netherworld, appearance replaces reality. According to one investigator, Klegerman is the master and Yanover the poor pupil. "Chuck Yanover doesn't think things out clearly," he says. "He's caught up with the spirit of adventure with a sparkle in his eye ... but Nate Klegerman thinks it all out."

So when Klegerman is asked by Yanover where the money is, he will simply tell him that the money is gone, and that together they can work on a new scam, that will once and for all make them both so rich that they can go off and live happily ever after. But somehow this never happens, and the con goes on.

Source List and Selected Bibliography

Bell, Daniel. *The End of Ideology*. Glencoe, Ill.: Free Press, 1960.

Block, Alan, and Scarpitti, Frank. *Poisoning for Profit: The Mafia and Toxic Waste in America*. New York: Morrow, 1985.

Bonanno, Joseph, with Sergio Lalli. *A Man of Honor: The Autobiography of Joseph Bonanno*. New York: Simon and Schuster, 1983.

Breslin, Jimmy. *The Gang That Couldn't Shoot Straight*. New York: Viking Press, 1969.

Charbonneau, Jean-Pierre. *The Canadian Connection*. Translated from the French (*La Filière Canadienne*) by James Stewart. Montreal: Optimum, 1976.

Cressey, Donald R. *Theft of the Nation: The Structure and Operations of Organized Crime*. New York: Harper and Row, 1969.

Demaris, Ovid. *The Last Mafioso: Jimmy "the Weasel" Fratianno*. New York: Times Books, 1981.

Freeman, B., and Hewitt, M. *Their Town: The Mafia, the Media, and the Party Machine*. Toronto: Lorimer, 1979.

Gage, Nicholas, ed. *Mafia, U.S.A.* New York: Dell, 1972.

Hammer, Richard. *Playboy's Illustrated History of Organized Crime*. Chicago: Playboy Press, 1975.

Hawkins, Gordon. "Organized Crime and God," *The Public Interest*, #14, Fall, 1969.

————, and Morris, M. *The Honest Politician's Guide to Crime Control*. Chicago: University of Chicago Press, 1970.

Horwood, Harold, and Butts, Ed. *Pirates and Outlaws of Canada, 1610-1932*. Toronto: Doubleday, 1984.

Ianni, Francis. "Mafia and the Web of Kinship." *The Public Interest*, #22, Winter, 1971.

Kwitny, Jonathan. *Vicious Circles: The Mafia in the Marketplace*. New York: Norton, 1979.

Mayhew, Henry. *London's Underworld*. Edited by Peter Quennell. London: Bracken Books, 1983.

Nelli, Humbert S. *The Business of Crime: Italians and Syndicate Crime in the United States*. Chicago: University of Chicago Press, 1976.

Organized Crime and the World of Business. Report of the Commission of Inquiry. Montreal: Government of Quebec, 1977.

Phillips, Alan. "The Mafia in Canada," *Maclean's*. A five-part series: August 24, 1963; September 21, 1963; October 5, 1963; December 2, 1963; and March 7, 1963.

Le Rapport de la Commission de Police du Québec. Quebec City: Government of Quebec, 1975. English translation, 1976.

Report of the Royal Commission into Certain Sectors of the Construction Industry (known as the Waisberg Commission). Toronto: Government of Ontario, 1974.

Report of the Royal Commission on Gambling (known as the Roach Commission). Toronto: Government of Ontario, 1962.

Rowland, Wade. *Making Connections*. Toronto: Gage, 1979.

Smith, Dwight. *The Mafia Mystique*. New York: Basic Books, 1975.

Sondern, Frederic, Jr. *Brotherhood of Evil.* New York: Farrar, Straus, and Giroux, 1959.

Teresa, Vinnie, and Renner, Tom. *My Life in the Mafia.* New York: Doubleday, 1973.

U.S. Senate Hearings, Permanent Subcommittee of Investigations, Committee of Government Operations. *Organized Crime and Illicit Traffic in Narcotics* (known as the Valachi hearings). Washington, D.C., U.S. Government Printing Office. (In five parts with a volume containing the index, 1963-4.)

INDEX

Niagara Peninsula region, 31-42, 50, 102, 273, 279
Nickle, W. F., 273
Nicoletti, Vince, 245
North Bay, Ontario, 170
North Koreans, 155-6, 225, 287, 289, 293-303
North York (Toronto), 123
Notto, Sebastino, 37-8

Oake, Al, 297-8
Oakville, Ont., 39-40, 189, 244-6, 273
O'Brien, Tommy, 13
Obront, William ("Obie"), 101, 193
Off, Bonnie Rae, 168-70, 172
"old" Mafia, 113, 123, 185
Olson, Clifford, 215
Olympio, Sylvanus, 288
omertà, ix, 2, 186
"One-Eyed Connelly", 27
Onoratà Societa, L'. *See* Honoured Society
Ontario, 5-6, 15; history of organized crime in Ontario, in 1906-1920s, 31-42; in the 1930s and 40s, 265-86; in the 1950s and early 60s, 43-56; in the mid to late 1960s, 57-65, 76-84; in the 1970s and early 80s, 85-264, 287-303
Ontario Criminal Injuries Compensation Board, 222
Ontario Police Commission, 114-15, 117, 192
Ontario Provincial Police. *See* OPP
Ontario Temperance Act (OTA), 39, 85, 149, 266, 268, 273-4, 276, 278
"Operation Arrow", 257
"Operation Condor", 174-5, 239-40, 242
"Operation Oblong", 106-7, 109, 111, 152, 156, 159
"Operation Overlord", 152
"Operation Rough Rider", 258
"Operation Top Hat", 152, 159
OPP, 141, 144-6, 149-50, 217, 226, 242, 257, 268, 290, 292-3, 299
Orde Street Public School, 20
organized crime: definition of, 1-17; in Canada, 31-303. *See also* Mafia
"Organized Crime and God", 4
"Organized Crime and the World of Business", 101
Osborne, Coulter, 250-1

OTA. *See* Ontario Temperance Act
Ottawa, Ontario, 85, 88-90, 116, 148, 150, 284
Ottawa Police Department, 150
Outlaw Motorcycle Club, 256-8
Overbury, Stephen, 293
Oxford English Dictionary, 8

Pagano, Clinton, 161, 173-5, 239-41
Palermo, Sicily, 32, 255
"Palmer, Mr.". *See* Natarelli, Pasquale
Papalia, Anthony, 45
Papalia, Domenic, 45
Papalia, Johnny "Pops", 13, 40, 44-8, 50-5, 68, 76, 95-6, 147-9, 179, 232, 253-4
Paris, France, 288-9, 298-9, 303
Park Plaza Hotel (Toronto), 76, 79, 81, 170
Pasquale, William, 38
Patriarca crime family, 70
Peel Regional Police, 108, 226-36, 239
Penna, Joe, 274-5
Peoples Jewellers, 153
Perdue, Michael, 292
Perri, Bessie. *See* Starkman, Bessie
Perri, Rocco, 20, 21n, 23-4, 24n, 95, 179, 265-86; physical description, 269-70; early years, 265-71; murders, 268, 270-3; interview with *Toronto Star*, 271-3; Royal Commissions, 273-6; in jail, 268, 276; corruption of Customs officers, 279-86; disappearance, 286
Perskie, Steven, 161
Petrosino, Joseph, 33
Phelan, Tom, 281
Philadelphia, Pa., 15, 161, 165, 175, 229
Philadelphia Bulletin, 173
Philippines, 288, 294-8
Phillips, Alan, 47, 52
Piccininni, Joseph, 186
Pickford, Mary, 20
Piersante, Vincent, 17
Pinheiro, Antonio, 186
Pirates and Outlaws of Canada, 1610-1932, 2
Plasterers' and Cement Masons' Union, 88
Poe, Edgar Allan, 41
Poisoning for Profit: The Mafia and Toxic Waste in America, 172

Western Guard, 291-2
Wetston, Sam, 237-8
Whalen, Michael, 22
Wheatley, Randolph, 86, 95
Whitney, Sir James, 34
Williams, General, 273
Williams, Harrison, 160
Wilson, Woodrow, 267
Windsor, Ontario, 231, 267, 279-86
Wingate, James, 229, 236
Winters, Robert (Bob), 174-5
Witness Protection Program (U.S.), 5,
    151-2, 166, 262
Wolfe, Sam, 33
Wood, Charles, 268-9, 274, 276-7
Woodbridge Mall, 224, 226

Yanover, Charles Stephen, 86-7, 90-4,
    101, 107, 146-7, 153, 162, 225, 265,
    287-303; early years, 90-4, 302; physi-
    cal description, 91; character, 91-2,
    287-8, 293-4, 301-3; as "Chuck the
    Bagel", 92; enforcement work with
    Volpe, 90-7, 302; bombing, 90-7,
    287; on Volpe's co-operation with
    police, 211, 228; and Togo, 287-90;
    and Dominica coup, 291-4; and
    Korean assassination plot, 155-6,
    287, 294-303; Veronac extortion
    108-10, 291; and Ian Rosenberg's
    murder, 110; on Volpe's death 228;
    on Cecil Kirby, 301-2
York Lathing, 193
Yorkville, 100
Yugoslavia, 66, 82, 136, 253

Zahler, Maurice, 153-5
Zappia, Domenic, 94, 96
Zappia, Joseph, 96
Zentner, Max, 189
Zito, Rocco, 131, 255